In Times of War

In Times of War

AN ANTHOLOGY
OF WAR AND PEACE
IN CHILDREN'S
LITERATURE

Edited by Carol Fox,
Annemie Leysen and Irène Koenders
with Rob Batho, John Clay, Manuela Fonseca,
and Annemie Devynck

PAVILION

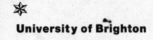

First published in Great Britain in 2000 by
PAVILION BOOKS LIMITED
London House, Great Eastern Wharf
Parkgate Road, London SW11 4NQ

In co-operation with:
University of Brighton (UK)
University College Chichester (UK)
Katholieke Hogeschool Leuven – Departement Lerarenopleiding (BE)
Escola Superior De Educação Setubal (PT)

Editors:
Carol Fox, Annemie Leysen and Irène Koenders

With the assistance of:
Rob Batho, John Clay, Anne-Marie Devynck and Manuela Fonseca,

Design and layout © Pavilion Books Ltd.

The moral right of the authors and illustrators has been asserted

Designed by Bet Ayer

A CIP catalogue record for this book is available from the British Library.

ISBN 1 86205 446 0

Set in Times and Galliard
Printed in Spain by Bookprint

2 4 6 8 10 9 7 5 3 1

This book can be ordered direct from the publisher. Please contact
the Marketing Department. But try your bookshop first.

Website: http://www.pavilionbooks.co.uk

Contents

Foreword

WORDS OF WAR

This anthology is the result of a collaboration by teacher educators in three European countries, Belgium, Portugal and the UK, a project which has been funded for four years by the Comenius section of the EU Socrates programme. The EU was based on the desire of war-torn European countries never to repeat the horrors of the two world wars of the last century, a desire that has become more urgent as we enter a new millennium in a Europe that still cannot call itself peaceful.

The aims of the project were simple – to collect, translate, and disseminate the very rich literature for children around the topic of war and peace. First we identified, collected and read examples of children's literature about war, and then we published a tri-lingual catalogue of 200 works for children. The catalogue is available on the internet at :http://intranet.bton.ac.uk:7776/education/default.htm At this stage we discovered that there were so many children's stories on conflicts of the twentieth century that on the whole it seemed sensible to limit ourselves to those. We also found that in the last 10-15 years of the twentieth century there had been a great burgeoning of this kind of literature in Belgium, Holland and the UK, though not so much in Portugal whose relationship to the two world wars is different.

Our second stage was for each participating country to produce an anthology of extracts from picture books and novels together with poems and other literary genres, for use in schools. This meant that each of us would for the first time be introducing literature in translation that erstwhile had not been available to young readers. This was particularly true for this UK anthology In Times of War, partly because the English language publishing industry in Britain is comparatively so extensive that translations from other languages are not as frequent as they ought to be. A major aim of this book is to make teachers and young readers aware not only of what is being written and read in other countries, but also of what there is to gain from seeing a war through other eyes in different contexts.

While we understand that it is very important that children receive history teaching about the conflicts of the twentieth century, we came together in a collective belief in the power of imaginative literature to help children to think about war through the virtual experiences and powerful images provided by stories and poems. In this book children may enter the terror of First World War trench warfare, become the young girl who waves good-bye to a Georgian soldier who found himself on the Dutch island of Texel at the end of World War Two, hide out in the forests outside Warsaw with the Polish partisans after the fall of the Warsaw ghetto, or journey from Bosnia to Croatia with young refugees from the recent war in the former Yugoslavia. And the reader will find here many other conflicts, taking the characters in the stories to lands as far apart as Kazakhstan, Mozambique, Iraq and Northern Ireland.

We have selected our passages on the basis that children are likely to enjoy them and want to read more, rather than on any shared ideology about war. However, we have not come across any children's book that promotes war or glorifies it. We hope that by their reading of these extracts from stories children will be encouraged to make connections between the past and their own lives and situations; indeed many children's authors help them to do precisely that.

The passages in this anthology have been chosen to appeal to young people of different ages and different levels of reading experience, though its readership is probably most accurately designed to be between KS2 and GCSE. At least three of our extracts were not intended primarily for child audiences, Spiegelman's *Maus*, Tardi's *Trench Warfare* and Briggs' *Ethel and Ernest*. Nevertheless these stunningly powerful and very different representations of war speak to readers of all ages. We have included extracts from graphic novels and picture books not as an appeal to beginning readers, but to give more experienced readers a chance to compare and think about the different and complex ways that stories of war can be told visually, important in an age when most young people experience representations of war through film and newsreel.

Although three European countries might seem to have a lot in common we all found that we were working against a background of different histories, different contexts for education and different languages. The UK participants have benefited from the great linguistic skill of their Belgian and Portuguese counterparts, who have had the burden of providing two-way translations constantly. The project has been led in an inspiring way by Annemie Leysen of the Katholieke Hogeschool in Leuven in Belgium, to whom we are all indebted for bringing and keeping us together and for taking the organisational burden. A list of the other participants, all of whom have worked tirelessly to produce the three anthologies, follows. In particular we owe thanks to the translators of the Belgian/Dutch and Portuguese extracts. Finally we are indebted to all the authors and their publishers included here, the great majority of whom have generously given permission to publish their work gratis.

Dr Carol Fox,
University of Brighton, February 2000

Play, Dreams
and Reality

AN IMAGINED EXPERIENCE OF THE GULF WAR

This novel is narrated by Tom who tells the strange story of how his very imaginative twelve-year-old brother Andy (alias Figgis) starts every night to dream himself into the persona of Latif, a young Iraqi soldier. Latif comes to inhabit more and more of Andy's life as the Gulf War of 1990 continues. Through this storytelling device Robert Westall is able to help his readers, too, to imagine what it must have been like to be a very young soldier fighting for his country. In this extract there are two ways of seeing what is happening in Iraq – through the television which broadcasts the action live world-wide, and through what is happening to Latif as he takes over Figgis' s life. The usual view of war as heroic and interesting is represented in this extract by Tom and his father, but through the character of Latif Figgis is able to experience its horrific reality.

Underneath, things were moving. I mean, in Figgis's dream-life. Almost every night now, I'd waken about four, and he'd be sitting on his bed, muttering in that strange dream language. And I got into the habit of getting up and sitting next to him. And I made a discovery.

You couldn't get anything out of him while he was deep in the dream, talking the strange language. And you couldn't get much out of him once he'd wakened up properly. He was just Figgis, with a few vague memories of carrying heavy wooden boxes or eating rice out of a tin with a wirehandle.

But there was an in-between stage, when he was just starting to come out of it. And then he still seemed to be somebody else, but understanding and talking English.

'What's your name?' I asked him once, as the hot, flushed, shifty-eyed face turned towards me.

He said something that sounded like 'Latif'.

After that I could sort of summon him out of the dream by calling, 'Latif! Latif!' Then I'd get some really hairy stuff out of him. He said he lived in a place called Tikrit, and his father repaired cars for a living. 'German cars are good,' he said. 'And Russian cars. Yankee cars are rubbish. My father says.'

And he spat on our bedroom carpet. I sat there staring at the little bubbly bit of spit, soaking into the pile. I'd never seen anyone spit before: except into a hanky when they had a cold.

I looked up Tikrit in our atlas; it was north of Baghdad. Then I read in the paper it was where Saddam Hussein himself came from.

But that didn't prove anything. I mean, if I could look it up in the atlas, or the newspaper, so could Figgis. I mean, at that stage, I still reckoned he was making it all up. Another typical Figgis-game. I couldn't be sure he wasn't having me on deliberately. Another deep Figgis-joke... How wrong I was...

But I enjoyed the performance; he could always give a good performance, could Figgis. What an imagination he had!

I would ask him about Saddam Hussein.

'He is our hero. He is not afraid of the Americans. He is the only Arab who is not afraid of the Americans. The Americans will not bribe him into silence. He will make fools of them, by the force of his will!'

But I learnt to keep off the topic of Saddam in the end. One night he got so worked up he leapt to his feet and began yelling, 'Saddam, Saddam, Saddam!' so loud it brought my mother through in her dressing gown, before I could get him out of the dream.

He wakened up when she spoke to him; looking all dazed and lost as usual. She talked to him softly, in a way that made me feel a bit jealous. Cuddled him, then got him back to bed. Then she turned on me. 'I want a word with you, Tom!'

We sat down in the cold kitchen. The central heating was off, and I began feeling a bit sorry for myself, and wanting to get back to bed.

'Look, Mum, he was only having a bad dream. You know what Andy is. He's always had them.'

Her eyes were too sharp for my liking. 'How often is this happening?'

I shrugged and lied, because I wanted to get back to bed. 'Once or twice.'

'Why didn't you tell me?'

I just shrugged.

'I heard what he was shouting. Is he worried that there's going to be a war?'

'No more than anybody else.'

'A lot of kids are having nightmares about the war. I was talking to Nancy Tarbet in Sainsbury's. Her two are having nightmares. About being burnt alive!'

'They're just little kids. Andy's twelve...'

'So that makes him a big tough-guy, I suppose! Like you and your father! You know how Andy *feels* things...'

'What do you think Dad and I are? The Magnificent Hulks? Hairy apes?'

'Well, you're not losing much sleep over it, either of you!'

I shrugged again.

'It's all that telly,' she said viciously. 'They have nothing new to say. But they go on saying it. Night after night after night, 'til you could scream. And your father has to listen to every single word. He seems to have forgotten where the "off" switch is.'

I could've said something sharp then. I won't hear a word against my dad. But I just said, 'Are we going to sit here all night? I've got school tomorrow.'

'*Goodnight!*' she said, and stalked out, putting the lights out as she passed the switch, and leaving me to find my way to bed in the dark.

She's not normally spiteful. It came as a shock to me, just how upset she must be.

It was unfortunate that Dad insisted on having the kitchen telly on for the six o'clock news, during supper the following night. I mean, it *was* dead boring. There was nothing new; just that the Americans were pouring in more and more stuff; with the same old video recordings of orange tanks moving through pink dust clouds into a mauve sunset.

'I'm switching this rubbish off!' said Mum.

'No,' said Dad. 'I want it. I want to know what's going to happen.'

'You know damn well what's going to happen,' snapped Mum. 'A lot of people are going to get killed. Because the world is run by *men*! Mrs Simpson's lad's out there. I had her in tears this morning, in the post office.'

'I know what they're going to call this,' said Dad. 'The crying war. Remember when those two Aussie frigates sailed for the Gulf? It wasn't just the sailors' wives crying. It was the flippin' sailors as well. The whole world's gone soft. As for that Gulf Mums' Association, going on about our lads being homesick... it's enough to make you weep. How do you think our parents coped in World War Two? When my father went to Korea, my mother didn't twitch a muscle. Or she cried in *private*.'

'So we do nothing? And let our lads get killed for *nothing*?'

'It's not nothing. Saddam's nearly got the atomic bomb. Better to lose ten thousand now than a million later.'

'*Ten thousand?*' My mother was nearly screaming. 'You're very free with your ten thousand. When you nearly broke your heart over that baby squirrel on the lawn. I think you're stark raving mad, Horsie. All you men have taken leave of your senses. Suppose it was you who had to go? Or Tom?'

My father's face went as still as a stone. 'I hope I would do my duty,' he said coldly. 'Are you calling me a coward?'

'And I hope I would do my duty as well,' I added, moving about a quarter of an inch closer to Dad.

'Men,' said Mum. But she flushed crimson. She knew she'd gone too far.

'Anyway,' said Dad, in a softer, making-it-up sort of tone. 'It won't be our lads that'll get killed. We'll bomb them to bits before we send our lads in. That Schwarzkopf knows what he's doing.'

'Bomb them to bits?' Mum went up like a rocket again. 'Don't you think the Iraqi soldiers have mothers as well? Or do you think they're made out of metal, like Daleks?'

I looked across at Figgis, who hadn't said a word. He was just staring at film of apricot-coloured Tornados taking off, leaving clouds of puce smoke. I couldn't read the look on his face at all.

I don't know why I pushed Figgis so hard, with that night-time game of ours. I suppose in a way, I'd always envied him. Figgis the dreamer, lost in a world of his own. Figgis, who was never bored with his own company, his own thoughts. Me, I need my mates. If I'm left alone for an evening, I stuff myself with grub from the fridge, I stuff my head with rubbish from the telly, and end up going to bed in a right bad mood. I've got to have things happening; got to have some action.

I suppose this Latif Thing was like a new toy. And I made the most of it, night after night. *Was* Figgis just making it up? If so, I wanted to push him to the far end of it, to catch him out in something stupid that I *knew* was wrong. I'd read a lot about the coming war myself by that time – everything I could lay my hands on.

But whereas I was reading about big military stuff – bunkers and sand berms and oil-filled ditches waiting to be set alight, I never got that kind of stuff from the Latif character. He went on about playing football, 'til the old ball burst and they couldn't repair it. About the little creatures of the desert; and how the men caught and ate them, because they never had enough to eat. About having his mess-tins stolen, and being in trouble with the major; until his mate Akbar, who was a shepherd and could move silently, stole some new ones for him, from the new crowd further along the line.

And about never getting letters from his mum. And those lice again. He was always trying to get rid of lice; either with a bar of wet soap, or by running a match along the seams of his uniform. Only one thing worried him more than lice. A different major, who had a taste for young boys, if he could corner them alone...

Cunning stuff – or was it *true*? I could never make my mind up. It was middle-of-the-night stuff, and the rules are different, somehow, in the middle of the night.

So I didn't notice for a long time that the Latif character was getting stronger and stronger; and I was getting more and more caught up with him.

Until one day in school, I fell fast asleep in the middle of a history lesson. I jolted awake and the teacher and all my mates were laughing at me. I remember the history master, who was a nice bloke called Giddings who I liked, quoted a verse from Thomas Hood at me:

'My candle burns at both its ends
It cannot last the night
But oh my foes, and oh my friends
It gives a lovely light...'

It should have been a warning to me. But I just told myself the history room had been overwarm – it was nearly Christmas by then, and the school boilers were working full out. And all my mates asked if I'd been up half the night boozing at some party, or getting off with some girl. So I didn't take it seriously.

I didn't even take it seriously when Figgis came home with the worst school report he'd ever had. He'd dropped from first to tenth in the end-of-term exams. Mind you, tenth in the top stream at Elmborough Grammar School was still pretty good. But it wasn't Figgis.

Mum went on at him, and then Dad came home and went on at him, then they both went on at him over supper. Oh, they were very liberal, very understanding. Was he worried about something? Was he being bullied? That sort of enlightened parents' crap.

Figgis didn't seem worried, somehow.

And that should have been the biggest warning of all.

That, and the scratching. He developed this terrible habit of scratching. His hair, his armpits, all over. But especially his hair and his armpits. Even when we had people in over Christmas... Mum nagged him cruel, made him have baths, even took him to the doctor. The doctor found lots of raw red marks all over him, the results of the scratching. But no *reason* for the scratching. He booked him in to have tests done by some sort of skin specialist, after the New Year.

Figgis never got to have those tests.

From *Gulf* by Robert Westall

CHICKEN COOP

In Op het puntje van mijn tong (On the Tip of my Tongue) *the Jewish poet-ess Louise van Santen gives example after example of what it must be like to be young in times of war. Between the lines of this poem too, the war and holocaust loom.*

At the end of the garden
of the house I was born in
was an abandoned chicken coop
with wood with clinging flakes of paint
and chicken wire that had lost its holes
and inside, for a rooster
a dangling crooked perch
swinging loose on rusty rings.
For us five kids the coop was home
or a stockade with sentries
standing guard over baddies
or a churchyard for funerals.
My grandfather was laid out once
in a shabby coffin in our front room
the whole family stood around
but none of us children knew
what they were going to do with that coffin
– take it to our coop in the garden?
but maybe nobody thought that but me.
And later we moved
and later still we were driven out
and banished to an unknown Uz –
we weren't even fully grown
and behind bars in the stockade
I sometimes thought of that abandoned coop
where play and fantasy were part of life
where barbed wire and cutting hinges
were not the stuff of nightmares –
suddenly the baddie was on the outside

staring in at Job and taking the crooked perch
to thrash those rusty rings –
and later still, when there was next-to-no food
and the indescribable had happened
– I had forgotten our chicken coop.

From *On the Tip of my Tongue: Poems*
by Louise van Santen

PLAYING FOOTBALL WITH THE ENEMY

This comes from a picture story book about the First World War. In the story four young Englishmen volunteer to fight, and find themselves in the battlefields of Flanders. In this extract it is Christmas and the English and German soldiers greet one another in No Man's Land (the area between the English and German battle trenches). The soldiers on both sides are able to bury their dead and then somebody starts a football game... Although the characters are fictional this is based on real events.

A small group of men from each side, unarmed, joined them. They all shook hands. One of the Germans spoke good English and said he hoped the war would end soon because he wanted to return to his job as a taxi driver in Birmingham.

It was agreed that they should take the opportunity to bury the dead. The bodies were mixed up together. They were sorted out, and a joint burial service was held on the 'halfway line'.

Then, from somewhere, a football bounced across the frozen mud. Will was on it in a flash. He trapped the ball with his left foot, flipped it up with his right, and headed it towards Freddie.

Freddie made a spectacular dive, caught the ball in both hands and threw it to a group of Germans.

Immediately a vast, fast and furious football match was underway. Goals were marked by caps. Freddie, of course, was in one goal and a huge German in the other.

Apart from that, it was wonderfully disorganized, part football, part ice-skating, with unknown numbers on each team. No referee, no account of the score.

It was just terrific to be no longer an army of moles, but up and running on top of the ground that had threatened to entomb them for so long. And this time Will really could hear a big crowd – and he was playing for England!

He was playing in his usual centre forward position with Lacey to his left and little Billy on the wing. The game surged back and forth across No Man's Land. The goalposts grew larger as greatcoats and tunics were discarded as the players warmed to the sport. Khaki and grey mixed together. Steam rose from their backs, and their faces were wreathed in smiles and clouds of breath in the clear frosty air.

From *War Game* by Michael Foreman
(illustrations in colour section)

VLAMERTINGHE
(PASSING THE CHATEAU, JULY 1917)

'And all her silken flanks with garlands drest' –
But we are coming to the sacrifice.
Must those have flowers who are not yet gone West?
May those have flowers who live with death and lice?

This must be the floweriest place
That earth allows; the queenly face
Of the proud mansion borrows grace for grace
Spite of those brute guns lowing at the skies;

Bold great daisies' golden lights,
Bubbling roses' pinks and whites –
Such a gay carpet! poppies by the million;
Such damask! such vermilion!
But if you ask me, mate, the choice of colour
Is scarcely right; this red should have been duller.

by Edmund Blunden

RUANDA (*RWANDA*)

In Wat de ogen niet horen (What the Eyes Do not Hear) *Daniel Billiet published a series of harrowing poems – and other texts – about war and violence in Sarajevo, Somalia and Rwanda.*

1.

With a filthy machete
the man carved
a flower
out of a piece of wood.

A red flower.

It smelled of fear for his family.

2.

With a machete
the man carved
a gun
out of a piece of wood.

His son is now
playing at war, jubilant.

From *Wat de Ogen niet Horen (What the Eyes Do not Hear)*
by Daniel Billiet

A YOUNG FREEDOM-FIGHTER
MAKES USE OF HIS GUN

Paul Kagomi is a teenage freedom-fighter who has spent most of his childhood fighting for democracy with a rebel group. After the revolution has been won Paul's adoptive father, Michael, takes power in the new government; but there is a coup and Michael Kagomi is imprisoned. Paul returns to the city to work for his father's freedom. With him is his companion, a young girl called Jilli. In this chapter Paul is involved in helping the traders and stall holders in a local market to fight against a gang of thugs called the Deathsingers. The Deathsingers run a protection racket in the market and bully and intimidate the people. Paul has brought his AK rifle with him from the old days when he was a freedom fighter in the bush. In this scene the fact that Paul is armed is very important in defeating the Deathsingers, though he does not use his gun to kill with.

As they made their way down through the market the hot noon air seemed heavier and stiller than usual. The music still blared away, but the other noises were different – few of the traders were sleeping, and many sat in groups, smoking and talking in low voices. Paul himself felt listless and uncertain, longing for the clean air and clear purposes of the bush. The basket weighed on his head. The gun was no use here, on this mission, but he couldn't have risked leaving it among Efoni's inflammable stock.

A drowsy woman sold them lemonade and they settled in a place from which they could see several liquor-stalls, where they dozed in turn. Nothing happened for a good two hours, then Jilli nudged Paul's side and woke him.

'Men coming,' she muttered.

Two traders appeared with a bottle-stacked barrow, and a third man strolling arrogantly beside them. He watched while the traders opened a stall and stacked the bottles on to their trestle. Before they'd finished a similar team had arrived, and then two more, and by now there were customers drifting in in two and threes, buying drinks and settling into groups. Hours before normal the liquor-stalls were busy. The customers sat on the ground, a dozen men together, and talked among themselves with anger in their gestures. In one group a man jumped to his feet and performed the sort of boast-chant Fodo sometimes used to do before action, with a foot-stamping dance to the rhythm of his friends' handclaps.

Paul was wondering whether it was worth the risk of wandering along the stalls and counting the drinkers when a tall thin man in a fawn suit strolled up and squatted down with a group. They stopped their talk to listen to him while he drew shapes in the dust, the way Michael would do to explain a plan of attack. He answered a few questions, gesturing directions with his hands, and moved on to the next group.

For the first time for several days Paul felt a stir of excitement. The man's face was in shadow under the brim of his straw hat, but his movements had the same spider-limbed jerkiness as those of the watcher at the bar on Curzon Street. The suit was the same. So the struggle for power in the market might have something to do with Michael, after all.

He bought a twist of mu-nuts, which they nibbled slowly. Time passed. Then an army truck backed in by the liquor-stalls and two soldiers unloaded wrapped packages, some soft and shapeless and others hard and narrow – blue T-shirts and bundles of truncheons, Paul guessed. They shared them out among the groups of drinkers who rose to their feet and started to move off up separate alleys.

'I'll go and find those fellows by the Coke-sign, shall I?' said Jilli. 'That way you can stay and see what they do.'

'OK,' said Paul. 'Wish we'd had you with us in the bush, Jilli.'

She laughed and strolled dreamily away, spitting the mu-shells over her shoulder as if going nowhere special. Any commando would have been glad of her, he thought – she'd known without telling that this was why Warriors worked in pairs, one to keep watch while the other reported. Oh for the day when Michael could meet her! Perhaps he'd make her his daughter. That would be great...

The Deathsingers were easy to follow. The market sounds

changed as they went by, laughter and argument dying into silence and rising back to mutters of alarm once they'd passed. The group Paul had chosen elbowed their way through a crowd of young men who'd gathered round a music-stall (the word seemed to get round in minutes whenever a trader had a fresh consignment of tapes, and fans flocked in from all over Dangoum). One of the shoppers must have protested at being pushed. There was an explosion of violence, too quick to follow, but ending with the Deathsingers swaggering on while the music-lovers crowded round two of their friends who lay on the ground, writhing and moaning.

The group Paul was following stopped among the leather-sellers. Two of them looked at their watches. Others picked over a pile of goat-hides, obviously not intending to buy anything but commenting contemptuously to the trader on the quality of his stock. Every move they made, every pose they struck, the angles of their necks, their gestures, their voices – raucous enough to penetrate the battering music from the palms close by – all were charged with an aggressive anger that seemed to flash between them like noiseless flickers of lightning among massed clouds before a storm breaks at the beginning of the rains.

Paul squatted down a few yards off and pretended to re-roll one of the lengths of cotton that hid the AK. He had no plan, but he was a Warrior, his job to keep in touch with the enemy. As he waited the man in the fawn suit came gangling in from the left, spoke briefly to two of the men and moved on. At once Paul's task became clear. When he picked the gun-basket up it seemed lighter than before, as if the AK too understood its purpose. The man in the fawn suit was Michael's enemy, a single, simple target.

Paul trailed him between the stalls to the next group of Deathsingers, who were already sharing out the T-shirts. The group beyond were dressed, swinging their truncheons and quietly humming the Deathsong. Around them the stalls were silent. The man picked out three of this group and slouched with them over to the palms, watched by the stall-holders. This was the tourist area of the market, the prime sites where the stalls sold carved spirit-figures and chiefs' stools and grass-and-bead dance-masks and zebra-hair fly-switches and things of that sort. The stall-holders were rich and greedy, greatly disliked by the ordinary traders. Paul could feel their fear.

The man looked at his watch and nodded. One of the Deathsingers turned to the deaf old legless man who played the tapes and gave him a violent shove which toppled him off his stool. Another swept his pile of tapes from the upturned crate he used as a table. The man in the fawn suit studied the tape-deck, pressed a switch and ejected the tape it was playing. The whole market fell still. Some hens cackled, as though they too recognized the alarm, the moment before the storm broke.

The man in the fawn suit took a tape out of his pocket and pressed it in. Into the hush rose the Deathsong, a ghost-wail louder than human, throbbing from the big loudspeakers. Faint through its sound Paul heard the coppersmiths' gong beginning to beat in answer. Then everything was drowned by the clamour of simulated gunfire.

Paul looked at the stall-holder beside him, a Naga woman, her face grey-yellow with fear. She was piling grass masks in under the main trestle of her stall.

'Want me to guard your goods, missus?' he said.

'Clear out. What use are you?'

He lifted the basket down and eased the muzzle of the AK into view. She stared at it, then at him.

'How much?' she said.

'Twenty gurai. Ten now and ten when it's over.'

'OK.'

He helped her stack the rest of her stock away and slid in beneath the trestle between two piles of masks, where he lay watching the scene under the palms. The sounds of fighting were spreading behind him. He heard a yodelling noise, like the sound of Fulu farmers calling the news along the Strip, and guessed it was some kind of Oni-oni battle-cry. The man in the fawn suit was probably too close to the speakers to hear it, but now something went up in a crackle and roar of burning and he climbed on to the crate for a better view, then jumped down again to listen to the report of a Deathsinger who'd come running in from the fight. The messenger showed him an Oni-oni hat. The man shrugged. He wasn't worried. The Oni-oni could muster about thirty or forty fighters, Paul guessed, the Deathsingers six times that. There'd been about eighty of them down by the liquor-stalls, but they would not have been the only ones. Others would have mustered at bars along the edge of the shanties, to make a timed attack from all sides. It was a well-planned operation.

The man in the fawn suit was clearly in charge. But suppose he wasn't there. Suppose he got taken out...

Seemingly without his having told it his hand was feeling down through the rolls of cotton and working the AK free. All the uncertainties were gone. Everything had come together for this moment. This was why he had buried the gun all those months ago, instead of letting it be handed in for destruction. This was why the soldiers had come to Tsheba. This was why he had risked the appalling trek south to the railway, to dig the gun up again. This, just now, was why he had suggested to Major Dasu that Jilli should come with him, so that she could take the message back while he stalked his prey. It had all been arranged long ago, and he knew who had arranged it. Her voice whispered in his mind. *I love you, my son. Love me. Bring me alive with your beautiful gun.*

An easy, simple target. Three shots rapid, to make sure.

He slipped the safety down.

If only Jilli had been here, to share the moment, his fellow-Warrior.

The thought of her checked his hand on the cocking-lever, Jilli before she'd become a Warrior, standing in the rocking boat and craning over the reed-beds to watch her father's house explode in fire. A twist of petrol-soaked rag at the corner, a match, flames roaring through the sun-bleached stems, the tower of smoke, Jilli's screams...

The man was enemy. He was everything Michael and the others had fought against so long. But Paul knew with absolute certainty that if he pulled the trigger to kill him those shots would be the match which set Nagala on fire again. *Bring me alive with your beautiful gun.* No. Bitch.

He raised the safety and laid the gun on its side. *You've been lucky this time mister*, he thought. *But if anyone else starts shooting, you're dead.*

Black ashes of burning floated through the hot, slow-moving air. Beneath the stall something stank and flies whined between the stacked masks, seeking it out. The man in the fawn suit leaned against one of the trees and lit a thin cigar, just like the ones Michael used to smoke. Runners came and went. The Deathsong filled the air, but through it Paul could hear the smiths' gong still beating, and the shouts and screams, and the roar and crackle as another stall went up in flames. And then the clatter of imitation gunfire would drown everything.

He waited, ignoring the flies, controlling his tension, taut in him like the spring of a trap. Battles were like this. Watch that flank, Michael would say, be ready to shoot on that fireline, creep forward to those ant-hills if you get the chance... and then the action was all on the other flank and no-one crossed the fireline and no shot was fired as you snaked towards the ant-hills, but your task was still part of the battle. So, now, the man in the fawn suit was Paul's task. In intent poised stillness he watched him, like a leopard watching a grazing antelope. The man was still very near his death.

A couple of market police hurried up to the palms and spoke to him. They were a useless lot – all they did in the market was see they got their cut from the hash-sellers. Now they looked anxious, but he laughed at them and patted them patronizingly on the shoulders before turning to a runner who had just arrived. They strolled away. The runner clearly had good news – Paul could see it in his gestures, and the way he laughed as he gave his message, and the way the man in the fawn suit replied, then pointed up at the speakers and patted the tape-deck. *I've an answer to that, mister*, thought Paul.

Again he picked up the gun, cocked it, lowered the safety and took aim, then waited. Just as the imitation gunfire burst out once more he pulled the trigger. The lovely familiar jar of power ran through his forearm as he held the barrel steady.

The man in the fawn suit leapt and stared at his hand, which he'd still been resting on the tape-deck, then at the smashed deck itself, then at the speakers above, then round at the stalls. As the brief gun-deafness cleared from Paul's ears he found he could hear the sounds of fighting, the shouts and screams and crashings, and through them all the coppersmiths' gong still beating. They wavered to and fro, became louder, and then as they swelled were joined by a sudden crashing yell of onslaught mixed with a yipping bark. The man in the fawn suit jerked himself out of his astonishment and climbed on to the crate, shading his eyes to gaze over the nearer stalls. It was only a minute before the first of the retreating Deathsingers ran by.

They took the man in the fawn suit by surprise, but he jumped down at once and stood in the path of the next wave, shouting at them, ordering them back into the battle. They argued, gesturing towards the fight, but before anything could happen another lot came pouring through, and by now the stall-holders seemed to have grasped that these were defeated men and were darting out between the stalls to yell at them and pummel their shoulders as they ran. Soon if any of the Deathsingers fell he was done for as a mob closed screaming round him, kicking and pounding like boys killing a snake till he lay still.

Now, thought Paul. Now someone will start shooting. They've got nothing to lose. He wriggled his way out to the back of the stall, cradling the gun ready, hoping the rush of people would offer him a clear shot when the moment came. The man in the fawn suit made three separate efforts to bar the route, but they swept past him without even stopping to argue. He was so furious with them that the traders must have thought he was on their side as he yelled and cuffed their enemies.

Now he gave up and stood clear of the rush in the slot beside the mask-seller's stall. Paul could have moved two paces and touched him as with quick but unflustered movements he rolled up his hat and stuffed it into the pocket of his jacket, which he then took off and folded over his arm. He turned, edged along the back of the stall behind and waited beside it to cross the next alley where a mob of blue-shirted fugitives were streaming by. His pose was easy, like a sightseer. Quietly Paul slid along between the stalls until he was directly behind him, just out of reach. He raised the gun and cocked it, firmly, making the metallic double click and slither good and loud. The man froze.

'Put your hands up,' said Paul. 'Turn round.'

The man did so. Their eyes met. He looked at the steady muzzle of the gun and smiled.

'Big toy for a kid,' he said.

'Man-size bullets in it,' said Paul. 'Want to find out? I've got the catch down.'

The man's eyes flickered as though something was happening behind Paul's back. Paul tensioned his finger on the trigger. It was pretty certainly only a trick, but there was no harm in the man seeing that if anything touched him the gun would fire.

'OK,' he said. 'Keep your hands how they are and turn round.'

The man let his hands drop to his side and stayed where he was, still smiling. Paul had guarded prisoners who'd thought they could try this sort of thing with children. He lowered the muzzle a few inches.

'Give you three,' he said. 'Then I'll shoot your leg off. One, two …'

The man nodded, raised his hands and turned.

'Walk,' said Paul. 'Play it safe, mister. Don't think I'm new to this. Go where that gong's being hit.'

The steady triumphant beat was now the loudest noise in the market. The fight wasn't over, but the sounds had scattered, mainly down towards the lower end of the market but coming from anywhere where the market people or the gangs had a few Deathsingers cornered. A lot of the stalls were wrecked, their goods spilt, their tables toppled, their awnings in tatters. When he reached the area where the Fulu women had traded he found nothing but piles of smouldering ash, and most of the space around was flattened. The coppersmiths' section was like a junkyard. Bodies, mostly with blue shirts, lay around. Women, many of them bloodied and weeping, wandered to and fro or helped others worse hurt than themselves. It didn't look like the scene of a victory.

In the middle of it hung the gong. Two boys still thumped it with alternate strokes. Beyond it a group of adults was gathered, with Major Dasu's tall figure among them. Paul marched his prisoner over.

'I see the black lion,' he called.

Major Dasu turned, let his eyes flick over the man and on to the AK. Paul could feel his anger. The man lowered his arms.

'Silly kid went and pulled a gun on me,' he said, easy, amiable, as if he were now among friends.

'He was in charge of the attack,' said Paul. 'He gave the Deathsingers their orders. I watched him the whole time. And six days back he was watching the house where Michael Kagomi told me to go if anything happened to him.'

'Kid's been dreaming,' said the man.

'That time he told me if I didn't clear off the Deathsingers would come to my hut,' said Paul. 'He might know what's happened to my father. And your cousin.'

'What's your name?' said Major Dasu.

The man shook his head. Major Dasu shrugged and called an order. Three men ran up.

'Take charge of this fellow,' he said. 'Search him. When you've done that get hold of a prisoner and tell him you'll let him go if he tells you everything he knows about this man.'

'He's got a flick-knife in his jacket pocket,' said Paul.

They led the man away. Major Dasu looked at Paul.

'I told you, no guns.'

'I didn't shoot anyone. I just took the sound system out, that's all.'

'You did that?'

'Sure.'

Major Dasu snorted – probably the nearest a Baroba ever came to a laugh.

'Deathsingers thought it was us,' he said. 'That's why they broke so easy.'

'It was us,' said Paul. 'Us Nagalai.'

'You're Kagomi's son all right. You don't let go of an idea. All right. But just keep it out of sight from now on. Off you go.'

'You'll tell me if you find out anything about my father?'

'Sure.'

He turned away. Paul folded the butt, unclipped the magazine, slid the gun up under his shirt and covered the muzzle with his forearm.

To account for the awkward posture he clutched his elbow with his free hand, as though he too had been hurt in the fighting, and made his way back to the mask-seller's stall. She refused to hand his basket over until he'd repaid the ten gurai she'd given him, saying he hadn't stayed to guard her stall till all the fighting was over. She was a mean woman. All around the market-people were rejoicing in the defeat of the Deathsingers, especially the traders who'd done no fighting and suffered no damage to their stalls. Paul hid the gun among the rolls of cloth and went to look for Jilli.

The Fulu women were standing in an excited group among their burnt-out stalls, twittering their triumph, bandaging each other's wounds but hardly seeming to notice their pain or loss. Efoni said she hadn't seen Jilli since she'd left with Paul to watch the Deathsingers assemble. By now a makeshift hospital for the badly hurt was being set up, but she wasn't there either. He tried the bar where Major Dasu's messengers had waited and questioned anyone who would listen to him, with no luck. Major Dasu was deep in conference with the other gang-leaders and Madam Ga, but one of his aides helped Paul find the actual messengers. One had bicycled off to fetch the Scorpions, but the one who'd stayed said Jilli had been going back towards the market.

It was dusk now. Paul worked systematically along the stalls, searching and asking. He found her well after dark. At that edge of the market, traders dumped their broken stuff and rotten fruit and other trash for the shanty children to pick over. Paul heard the cry of discovery, the clack of children's voices, the note of both shock and thrill. Sick with certainty he went to look.

The children had pulled her out from the garbage and laid her on the ground. Paul shoved them aside and knelt. There was light from a stall near by, but the shadows of the jostling children covered her and he could barely see. Touch told him that her face was all drying blood, her eyes glued tight so that he couldn't lift the lids. There seemed to be no pulse or breath. He slid his arms beneath her thighs and shoulders and with the children's help staggered to his feet.

'Bring my basket. Two gurai,' he said and lurched towards the market. It was no use. She must be dead.

It is my doing, he thought. *Mine and my mother's. It is because I sent her with the message. It is because I used my gun. It is because I remembered her and saw the burning hut. My mother didn't like that. She's a jealous bitch. She wants me for herself, alone. Soon as I'm learning to love someone else...*

His right arm was slipping from its hold. With an effort he shrugged Jilli's body into a new position. At the jar of movement he thought he heard her moan.

From *AK* by Peter Dickinson

BOYS AND GIRLS

East Timor remained Portuguese until 1976, when it was annexed by Indonesia. Its first free elections were held in 1999. This story tells of how the population lived under violent oppression and feared what lay ahead.

We've all seen
in books, newspapers, at the cinema, on television
pictures of girls and boys
defending freedom with guns in their hands.

We've all seen
in books, newspapers, at the cinema, on television
pictures of the corpses of girls and boys
who died defending freedom with guns in their hands.

We've all seen it!
And so?

From *Primeiro livro de poesia*
by Fernando Silvan

THE BRIDEGROOM

Eight writers from former Yugoslavia and eight writers from The Netherlands and Belgium struck up a friendship and together they wrote stories and poems. The Bridegroom is about a boy who flees the war in Bosnia with his mother.

'If the country I lived in had been on fire, I would be amazed to see stories come flying into my room. Some kind of flutter from another world. I'd be flummoxed, to say the least. Maybe I would have forgotten that there are other countries too, thinking of my own country only. This had better be a good story, in other words.

Alem was in the second year of primary school when the war started, not just started, but broke out – and when war breaks out, it shoots at everything, at people and buildings, it sets houses and trees on fire and poisons the water. War incites people to defend themselves tooth and nail. It incites them to flee, to hide, to shriek. It makes people die before their time.

Aunt Biba occasionally told people's fortunes in the shelter, by the light of an oil lamp, since war also makes electric light go out.

Everybody wanted Biba to tell them whether or not they would survive. Biba said: 'I'm not God! That sort of information is not on my cards. I will only read the fortunes of people who are interested in love. You must all tell me honestly what you wish to know. About love and devotion, I mean.'

That's what Biba said. Any old excuse was used by those who wanted to have their fortunes told, but all they were really interested in was whether or not they and their loved ones would survive the war.

Alem asked Biba to check if one day he'd be happily married and if his wife would be beautiful.

Biba looked at him and said 'Look at you, just look at you, barely the size of a hare, and you're talking marriage already!'

'Aunt Biba,' Alem said, 'Please. I must know. I so want to have a beautiful wife.'

'If you insist, sweetheart,' Biba sighed and she started arranging the cards. Alem looked at the cards, wide-eyed, as if he was a specialist himself.

Biba told him: 'Your mother will find you a beautiful girl whom you'll marry. You're going to live abroad. And have lots of children.'

Alem was over the moon much to the amusement of the people in the shelter.

He said to himself: Since I'm going to have children, I'm also going to grow up to be an adult. I'll continue to live. I'll survive. I'll live on. And play football...

He's been nicknamed bridegroom ever since.

'My own little bridegroom...', his mother teased him about it. A few days later his grandad was killed. He was on his bike when a mine exploded near him. The blast knocked him off the bike. Potatoes – he'd brought a basketful along for his grandchildren – were found all around his body.

When Alem's mother heard the news, she decided she'd get the children out of this hell. War is hell on earth, that is a fact.

Mother occasionally left Alem and his brother Amir on their own in the shelter. Then she visited all sorts of offices and asked for permission to take the children to a place where there was no killing.

Alem and Amir would sit waiting, ears pricked. They wondered whether their mother had been successful at all. They begged God not to let her be hit by a bullet. After a few months they finally got their papers to go abroad.

They went by bus. Shots could be heard, and exploding mines. The shooting eventually stopped. They were in unoccupied territory. They rode on, tired and sleepy.

A shiny and glistening thing suddenly loomed: a tall, very tall princess was coming towards Alem. She was as beautiful as his mother. Her hand came out from under her transparent, white veil and caressed his hair: 'You're my favourite. Here's a golden ball for you. We'll muster up an entire team for you, with the best players and all. You will play matches in all the stadiums of the world. You'll always win.'

'I'd rather have an ordinary ball, Princess, like the one me and my friend Marco used to play with. We even played inside his flat, under the painting of Jesus, which I kept staring at, for fear we might break something. Mario winked at me and at Jesus. Mario was killed when his mother took him to the doctor to be examined. He had this terrible cough. Please, Princess, do make him alive again. He was my best playing partner.'

Alem looked at the sky; where a huge flying carpet slowly started moving. It was packed with people.

'Who are you?' he asked when he realized he was flying too.

'We're the inhabitants of an occupied town. Your town.'

Alem took a closer look and spotted his friend Marco on the outer edge...

'Alem, Alem,' his mother shouted. This was where they changed buses. To cross yet another border...

From *Never Trust a Dragon: Stories and poems by writers from the Netherlands and former Yugoslavia*

THE SACK OF *NOUDAY*

Fernão Mendes Pinto must have had an elephantine memory. His book, The Travels of Mendes Pinto *(published in 1614), was written after more than twenty years on the go 'during which I was imprisoned thirteen times and sold seventeen times, in regions stretching from India, Ethiopia, Arabia Felix, Tartary, Makassar, over Sumatra and many provinces of the Eastern archipelago in outer Asia'. He was commonly referred to as Fernão Mendes Minto (=the liar), since his adventures sounded too fantastic to be true.*

The following morning, shortly before daybreak, António de Faria sailed up the river with the three junks, the *lorcha*, and the four fishing barges he had seized, and dropped anchor in six and a half fathoms of water right up against the walls of the city. Dispensing with the noisy salvo of artillery, he lowered the sails and hoisted the flag of commerce in keeping with Chinese custom, intent upon observing all the outward signs of peace and leaving nothing undone by way of complying with the formalities, though he knew full well, from the way matters stood with the mandarin, that it would do him no good.

From here he sent him another letter which was extremely polite and friendly in tone, offering to raise the ransom for the captives; but it made that dog of a mandarin so angry, that he had the poor Chinese messenger crucified on an X-shaped cross and exhibited from the top of the wall in full view of the fleet. The sight was enough to make António de Faria abandon the last shred of hope to which some of the men still made him cling, and at the same time, it made the soldiers so furious that they told him that, as long as he had decided to go ashore, there was no point in his waiting any longer because he would just be giving the enemies time to increase their strength.

Since this seemed like good advice to him, he embarked immediately with all the men who were determined to go ashore, leaving orders behind for the junks to direct a steady barrage of fire against the enemies and the city, wherever major gatherings were to be seen, provided he was not engaged in battle with them. And after disembarking at a spot about a culverin-shot's distance below the roadstead, without encountering the slightest opposition, he marched along the shore in the direction of the city where, by this time, many people were stationed on top of the walls, waving an enormous number of silk banners, trying to put on a brave show by shouting and playing their martial music and generally carrying on like people who put more stock in words and outward appearances than in actual deeds.

As our men came within a musket-shot's distance of the moat surrounding the wall, about 1,000 to 1,200 soldiers – a guess hazarded by some – sallied forth from two gates; and of this number, about 100 to 120 were mounted on horseback, or to put it in a better way, they were mounted on some rather sorry-looking nags. They began by putting on a fine show of skirmishing, running back and forth just as free and easy as you please, getting in each other's way most of the time, and often colliding and falling down in heaps of three and four, from which it was obvious that they were country bumpkins who were there not so much out of a desire to fight, but because they had been forced to come.

António de Faria gaily spurred his men on, and after signalling to the junks, he waited for the enemy out in the field, for he thought that they would want to engage him there, judging by the brave show they were putting on. But instead, they went right on with their skirmishing, running around in circles for a while, as though they were threshing wheat, thinking that this alone would be enough to scare us off. However, when they saw that we would not turn tail and run as they thought or probably hoped we would, they got together in a huddle and remained that way for a while, in a single body, in great disorder, without coming any closer.

Seeing them that way, our captain ordered all the muskets, which had been silent until then, to fire at once; and, as God willed, they hit the mark so well that more than half of the cavalrymen, who were in the vanguard, were knocked to the ground. Off to a good start, we rushed at them all together, calling on the name of Jesus as we went; and he, in his mercy, caused the enemy to abandon the field to us and sent them fleeing so wildly that they were falling on top of each other; and when they reached the bridge spanning the moat, they got themselves jammed in there so tightly that they were unable to move either backward or forward.

At this juncture, the main body of our men caught up to them and handled them so efficiently that, before long, more than three hundred of them were lying on top of each other – a pitiful sight indeed – for not a single one of them ever drew a sword.

Exhilarated by this victory, we made a dash for the gate, and there in the entrance we found the mandarin, surrounded by nearly six hundred men, mounted astride a fine horse, wearing an old-fashioned gilt studded breastplate of purple velvet, which we found out later had belonged to a certain Tomé Pires, whom King Manuel, of glorious memory, had sent as an ambassador to China on board Fernão Peres de Andrade's *nao* in the days when Lopo Soares de Albergaria was governing the State of India.

The mandarin and his men tried to stop us at the entrance, where a cruel battle ensued, during which, little by little, in the time it would take to recite four or five Credos, they began to drive us back with a lot less fear than the ones on the bridge had shown, and they would have given us a difficult time had it not been for one of our slave boys who knocked the mandarin off his horse with a musket ball that struck him right in the chest. At that, the Chinese became so frightened that they all spun around immediately and began retreating through the gates in complete disorder, and we along with them, knocking them down with our lances, while not a single one of them had enough presence of mind to shut the gates. And off we went, chasing them before us like cattle, down a very long road, until at last they swept through another gate that led to the forest where every last one of them disappeared from sight.

Next, to prevent disorder, António de Faria gathered his soldiers together and, in a single corps, marched with them straight to the *chifanga*; which was the prison where they were holding our men, who at the sight of us let out such a loud and terrifying cry of "Lord God, have mercy on us!" that it was enough to send the shivers down one's spine. He immediately had the prison doors and bars broken with axes, a task that our men threw themselves into with such great enthusiasm that it took but a moment to smash everything to bits and to remove the prisoners' shackles, so that in a very short time, all our companions were unfettered and free.

The order was given to our soldiers and the others in our company that each man was to lay hold of as much as he could for himself, because there would be no sharing of the spoils, and everyone was to keep whatever he could carry; but he asked them to be quick about it, for he would allow them no more than the brief space of half an hour in which to do it. And they all answered that they would be perfectly satisfied with that.

And then they all disappeared into the houses, while António de Faria headed straight for the mandarin's, which he had staked out for himself, and there he found eight thousand taels in silver alone, as well as five huge jars of musk, all of which he had gathered up. The rest, which he left for the slaves accompanying him, consisted of large quantities of silk, yarn, satin, damask, and fine-quality porce-

lain packed in straw, which they carried until they were ready to collapse.

As a result, the four barges and three sampans that had been used
as landing craft had to make four trips to transfer the loot to the
junks, and there was not a slave or sailor among them who did not
speak of his booty in terms of whole cases and bales of piece goods,
to say nothing of the secrets each one kept locked in his heart.

When he saw that more than an hour and a half had gone by,
António de Faria quickly ordered the men to return to the ships, but
there was absolutely no way of getting them to stop their looting, and
this was especially true of the men of most account. But with night
coming on, he was afraid some disaster might befall them, and he
had the torch put to the city in ten or twelve different places; and
since most of the buildings were constructed of pine and other
woods, the fire spread so fiercely that in less than a quarter of an
hour it looked like a blazing inferno.

Withdrawing to the beach with all the men, he embarked, with not
a murmur of protest from any of them, for they were all leaving very
rich and happy; and they had many pretty girls in tow, which was
really pathetic to see, for they were tied up with musket wicks by
fours and fives, and they were all crying while our men were laughing and singing.

From *The Travels of Mendes Pinto* by Fernão Mendes Pinto.

THE NUREMBERG RAID

*In this very funny yet very serious novel Conrad is a young boy
living in post-war Britain who is enchanted by the daring exploits
of fighter pilots in the Second World War. Conrad has two levels of
experience: in one he is a real young boy who goes to school and
feels a lot of contempt for his father, also known in the story as the
Great Writer because he is a playwright; but in his imagined
experience Conrad is a Great Aviator, flying a Lancaster bomber*

on a raid to Nuremberg in Germany. The plane is uncannily like
Conrad's plastic airfix models which he had glued together less
than perfectly. His navigator is a plastic figure who has no legs,
and the rear gunner turns out to be Conrad's father. Towzer the dog
has also come along for the ride. Although this scene is very funny,
Conrad's imagined bombing raid is realistic enough to make him
think about what it must really have been like to fly on bombing
raids at night.

The war was extremely cold, dark, uncomfortable and bumpy, and
it was making Conrad feel sick. This was one thing those stupid war
comics left out entirely, he thought to himself as he clung to the controls of the great clumsy bomber as it thundered through the night.
There were draughts everywhere, every piece of metal he touched
was so freezingly cold he was afraid his skin would come off on it.
Even though his leather flying jacket came up to his ears, and his flying boots almost up to his knees, he was teeth-rattling cold; it was
worse than football in the January sleet with Mr Hopkins.
'I thought aeroplanes were supposed to fly straight and steady,' he
shouted to his navigator over the howl of the engines. 'That's what
they look like from down below. This thing is like a Donkey Derby.'
Conrad was not exaggerating. The plane seemed to proceed in a
series of lurches, then suddenly drop what seemed the height of a
house, lurch again, and only a heavy dose of throttle would get it to
stagger along again.
   'I said it's like a Donkey Derby' he shouted again. The navigator
made no reply. Strong silent type. Conrad sneaked a look at him as
he sat there like a plastic dummy staring straight in front of him as if
he'd just been knocked out. 'You know,' said Conrad, 'you remind me
of my Dad, you do.' Silence from the navigator. 'You remind me *very*
strongly indeed of my Dad,' said Conrad. The navigator was not pro-
voked.
   Conrad peered into the darkness, a great aviator concentrating on
his task. They were supposed to be flying in close formation, which
was a) safer, b) more devastating in attack, c) looked smart on the
photos. Just like all the school getting up and sitting down at the

same moment instead of all higgledy piggledy, the way they liked to do it. The only trouble was that Conrad didn't know whether he was flying in close formation or not because it was too dark to see any other planes. He had a prescribed height to keep to, but what with all this lurching about it was quite likely that he'd drop on someone's head at any moment, or vice versa. Or run into the back of someone, or have someone run into the back of him. On the whole Conrad hoped that he was not flying in close formation, and that there were no planes within miles. Why didn't the books mention how difficult it was to see through the dark? When he got back he would certainly have something to say to Harris about it.

'Harris!' he would shout. 'You have no sympathy or consideration!'

Harris would shuffle and mutter and go red.

'Like to see you fly one of your Lancasters in the dark and the cold,' he'd say. 'Anyway you'd be too *fat* to get in the *cockpit!*'

Harris would cringe and apologise and promise to do better next time.

'Not good enough!' Conrad would shout. Yes, he'd certainly have a good time telling Harris off when he got back. He'd tell him about the navigator too.

'Worse than sitting next to Nigel Creamer!' he'd say. 'Just sat there like a dummy all the time! I've seen better navigators in Airfix kits!'

The Lancaster lurched again and the navigator slipped sideways.

'What's the matter with you then?' said Conrad. 'Gone to sleep?'

'You're supposed to be navigating this plane, can't do everything myself, can I?' The navigator didn't answer. He was leaning over at a funny angle. For a second Conrad thought he might have been shot. Then he took a close look at his navigator. The man's face was grey and expressionless. Somewhere Conrad had seen that face before. A dummy in a shop window? He gave the man a shove. He felt light and hollow and he rattled.

Funny sort of navigator.

'Hey, Harris,' he'd say. 'You've given me a dud navigator. He rattles.'

Conrad looked again. The navigator was in worse shape than he thought. Not only was he hollow and he rattled, but his legs only went down to the knee. This was definitely not good enough for combat aircrew. Then Conrad realised what had happened. His navigator had come out of an Airfix kit. Well: a plastic navigator was no good. He gave the grey expressionless gentleman a good kick to relieve his feelings and the hollow man shot out of his seat and tumbled over and over towards the dark cavern at the back of the plane.

'Oy,' said a strangely familiar voice. 'Steady on, Conrad. You're disturbing my train of thought. I was trying to do a bit of Yoga meditation back here.'

Oh, no. It couldn't be true. The rear gunner was his Dad. Conrad was lumbered not only with a useless hollow plastic navigator but a dozy writer of soppy plays to man the guns and shoot the nightfighters out of the sky. Shoot the nightfighters? His Dad couldn't even hit his pop posters at six feet with a set of darts. What sort of op was this going to be, Conrad asked himself. Good job somebody knew what was going on anyway. Conrad was going to have to run the whole show himself. As usual.

'It's not *time* for Yoga breathing!' he shouted. 'You're supposed to be looking out for Messerschmitts.'

'What do they look like?' called the great writer.

'They've got twin engines. Anything with twin engines is one of theirs.'

Fancy not knowing what a Messerschmitt looked like.

'What do I do when I see one?' shouted the great writer after a typically long pause.

'Blast it out of the sky!' What did he think you did with Messerschmitts? Ask them over for a drink? Another long pause. Doubtless the rusty brains were turning in the rear turret.

'But I can't stand violence.'

'Well you're going to have to get some in, aren't you?' shouted Flying Officer Conrad Pike. 'We all have to do things we don't like doing. I have to go to school and have my brain rotted in the classroom and play football in the sleet till I get pneumonia. The least you could do is blast a few Messerschmitts out of the sky!'

'Well, I'm afraid I can't see anything, Conrad,' said his Dad in a suitably humble voice.

'All right,' said Conrad. 'Just keep a look out and don't go into any of your trances.'

Conrad couldn't see anything either. They had been flying through thick cloud all the way. The Met Office had been dead right. They had said there would either be ten-tenths cloud cover, or alternatively a clear sky and a following wind. They had to be right one way or the other. Seemed like a nice easy job, doing weather forecasts. They couldn't give you a forecast for a bombing raid any more than they could tell you whether it would rain enough to get you out of football. Daft twits.

But Conrad had to admit it, it had been a picnic so far. A milk run. They might have been totally alone in the sky, no other plane in the universe, no ground below, no sky above. Just Conrad and his Dad and the plastic navigator, skidding and lurching through cloudy blackness in the huge roaring draughty cavernous Lanc with its load of blockbusters for Nuremberg.

The plane gave another lurch. A big one. Conrad checked his dials. One of the port engines was feathering. It would run fast, then hesitate for a split second, then feather round slowly, then pick up again. As if it was catching on something that was clogging it. Conrad felt a nasty cold feeling creep up his legs into his stomach. Something clogging it? Something, maybe, like polyurethane cement? If the navigator was made of hollow plastic, and the port engine was feathering, could it be that the Lanc he was flying was some sort of full-sized version of the less than perfect Airfix model he slept with every night? Conrad fervently hoped not. As a model kit it passed muster all right, but as a combat aircraft – well, he wished he'd spent a bit more time on some of the details. He had rather a nasty apprehensive feeling about the bomb bays. They had been one of the trickiest parts of the kit, and in the finish Conrad had got fed up with them and jammed them in anyhow, using more cement than was strictly desirable. They were probably jammed solid.

No. It couldn't be. That Lanc would never fly. It was just a coincidence. Conrad was in charge, the great aviator was at the controls, everything was responding perfectly except that port engine, and Conrad would pull them through. He forced the cold feeling down, out of his belly, down through his legs and out through his flying boots. He felt strong and capable and proud of himself. Conrad the invincible.

Something was touching his ear. Was it his fur collar? It tickled. He put his hand up and felt something damp and cold. Like a dog's nose. He jerked his head round.

'Towzer' he said. 'What d'you think you're doing here?' Towzer wagged his tail. He seemed to be quite pleased to be on the Nuremberg raid, and sniffed all the instruments with keen interest. 'Well, I don't know,' said Conrad. 'This is going to look pretty funny in the official histories of World War II.'

Towzer looked as if he didn't give a damn. He sat in the navigator's seat and had a good scratch. Conrad reached in his pack for the emergency rations and gave Towzer and himself a bit of chocolate. Towzer swallowed his bit with the speed of light and barked for more. 'No,' said the aviator firmly. 'This has got to last us to Nuremberg and back.' Towzer flopped his heavy warm body across Conrad's legs and began to settle himself for sleep. Conrad tried to push him off but Towzer exercised passive resistance. Conrad gave up and let him stay. It was against Air Force regulations to take a dog on a mission, and a violation of safety regulations to let him sleep on your legs, but Conrad felt prepared to take responsibility. Towzer's rich doggy smell began to take over the cockpit and make it snug and safe.

Suddenly the cloud cleared. Conrad stared through the windscreen and saw the sky full of aircraft. They had all been there all the time. Up above on the port bow were the vapour trails of two Halifaxes, and over on the right, too close for comfort, was another Lanc. Conrad could even read the identification markings. Far above and ahead and all around the night sky unrolled like an enormous dark blue bedspread studded with stars. It was an amazing sight; hundreds and hundreds of heavy bombers in the dark night sky.

Not dark enough. Not dark enough for safety. They were into the second half of the Met Office's brilliant forecast: clear skies and a following wind. Just what they didn't need, now they were over occupied territory. Now the German fighter pilots would be getting into their planes, the nightfighters which were faster, more manoeuverable, and had more powerful and longer range cannons than the lumbering Lancasters. In a few minutes, maybe less, they would be weaving in and out of the squadrons, picking out targets at their leisure. Conrad suddenly recalled the shooting booth at the fair. A long row of battered metal ducks flew with the speed and panache of a snail's funeral from left to right across a black background. You lined your gun up, and waited for one to cross your sights. There was plenty of time to squeeze the trigger slowly. Even Conrad's Dad had hit one or two. That's what they would look like to the Messerschmitts, Conrad thought. The ducks would clang over backwards and disappear from view. He didn't want to clang over backwards and disappear from view. He wasn't frightened yet, but he felt angry and cheated. Wars should be fair. It wasn't right for one side to be like the ducks and the other side like the customers.

'Plane coming up behind!' The voice came from the fat writer. So his Dad had stayed awake.

'What sort of plane?'

'Four engines.'

'Don't shoot!' yelled Conrad. The next second a huge dark shape passed right overhead and veered away to the right. A Halifax going out of control with smoke coming out of its port wing.

The nightfighters had got up amongst them already. Conrad and Towzer scanned the sky from left to right. No Messerschmitts to be seen. But far off to the left the sky lit up as flames burst from another Halifax and Conrad leaned over to see it spinning down through the flak, with tiny figures leaping out of the cockpit, the parachutes blossoming like puffballs.

'Log it,' said Conrad to Towzer, just to see what he'd do, and Towzer gave a gruff low bark.

Bombers were going down all over the sky, a few running straight into the box barrage aimed at random from the ground, but most falling to the invisible nightfighters. On a clear night, Conrad knew, the Messerschmitts would come from the left low down, fire for the port engines, and veer away at the last minute and avoid the flying debris. He'd be lucky to see one before he was hit. If the fat gunner got one in his sights it would probably be too late. Conrad flew steadily on. There was no point in trying to avoid the box barrage. You just had to put your nose down and go straight on. They had been lucky so far; they ought to be on target soon.

Suddenly Towzer started to yelp hysterically, as if he'd seen a cat in the garden. Conrad glimpsed something out of the corner of his eye and pulled the Lancaster into a steep dive to starboard. A black shape hurded across their bows from right to left and Towzer flung himself against the perspex as if he thought he could take the Messerschmitt by the scruff of the neck and shake it. Conrad caught a glimpse of two startled faces. Then it was gone and a split second later he heard the sounds of their own machine gun.

'Missed it,' came the apologetic voice of the great writer in the gun turret. Towzer growled and grumbled to himself and settled down in his seat.

In a German plane a white faced German pilot turned to his white faced German friend.

'Donner und Blitzen! Ein Hund in dem Lancaster!' With shaky hands he returned to base for a medical checkup.

The sky was empty now, though Conrad could see flak ahead, hurtling up and exploding uselessly in the black emptiness. He had no idea where he was; dogs and plastic Airfix men were not to be relied on for accurate navigation. Still, he'd drop his blockbusters somewhere, and he hoped he was over Germany.

Then he saw the flares, failing in vivid cascades of dazzling red and swinging gently under their parachutes like Christmas trees on fire. They were beautiful. They were better than anything he'd seen on Guy Fawkes night, they were like dream fireworks. Towzer stretched his neck and looked down with mild interest. He had never been one for fireworks himself. But Conrad was thrilled to the marrow. Not just because of the firework display.

He knew that the flares meant something. They were over target! Somehow he had piloted the cranky old Lanc all the way to

Nuremberg. There was something he had to say and just as he was wondering what it was he heard his own voice, crisp and curt like the pilots in the films.

'Bombs away!'

'Eh?' said the voice from the back.

'Bombs away, I said!'

'What am I supposed to do, then?'

'Can you see the drift handle on the bombsight?'

'Um... ummm... oh yes, there's some sort of handle here, Conrad.'

'Push it forward!'

'Can I go back to my turret now?'

'NO!' yelled Conrad. 'Slap down the selector switches!'

'How do I know what a selector switch is?' came the mournful voice.

Had there ever been such a dozy bomb aimer? They'd be back over England before they dropped their blockbusters.

'Slap down all the switches you can see then!'

'Switches all slapped down, sir!'

There was a long pause. Then the great writer said, 'I'm feeling a bit sick, Conrad. Can I go back to my little turret thing?'

'No!' screeched Conrad. Why hadn't the doors opened? What had gone wrong? Those bombs should be plummeting down now. It wasn't fair. But deep inside he knew what was wrong. Too much glue again.

'You're going to have to jump up and down on the doors,' he said.

'You must be joking, Conrad.'

'Jump!'

'But I'm not an active man, Conrad.'

'Jump! Those bombs are fused now; d'you want them to go off in the plane?'

'No, Conrad.'

'Shut up and jump then.'

The fat bomb aimer, shortsighted rear gunner, and self styled greatest writer in the world shut up and jumped.

'Nothing's happened, Conrad!'

'Jump again!'

The plane vibrated to the repeated clanging as the fat writer bounced on the bomb doors, puffing and wheezing. BONG *wheeze* Bong *wheeze* BONG BONG cough cough cough *wheeze* bong BONG BONG!

There was a sudden rush of air, a shrill squeal, the red light went on, and a great surge of power as the Lancaster, free of its load of bombs, leapt forward joyfully. Towzer yelped and whined and jumped on to Conrad's knees.

They had done it! They had bombed Nuremberg!

'Conrad!'

'What now?'

'I'm afraid I've got stuck, Conrad!'

Conrad turned.

The great writer was wedged in the bomb bay with his legs dangling in the slipstream. Somewhere down below his boots were on their way down to enemy territory, a fiendish new weapon in the Allied armoury.

Conrad gnashed his teeth.

'Can't you do *anything* right?'

'I'm sorry, Conrad. You know war's not really my thing. Er...d'you think you could get me out?'

Conrad wedged the controls and handed them over to Towzer, who sat in the pilot's seat staring ahead with a pleasing air of grim concentration. Back in the belly of the plane the plastic navigator was whirling around in the gale like a drunken gymnast.

It was a tricky situation, but Conrad felt capable of anything now. He held on to the guard rail to avoid being sucked out himself, and felt the mighty power surge into his muscles as it had done on the night of the tank. He grabbed his Dad's arm and pulled.

'We'll never make it, Conrad. Oh dear, this is terrible.'

'Push with your other hand,' snapped the mighty aviator.

'You know, you should be glad you're so greedy. You're just slightly fatter round the waist than a blockbuster.'

'This is no time for personal remarks,' said his Dad. Conrad shut his eyes and heaved, and with a slow sucking noise the great writer came out of the bomb bay and whirled about the plane with the plastic navigator like a couple of mad Apache dancers. Conrad pulled the lever twice, the bomb doors creaked shut, and the mad Apache dancers subsided and rolled gently to and fro on the floor of the plane. Conrad's Dad looked in some distress, but the plastic navigator seemed unmoved by his experience. The roar of the engines seemed like silence after the howling of the gale.

'I've got all glue on my uniform,' said the writer.

Conrad said nothing but thought: if I hadn't used too much cement my Dad would have bombed Nuremberg in person. Conrad didn't feel strong any more. He felt weak and shaky.

'Hey. Thanks very much,' said his Dad. 'You saved my life then, you know.'

'That's all right,' said Conrad. He felt a bit like crying, he didn't know why. He wanted to be home in bed; he wanted to leak back.

He made his way back to the pilot's seat and relieved Towzer at the controls. He read the flickering instruments and turned the great lumbering bomber on its homeward route.

The sky was dark and empty again after the Christmas trees of Nuremberg. The great plane buzzed slowly through the empty sky; the wind was against them now.

Nuremberg, Nuremberg. They had bombed Nuremberg and now they were coming home. Conrad felt very tired. Nuremberg, he thought. A city bigger than Edinburgh, smaller than Leeds. His Gran lived in Leeds. He thought of bombers, German bombers bombing Leeds. German bombs crashing through his Gran's roof. She wouldn't know what was happening. They wouldn't be aiming for his Gran, but they might hit her all the same. Stop thinking, he said to himself, but he couldn't help it. There had to be grandmothers in Nuremberg too; Conrad wasn't stupid. Had one of his bombs fallen through someone's gran's roof? It was a bad thought, and it wouldn't go away. How did bomber pilots stop themselves from thinking bad thoughts on the slow journey home through the quiet empty sky? He reached for Towzer and sank his hand into the comforting warm fur.

'Plane coming up behind!' It was the great writer.

Conrad didn't have time to do anything. A burst of cannon fire-crashed into the wing of the Lancaster from the unseen Messerschmitt. Then they were alone again, left by the nightfighter to struggle and crash. Conrad checked the controls. The oil pressure was falling rapidly on the one good port engine, which was rapidly overheating. If he didn't shut it down, he'd have a fire on his hands. He pulled the feathering toggle and leaned out to watch it splutter to a halt. They were losing height already, at the rate of five hundred feet a minute. They weren't going to get back. They had bought it.

'Get your parachute on Dad,' he said.

'We're going to have to jump.'

'Oh no,' said his Dad. 'Do we have to?'

'You'll like it,' said Conrad. 'People pay money to do it. It's a healthy hobby Dad.'

'Oh, leave off,' moaned his Dad, struggling to get the straps round his fat body. 'Bags I go first.'

'You are first,' said Conrad. 'We've got to jettison the heavy stuff first, and you're the heaviest stuff here.'

'But I don't speak German. Can't we wait till we get to France?'

'You'll soon pick it up,' said Conrad. To his surprise, he felt quite wide awake and cheerful again. 'Open the emergency door.'

'Right,' said his Dad. 'Er, what do I do?'

'Well, you sort of jump out of the plane,' said Conrad in a sarcastic voice.

'I was afraid it might be something like that,' said the great writer. 'Then what?'

'You count up to five slowly and pull.'

'Well, I can do that all right, I think.'

'Get on and do it then,' said Conrad.

'Right. Right,' said his Dad. 'See you later then.'

'Right,' said Conrad.

'Right,' said his Dad. 'Right, I'll just, er... I'll just do it now, shall I? Just sort of leap bravely out, eh?'

'YES!!!' howled the exasperated pilot.

'Right, okay then,' said the writer. Conrad turned and saw his Dad leaning gingerly out.

'I didn't really much fancy the look of it down – waaaagh!' Conrad's Dad had made his first parachute jump.

The plane leapt forwards as the great weight departed, but was soon losing height again. Conrad scrabbled under the seat. One parachute. He scrabbled under the navigator's seat for a parachute for Towzer. And found a moulded grey plastic model of a parachute.

'Oh, Towzer,' he said.

Towzer whined and nuzzled him. Conrad couldn't stand it. He thrust the protesting hairy legs through the straps of his own parachute and tightened them.

'You look like a bundle of old washing, Towzer' he said. Towzer looked seriously alarmed, much as he did when trapped in the kitchen with an imminent bath in store for him.

'It's not a bath, Towzer,' said Conrad. 'It's more a sort of a walk.'

Towzer pricked up his ears and wagged his tail. Before he could do anything else Conrad shoved him through the door and with a startled yelp Towzer shot out into the night.

Conrad was alone in the plane with nothing but a plastic model parachute, losing height with every second. He might never see his Dad or his Towzer again. He didn't know whether he was over the town or the country, land or water; he didn't know whether there was any chance of surviving a crash landing. He didn't know anything and it wasn't fair. The war was asking too much of him. He was only a boy.

He peered ahead. Pitch black. Nothing to be seen below. But he must be near the ground now. It would all be over soon. If he died in the crash, did that mean he'd be stuck forever in the war, an unknown casualty, and never leak back into his own world of Parkin and Creamer and the Airfix models? If he died in the crash, maybe he would leak back dead, be found in his bed stone cold with dreadful and mysterious fatal injuries. Well: somebody would be finding out soon.

He checked his instruments. Five hundred feet. He switched on the landing lights. Amazingly, they worked, and he saw the ground heaving and swaying in front of him. He had almost no control of the plane now; its strange lurches had no connection with the way he wrenched the control column to and fro. He saw sky. He saw an upside down river. He saw a forest standing on its side. He saw cloud, or was it snow? He saw sky again. He saw a road. He saw a snow-covered field, the right way up, rushing towards him at murderous speed. Height twenty feet. Ground speed a hundred miles an hour. He cut the engines and shut his eyes.

The jarring crash roared into his ears. He felt as if he'd been hammered into a dentist's chair with a pile-driver. He felt crushed all over, as if the whole world was trying to crash its way into his body. The roaring in his ears grew louder and louder and suddenly he was floating on a sea of darkness, weightless, beyond space, beyond time. Floating through the dark endless universe. He didn't know where he was or when he was or who he was. Then the blackness seeped round him like a big black glove and he lost consciousness.

From *Conrad's War* by Andrew Davies

THE DYING AIRMAN

This grimly humorous poem has echoes of Conrad with his Airfix model aeroplanes in the preceding extract

A handsome young airman lay dying,
And as on the aerodrome he lay,
To the mechanics who round him came sighing,
These last dying words he did say:

'Take the cylinders out of my kidneys,
The connecting-rod out of my brain,
Take the cam-shaft from out of my backbone,
And assemble the engine again.'

Anon

THE ENGLISH PILOT

Michiel is going on sixteen and is the eldest son of a country village burgomaster. His father is taken hostage and executed by a firing-squad. Michiel finds out how difficult it is to suss out close acquaintances. Dirk, the neighbours' son, asks him to deliver a letter to Bertus Hardhorend should a raid on a distribution centre fail. As it turns out, the attackers are ambushed by the Germans and Bertus is taken prisoner. From that moment on, Michiel becomes responsible for an English pilot who has been shot and who is hiding in a cave in the woods.

Michiel read the letter three times. Then he tore it up into tiny pieces and buried them. He suddenly felt very calm, in spite of the tight knot in the pit of his stomach. He was going to harbour an English pilot, a crime punishable by death. The only question was, how much had Dirk said? As little as possible, he was sure. Perhaps he had only mentioned Bertus's name and kept Michiel's secret. He would have to sneak home and find out if the Germans had been looking for him. But it was too early for that. He must first go to the pilot. He might not have eaten for two days. Where could he get food for him? At home? That would be unwise. Van de Werf lived near by and Michiel was popular there, so he got on his bike.

Mrs Van de Werf was busy cleaning the baking-house. They had been living in it all summer, but now that the weather was turning cold, they had moved into the kitchen and the baking-house had to be cleaned out.

'Morning, Michiel,' said Mrs Van de Werf.

'Good morning, Mrs Van de Werf. Fine weather today.'

'You're right about that. My word, you've grown! Take care the Boche don't take you off to work in Germany. How old are you?'

'Nearly sixteen.'

'Well, they took my brother's son in Oosterwolde last week. He was working in a factory. True, he was seventeen, but... you know, they take them younger every day.'

'I'll lie low.'

'What did you want? Something to eat?'

'Well, if possible.'

'And what would you like?'

'A piece of ham, if that's not asking too much?'

'Well, as it's you...'

They went into the house together. Hanging in the chimney were two big hams, and bacon and sausages. Mrs Van de Werf took a ham off the hook and sliced off a fair-sized piece.

'Here you are.'

'Thanks ever so much, Mrs Van de Werf.' Michiel paid and started to go.

'Wouldn't you like a nice piece of my bread-and-cheese?'

'Oh, yes, please!'

The woman cut a slice off a big round loaf which she held against her chest, put butter and cheese on it and handed it to Michiel. It was a meal in itself. Anyone from a big city would have been glad to pay a pound for it.

'Thanks, I'll eat it on my way home,' Michiel said. 'I must run now.'

'Off you go, then, boy.'

Once out of sight, Michiel opened the wrapping around the ham and put the bread-and-cheese in it as well. Then he went off towards Dagdaler Wood.

He found the north-east square without difficulty. Making quite sure that no one had seen him, he hid his bicycle some way off, for he had to go under the bushes. He made his way on foot for the last half-mile. The wood was silent, the autumn sun shone through the trees, and the silence was only broken by birds singing.

Michiel looked carefully around as he approached the young plantation. The young trees were so closely packed together that he could see no way through them. How on earth was he to get to the hide-out? Then he noticed that, close to the ground, there were fewer branches. He could crawl. It was hard work and his face and arms were scratched by the prickly branches. Every so often, he stood upright to see where he was and to check that he was still alone. At last, he was near the middle, but where was the hide-out? He struggled on trying not to make a noise, though he could not help snapping some small twigs.

'Don't move!'

Startled, Michiel stood frozen. The voice was very close. Lowering his own voice, he said, 'Friend.' Why he said that he didn't know. Perhaps he had read it somewhere. No, it was what Jannechin said to her dog!

'Who are you?'

He knew what that meant, from his English lessons at school.

'Dirk's friend,' he said.

'Where is Dirk?'

'In prison.'

'Come closer,' the Englishman demanded, and Michiel obeyed by crawling closer to the voice. Now he could see narrow steps going down. A young man, about twenty years old, was standing at the side of the entrance. Part of the trouser-legs of his uniform had been cut off to accommodate the plaster. His right arm was in a sling and his jacket was draped over his shoulders. He had a thick beard. In his left hand he held a gun. He gestured to Michiel to come down.

It was very dark inside, but once Michiel's eyes were accustomed to it, he saw how the hide-out was constructed. A broad, deep hole had been made and small tree-trunks supported the sides. A large wooden door, or something of the sort, formed the ceiling or roof. This was covered with earth. The little trees planted on this were scraggly. Perhaps there was too little earth for them. The hide-out was about ten feet long and six feet wide. Dirk had made a good job of it, but to stay in it day and night with a broken leg! In one corner was a heap of dry leaves and two plain blankets. Michiel also saw a bottle, a cup, and an old woollen shawl. That was all. Good heavens, to think this man had been here for weeks!

They started to talk with difficulty. The pilot realized that he had to speak very slowly and Michiel searched his memory to find the words he had learned at school. And they managed to communicate. The pilot was called Jack and was happy to have somebody to talk to, because with Dirk, who had never done languages at school, conversation had been even more limited. When he heard that Dirk had

been caught and might have started talking, he became very nervous.
The Englishman was anxious about Dirk and for himself. Had Dirk
revealed the hide-out?

In spite of his fears, he ate the ham with pleasure. He had nothing
to drink and Michiel realized that he should have thought of bringing water. Jack asked him if he could return tomorrow with drink and
more food.

'O.K.,' said Michiel, feeling very proud that he knew a real
expression in such a difficult language. He also thought, 'Providing
I'm not caught like Dirk.' But he said nothing of the sort, not only
because he did not know the English words.

The pilot showed him the path, or rather the little stairway, Dirk
had used to get in and out, and he was soon out of the fir thicket. 'Be
careful of snakes,' Michiel had once heard in Sunday School, so he
looked carefully around before removing his bike from the bushes.
As he emerged from the wood, he double-checked to make sure that
nobody had spotted him. Before going home, he went first to Dirk's
parents. They were still very upset, but he had no difficulty directing
the conversation around to the search of the house – the poor people
could talk of nothing else.

'Did the Germans search any other houses today?' he asked.

'Not that I know of,' Mr Knopper said.

'I'm always scared they'll take my father,' Michiel said.

'Now that they've taken our Dirk we can understand your fear...'
and he started all over again, talking about his own misery.

Michiel was now almost convinced that the Germans had not
been searching for him. His neighbours would certainly have known.
Nevertheless, he was rather nervous as he entered the house through
the back door after putting his bike in the barn. But his mother said
cheerfully:

'There you are, then, Michiel. What did you do with yourself
today?'

So it was all right.

'Nothing special. I went here, there and everywhere.'

His mother took no notice. The evening passed. He felt an irre-
sistible urge to take someone into his confidence – his father, his

mother or Uncle Ben – but he was able to suppress it. 'A good resistance worker works on his own,' he had once heard his father say. 'He is alone with his task and with what he knows.'

Michiel was well aware that his task was an adult one, and that from now on it was a question of life and death. Well, he had always hated being treated like a child and now he had his chance to behave like a man, so he said nothing. He expected his mother to read from his face that he had something on his mind and perhaps she would say, 'A penny for your thoughts.' He kept thinking he heard the police coming. He also wondered how he would manage to get enough food for Jack during the next few weeks. But he said nothing.

From *War Winter* by Jan Terlouw

LITTLE BOY

In Wat de ogen niet horen (What the Eyes Do not Hear) *Daniel Billiet published a series of harrowing poems – and other texts – about war and violence in Sarajevo, Somalia and Rwanda.* Little Boy *clearly refers to the atomic bomb that was dropped on Hiroshima in 1945.*

The Little Boy played such havoc
that for miles around
all trees and houses
and dreams and grouses
and people… were destroyed

As he had been taught

Adults?
Leave them alone for just one minute
and they destroy something.
or someone.

From *What the Eyes Do not Hear* by Daniel Billiet

HIROSHIMA

This anonymous poem manages to tell the story of Hiroshima in the most economical yet extremely vivid way.

Noon, and hazy heat;
A single, silver sliver and a dull drone;
The gloved finger poised, pressed:
A second's silence, and
Oblivion

Anon

RELATIVE SADNESS

Colin Rowbotham's poem, like Hiroshima *above, has the compression and elegance of a Japanese Haiku.*

Einstein's eyes
were filled with tears
when he heard about Hiroshima.

Mr. Tamihi
had no eyes left
to show his grief.

by Colin Rowbotham

In Flanders Fields

THE CLAY STAMPERS FROM LONDON

This book describes the lives of two boys – Flemish Serafijn and Welsh Daffy – during the bloody trench war near Passchendaele of 1917. Serafijn sells sweets and cigarettes to soldiers on their way back to or from the front. Daffy, a crafty thief and haggler, is a clay stamper. He has been brought in to dig tunnels under the German positions. The two boys become friends and try to forget the atrocities of the war.

The roaring of the guns died down. The Germans continued to fire until the barrels of their pieces were red hot. Time for a short break. A few minutes to let the murder weapons cool down and point them at another target. Serafijn crawled out of the basement. The rubble that had buried his tent-cloth was no longer there. The heap of bricks had turned into powder, a crater full of red dust. Daffy pointed at an old shellhole by the ruins.

'That's where I was when this bastard exploded,' he said.

'Yes,' Serafijn answered and then stalled; either you survived a bombing, fair enough. Or you were shot to bits, end of story.

'Come with me,' Daffy said, sounding like the boss.

'Where to?'

'To Poperinge.'

Serafijn couldn't help but think this was a joke. What made this brazen cad think he'd go to Poperinge with him? No way. He had to get to his mother's café in Dranouter as soon as possible. Get some rest. Stock up on new goods. Up and about again tomorrow. Selling cigarettes and tobacco to the soldiers on their way to the front at night. Providing the relieved troops with sweets and drink in the morning.

'You walk to Poperinge if you want,' he said, 'I'm going home. Adieu.'

'I'm going with you, thanks for the invitation,' Daffy answered without flinching.

The land looked as if it had been torn open by a huge plough. There were gaping bomb craters everywhere and the wafting stench of explosives. Dead bodies lay strewn all over the place. Stretcher-bearers were removing the wounded. Soon the gravediggers would appear. Their workload got heavier each day. Serafijn walked on in silence. Daffy followed just as silently. The morning mist lifted, they were in for another scorcher.

A column of lorries was bumping over the paved road. Sputtering engines, thick blue smoke from the exhausts, steam from the radiators. Every time they hit upon a row of horse-drawn carts, the lorries slowed down. The huge draught animals drew sparks from the cobbles. They were delivering ammunition for the guns in the fields, each gun with a wall of sandbags around it. Soldiers wearing blankets and overcoats were sleeping near the parts. A quick nap until the next bombing.

'What's your name then?' Daffy asked.

'Serafijn. Yours?'

'Call me Daffy. Everybody does.'

He suddenly seemed less brutal. Just a boy on the edge of the war, like him. 'How did you end up here?' Serafijn asked.

'I came here to stamp clay'

Serafijn stopped. He checked Daffy's face to see if the Welshman was pulling his leg. The lad stared back impassively.

'You're not a soldier then?' Serafijn asked.

'I'm a tunnel digger,' Daffy smiled, 'a clay stamper. Know what that is?'

'No,' Serafijn said and continued to walk.

Daffy came and walked next to him. He clearly needed a chat. A friend. Someone to confide in.

'I was working in London when the army asked for volunteers to dig tunnels under the front,' he said. 'Long corridors, all the way up to and under the German positions.' He indicated a point in the distance, in the fields between Kemmel and Mesen. Serafijn's eyes followed his hands. He could see the front. Fountains of greasy clay spouted up where shells hit the crest of the hill. They were at it again. For two months now, Britons, Australians, New Zealanders had been waging a devilish battle to conquer the next range of hills. They hadn't moved one inch. The Germans occupied the high ground to Geluveld and Zonnebeke. Day and night, their machine guns sounded from concrete bunkers. Whoever dared peep over the edge of a trench was mowed down instantly. Carrying out an assault against those positions was pure suicide.

Staying put was almost as dangerous, actually. Even the ones who hid underground like moles could be killed by a shell, just like that. The German guns were tucked safely behind the distant hills. Some pieces were so heavy they could easily shoot their deathly load far beyond Kemmel.

Possibly even worse was this other, new threat that quietly grazed the soil when the wind came from the east. Then the Germans opened cans of mustard gas. A slick, greenish-yellow cloud slid over the land, penetrated clothes, burned skins, scorched lungs.

Serafijn had to gasp every time he thought of gas. He was jolted out of his thoughts by a shriek.

'Make way! Make way! A driver was yelling.

A five-in-hand thundered past. Three horses in front, their bodies so close to each other that you could hear their bodies touch. Then two more horses and then the cart with the yelling driver, holding a long whip.

'More than a hundred cartloads of explosives went into the tunnels,' Daffy sighed, 'right under the Germans' arses. Did you hear the explosions when the attack started? June 7th, ten past three in the morning.'

'Yes. The earth in Dranouter shook so violently that I almost fell out of bed.'

'Well, those are the tunnels I dug. Me and my mates.'

'Sure,' Serafijn snapped back, not believing a word of it.

So Daffy told him what had happened, for he didn't want his new friend to consider him a brag and a liar.

'My father was a miner in Wales,' Daffy said, 'but he moved to London because he could earn a better living there, digging tunnels for the underground railway. And pipes for the sewers.
When I was twelve, he took me along to learn. Not easy. In London they have a special way of working, you see.'

'Sure,' Serafijn muttered, for he was convinced the Welshman was bragging again.

'You have to be a professional to understand,' Daffy reacted. 'The London subsoil is like the Flemish soil. Blue clay. Terrible stuff.

Hard and sticky. Ordinary pickaxes and shovels just won't do.

It took months before the army realized that. First they got miners in from Yorkshire. Champions in the coalmines, but useless out here. Their pickaxes got stuck in the clay. The soil they were supposed to remove stuck to their shovels. So they had a go at it with an electric excavator. It worked for a few days, but then it got hopelessly stuck in the clay as well. Still is. They'll never get it out, if you ask me.

That's when they thought of us. The London clay stampers. Men from Wales. Irishmen too.'

From *Serafijn's War* by Roger H. Schoemans

IN FLANDERS FIELDS

This is the famous poem of the First World War which first appeared in the English magazine Punch *and became instantly popular.*

In Flanders fields the poppies blow
Between the crosses row on row,
That mark our place; and in the sky
The larks, still bravely singing, fly
Scarce heard amid the guns below.

We are the Dead. Short days ago
We lived, felt dawn, saw sunset glow,
Loved and were loved, and now we lie
In Flanders fields.
Take up our quarrel with the foe:
To you from failing hands we throw
The torch; be yours to hold it high.
If ye break faith with us who die
We shall not sleep, though poppies grow
In Flanders fields.

by John McCrae

THE LIVES OF SOLDIERS IN FLANDERS IN THE FIRST WORLD WAR

This picture book takes John McCrae's famous poem of the First World War In Flanders Fields *and illustrates it line by line, as in the following extract.*

We are the Dead. Short days ago

From *In Flanders Fields: The story of the poem by John McCrae*

Loved, and were loved, and now we lie

We lived, felt dawn, saw sunset glow,

In Flanders fields.

ARMAGEDDON

*January 1918. Faucheux, Binet, Charpentier and Desbois. They are
dead or half-dead, ploughing through the muddy trenches. The
author gives a moving description of the senselessness of war.
Although Tardi avoids historical data, official figures, and clearly
sides with the cannon-fodder, he does manage to focus on the
absurdity and destructive aspects of The Great War in general.*

They had dumped us all in one long ditch.

Bodies...dead bodies...old ones and fresh ones. Why? WORLD WAR ONE, sir! 35 countries took part, from near and from far! The numbers? A 'historical' stock-take for future reference? 10 million dead! How many years of life buried forever in that mud? How many orphans? Cripples, widows? In France alone, 2,300 acres of military cemetery. Good beet soil, but all it grows now is crosses! If the French dead marched past in rows of four to celebrate the Fourteenth of July, it would take at least six days and five nights before the last one showed his ashen face...

11 departments, 2,907 communes, 1.2 million acres of woodland, 4.75 million acres of farmland devastated! 794,040 houses and flats, 9,332 factories, 36,854 miles of road and 8,333 works of art destroyed. 2.5 billion cubic feet of rubble!

It would take 11.6 billion cubic feet to fill the 490 miles of trenches on the front... and the cost? For cannons, shells etc... 2.5 trillion gold francs!

Enough to buy every inhabitant of Europe — not counting the Russians — a three-bedroom home... But what use are numbers?

It wasn't a good idea, taking position in a graveyard...

How could we have sunk so low? Catastrophic, scandalous, degradation...

Now we had to reach the aid station. I wasn't even wounded, but I followed the cripples, just like I'd always followed other people...unfortunately for me.

This guy gives everyone a laugh by making some poor bum carry him. He's probably a farmer like him, but he's German, so...

And you, Englishman? You had to help your neighbours, but I bet you're sorry now.

Poor Sikh, you were sent to slaughter, and you're thinking of home.

Troops from the United Kingdom, Canada, Australia, New Zealand, South Africa and India, more than 900,000 British subjects died protecting the interests of the English crown...but they didn't all fall in the land of the Frogs.

Senegalese, your ancestors the Gauls are proud of you. Half-frozen, you die for France.
The white man who flogs you and exploits your land also keeps you away from his women and tells the most ridiculous stories about you. They say that you are only too pleased to let yourself be killed, happy to be able to help the one who so kindly gave you his religion, his booze and his tuberculosis bacterium.

Poor slave, poor beast of burden, they load your shoulders with death!

...and it all ends at the aid station.

And you, Algerian, come from the Atlas Mountains to die in Artois.
We're not grateful to you, you are a Frenchman after all — for now at least.
Because you and your son will fight the colonist who grows grapes on stolen
land. You'll chase him away!

Cries of pain, the stench of blood and faeces...back at the aid station.

Soldiers from 'North Africa' — 36,000 casualties — even the ordinary soldier is scared of you. When he sees you advancing, he knows it's going to get tough. You go first, but then it's his turn.

Indochinese, you've seen a lot of the country thanks to the French, haven't you? Keep on digging...

From *Trench War* 1914–1918 by Tardi

STAR AND JOE JOIN THE ARMY

Ploon is ninety and has taken care of three generations of Dutch children of the same family. She eventually becomes a burden to everyone and is sent off to an old people's home. Twelve-year-old Roelien finds this unjust and secretly takes her home, where she hides and takes care of Ploon. Roelien is fascinated by the child this old woman once was. Ploon tells fantastic stories about her youth amongst Flemish farmers and with Star and Joe, the sweetest horses on earth, who were requisitioned by the army. The author ingeniously interweaves past and present: the looming war and the touching friendship between two generations.

The attic door still jammed, even though Roelien was lifting it higher than ever before and the steps creaked horribly, however light she tried to make herself. She sneaked into the attic room. 'Where are you?' she wanted to whisper, but her voice still wouldn't cooperate. She looked behind the door, and there stood Ploon, squashed against the wall, suitcase in band.

'Have they gone?' she hissed. 'I was so scared! Why didn't you stop them?'

The bed had been made and not a trace of Ploon's things was in sight.

'What brings them here in the first place?' Ploon muttered on, 'they have no right to be here!' She dumped the suitcase back where it belonged, clumped to her chair, sat down and said: 'Good riddance to bad rubbish.'

Roelien was still standing in the middle of the room; lips quivering, with spite this time. She cast an angry look at Ploon, who was scanning the room with a what-can-I-do-next face. Then Ploon extended her hand.

Keeping the noise down might help, Roelien had wanted to say. You'll only have yourself to blame if you get found out – the way you stumble around and all. You should be more careful too: this morning you left the TV on downstairs and cheese crusts all over the place, and yesterday…

She didn't say a word. Ploon bent down, groped under the low table cloth and conjured up one of the bars. She beckoned Roelien and put a huge piece of chocolate in her mouth, as if to a toddler who needed soothing.

Someone downstairs banged the front door: it was mum, rushing out to run some errands. Ploon liked that and nodded that Roelien should sit down where she'd just been sitting.

'I'm needed downstairs,' Roelien said, 'I was busy ironing,' but Ploon shook her head and decided otherwise.

September 1914
Stijn has just turned fourteen and is walking up and down the farm-yard with an iron pot on his head and a pointed stick in his hands. He is shouting strange words; 'toadsheessen!' When the refugees were still around, in the horse stables, Stijn snuck up to them at night to listen to their stories, even though Mum had expressly forbidden it. 'You must never believe everything people tell you,' Mum says. These are terrible stories and Stijn keeps telling them to Ploon. She covers her ears. 'Are they lies then?' she asks Mum. Mum hesitates; lies, no, terrible things do happen, but not everything is true, and she'd rather Ploon didn't listen.

Basil had run into a bunch of German troopers – they were grey, from head to foot, and wore gruesome pickaxe helmets, real murder-ers, with terrible weapons and massive horses! – and the refugees had made for the coast in a panic. You should go too, they said, but Dad answered: they'll never make it this far, the English could be here any day now.

The horse stables are empty again. Ploon and Petrus have cleared them and spread the straw out into the sun. Ploon is staring at the empty mangers and biting her lip.

She never says much to Petrus; Petrus and Stijn are always together, and she's just a girl, but now with the big brothers gone and Stijn acting so funny, Petrus prefers her company. He's only eleven, but one year older than her.

He looks at her face and asks softly: 'Is it because of the horses?'

She nods. Why didn't Dad stop them, she wants to ask, because that's what's been on her mind all this time, that's what she can't understand. But she doesn't speak. She's been thinking about the men who were shouting themselves hoarse and pulling on the reins, and who beat Star until she almost tripped. She heard it, and Marthe was holding her. She heard the angry trampling of hooves on the stones, and she thought: kick, Star, kick! And Marthe wiped her cheeks, because she thought she was crying. But she wasn't crying, she never cried over the horses. She did keep hearing the shouting of the men, though, and the clatter of the hooves and how Star and Joe grumbled angrily because they didn't want to go. All day long she kept hearing it, and all night.

They sit down on a patch of straw in a dark corner of the stables.

'It's for our mother country,' Peter says solemnly. 'For the army. All horses must serve in the army.'

'Gregoor has kept one, and Feys too,' Ploon says.

'Those bags of bones, you mean!' Petrus calls out.

They want the strongest ones in the country. And does Ploon have any idea how many horses are needed to pull one gun? Six! Six big, strong ones! They need horses this size to even stand a chance against the enemy.

'Ours were so big and so strong, so...'

A gun. Star and Joe in front of a gun. Ploon hardly even knows what a gun is. A shooting thing. The rumbling noise they keep hearing in the distance, those are the guns over Lille, Dad had said.

'Joe wants to stay with Star,' Ploon says proudly.

Petrus muses. 'They're much too beautiful for a gun,' he decides: 'You know what? I reckon they've been taken to the king!' He gives her an expectant look, maybe this will work.

'The king, what king?'

'Our king, of course! King Albert! Maybe they'll be put in front of his carriage! Surely they'll not stay in Brussels, now that the city has been occupied.'

Ploon nods and smiles, it's nice to imagine the king caressing the horses, and saying: 'What beautiful, strong animals, and so well groomed! I've decided to use them as saddle horses, one for me, and one for the queen. What are their names?'

'The mare is called Star, majesty. She has a bit of a temper, but she'll be all right, really The gelding is called Joe, Jo-ey. They get brushed every day and they adore apples. And they must stay together, always.'

Ploon nods and peers outside through the open stable doors. She caresses the straw on which she is sitting and tries to feel the manes in her hands once again, they used to be so hard and so rigid, and just wouldn't curl, however often she brushed them.

From *Star and Joe* by Martha Heesen

A FARM HORSE IS SOLD TO THE ARMY

War Horse is the story of Joey, a farm horse who finds himself involved in the action in Flanders in the First World War. Joey belongs to Albert, a young man who takes great care of him and values him very highly. In this extract Albert's father is tempted by the high prices the British army are prepared to pay to buy good horses for action at the Front, so he sells Joey to Captain Nicholls for forty pounds, which was a great deal of money in those days. Albert is very upset when he finds out that Joey has been sold, and swears to join the army so that he too can go and fight at the Front. In this way both Joey and Albert become First World War recruits. Joey is eventually separated from Albert, and even finds himself working for the German side for a while.

Tying a long rope to the halter he walked me out of the stable. I went with him because Zoey was out there looking back over her shoulder at me and I was always happy to go anywhere and with anyone as long as she was with me. All the while I noticed that Albert's father was speaking in a hushed voice and looking around him like a thief.

He must have known that I would follow old Zoey, for he roped me up to her saddle and led us both quietly out of the yard down the track and over the bridge. Once in the lane he mounted Zoey swiftly and we trotted up the hill and into the village. He never spoke a word to either of us. I knew the road well enough of course for I had been there often enough with Albert, and indeed I loved going there because there were always other horses to meet and people to see. It was in the village only a short time before that I had met my first motor-car outside the Post Office and had stiffened with fear as it rattled past, but I had stood steady and I remember that Albert had made a great fuss of me after that. But now as we neared the village I could see that several motor-cars were parked up around the green and there was a greater gathering of men and horses than I had ever seen. Excited as I was, I remember that a sense of deep apprehension came over me as we trotted up into the village.

There were men in khaki uniforms everywhere; and then as Albert's father dismounted and led us up past the church towards the green a military band struck up a rousing, pounding march. The pulse of the great bass drum beat out through the village and there were children everywhere, some marching up and down with broomsticks over their shoulders and some leaning out of windows waving flags.

As we approached the flagpole in the centre of the green where the Union Jack hung limp in the sun against the white pole, an officer pushed through the crowd towards us. He was tall and elegant in his jodhpurs and Sam Brown belt, with a silver sword at his side. He shook Albert's father by the hand. 'I told you I'd come, Captain Nicholls, sir,' said Albert's father. 'It's because I need the money, you understand. Wouldn't part with a horse like this 'less I had to.'

'Well, farmer,' said the officer, nodding his appreciation as he looked me over. 'I'd thought you'd be exaggerating when we talked in The George last evening. 'Finest horse in the parish' you said, but then everyone says that. But this one is different – I can see that.' And he smoothed my neck gently and scratched me behind my ears. Both his hand and his voice were kind and I did not shrink away from him. 'You're right, farmer, he'd make a fine mount for any regiment and we'd be proud to have him – I wouldn't mind using him myself. No, I wouldn't mind at all. If he turns out to be all he looks, then he'd suit me well enough. Fine looking animal, no question about it.'

'Forty pounds you'll pay me, Captain Nicholls, like you promised yesterday?' Albert's father said in a voice that was unnaturally low, almost as if he did not want to be heard by anyone else. 'I can't let him go for a penny less. Man's got to live.'

'That's what I promised you last evening, farmer,' Captain Nicholls said, opening my mouth and examining my teeth. 'He's a fine young horse, strong neck, sloping shoulder, straight fetlocks. Done much work has he? Hunted him out yet, have you?'

'My son rides him out every day,' said Albert's father. 'Goes like a racer, jumps like a hunter he tells me.'

'Well,' said the officer, 'as long as our vet passes him as fit and sound in wind and limb, you'll have your forty pounds, as we agreed.'

'I can't be long, sir,' Albert's father said, glancing back over his shoulder. 'I have to get back. I have my work to see to.'

'Well, we're busy recruiting in the village as well as buying,' said the officer. 'But we'll be as quick as we can for you. True, there's a lot more good men volunteers than there are good horses in these parts, and the vet doesn't have to examine the men, does he? You wait here, I'll only be a few minutes.'

Captain Nicholls led me away through the archway opposite the public house and into a large garden beyond where there were men in white coats and a uniformed clerk sitting down at a table taking notes. I thought I heard old Zoey calling after me, so I shouted back to reassure her for I felt no fear at this moment. I was too interested in what was going on around me. The officer talked to me gently as we walked away, so I went along most eagerly. The vet, a small, bustling man with a bushy black moustache, prodded me all over, lifted each of my feet to examine them – which I objected to – and then peered into my eyes and my mouth, sniffing at my breath. Then I was trotted round and round the garden before he pronounced me a perfect specimen. 'Sound as a bell. Fit for anything, cavalry or artillery,' were the words he used. 'No splints, no curbs, good feet and teeth. Buy him, Captain,' he said. 'He's a good one.'

I was led back to Albert's father who took the offered notes from Captain Nicholls, stuffing them quickly into his trouser pocket. 'You'll look after him, sir?' he said. 'You'll see he comes to no harm? My son's very fond of him you see.' He reached out and brushed my nose with his hand. There were tears filling his eyes. At that moment he became almost a likeable man for me. 'You'll be all right, old son,' he whispered to me. 'You won't understand and neither will Albert, but unless I sell you I can't keep up with the mortgage and we'll lose the farm. I've treated you bad – I've treated everyone bad. I know it and I'm sorry for it.' And he walked away from me leading Zoey behind him. His head was lowered and he looked suddenly a shrunken man.

It was then that I fully realised I was being abandoned and I began to neigh, a high-pitched cry of pain and anxiety that shrieked out through the village. Even old Zoey, obedient and placid as she always was, stopped and would not be moved on no matter how hard Albert's father pulled her. She turned, tossed up her head and shouted her farewell. But her cries became weaker and she was finally dragged away and out of my sight. Kind hands tried to contain me and to console me, but I was unconsolable.

I had just about given up all hope, when I saw my Albert running up towards me through the crowd, his face red with exertion. The band had stopped playing and the entire village looked on as he came up to me and put his arms around my neck.

'He's sold him, hasn't he?' he said quietly, looking up at Captain Nicholls who was holding me. 'Joey is my horse. He's my horse and he always will be, no matter who buys him. I can't stop my father from selling him, but if Joey goes with you, I go. I want to join up and stay with him.'

'You've the right spirit for a soldier, young man,' said the officer, taking off his peaked cap and wiping his brow with the back of his hand. He had black curly hair and a kind, open look on his face. 'You've the spirit but you haven't the years. You're too young and you know it. Seventeen's the youngest we take. Come back in a year or so and then we'll see.'

'I look seventeen,' Albert said, almost pleading. 'I'm bigger than most seventeen-year-olds.' But even as he spoke he could see he was getting nowhere. 'You won't take me then, sir? Not even as a stable boy? I'll do anything, anything.'

'What's your name, young man?' Captain Nicholls asked.

'Narracott, sir. Albert Narracott.'

'Well, Mr. Narracott. I'm sorry I can't help you.' The officer shook his head and replaced his cap. 'I'm sorry, young man, regulations. But don't you worry about your Joey. I shall take good care of him until you're ready to join us. You've done a fine job on him. You should be proud of him – he's a fine, fine horse, but your father needed the money for the farm, and a farm won't run without money. You must know that. I like your spirit, so when you're old enough you must come and join the Yeomanry. We shall need men like you, and it will be a long war I fear, longer than people think. Mention my name. I'm Captain Nicholls, and I'd be proud to have you with us.'

'There's no way then?' Albert asked. 'There's nothing I can do?'

'Nothing,' said Captain Nicholls. 'Your horse belongs to the army now and you're too young to join up. Don't you worry – we'll look after him. I'll take personal care of him, and that's a promise.'

Albert wriggled my nose for me as he often did and stroked my ears. He was trying to smile but could not. 'I'll find you again, you old silly,' he said quietly. 'Wherever you are, I'll find you, Joey. Take good care of him, please sir, till I find him again. There's not another horse like him, not in the whole world – you'll find that out. Say you promise?'

'I promise,' said Captain Nicholls. 'I'll do everything I can.' And Albert turned and went away through the crowd until I could see him no more.

From *War Horse* by Michael Morpurgo

Remembering and Forgetting

GRASS

In this poem the American poet Carl Sandburg uses the battles of the Napoleonic wars, and the American Civil war to show what will happen to the dead and to the memory of the First World War.

Pile the bodies high at Austerlitz and Waterloo.
Shovel them under and let me work –
I am the grass; I cover all.

And pile then high at Gettysburg
And pile them high at Ypres and Verdun.
Shovel them under and let me work.
Two years, and ten years, and passengers ask the conductor:
What place is this?
Where are we now?

I am the grass.
Let me work.

by Carl Sandburg

THE BIRCH TREE

All the stories in Uit de loop van een geweer *(From the Barrel of a Gun) are about war and violence – present and past – in Europe, South America and the Middle East. This story is about war in general, about the recurrence of war and violence.*

The tanks' turrets turned ominously towards the long row of houses, slums almost. The creaking was heard deep into the dead silent streets.

'Not the house with the white windows and the stables, on no account!', the commander shouted through the short-wave transmitter. He stared into space, to avoid the questioning looks of the tank's crew.

It was a strange house. Branches stuck out of two holes in the roof of the adjacent stables.

The commander peered at the door. It had been open, twenty years ago.

He's sitting down, staring into the night through the open door. The worst of the winter hunger is over, spring is in the air. The third spring since the enemy invaded and occupied the country.

He can't sleep, he knows his father is on the road. He often disappears into the dusk. Mother is given no details either. Maybe he's with the resistance, there are regular attempts in the area.

Maybe, one night, his father will not return.

The boy is fidgeting on his chair. Maybe his imagination is running riot. His father always returns with a huge bundle of wood from a nearby forest. Wood to cook the food on. Perhaps that's just an alibi, in case he runs into a patrol?

The boy sighs, wishing he were older than fourteen. What father takes a fourteen-year-old into his confidence anyway?

He suddenly hears his father's lightly shuffling step, he would recognize it anywhere. He's listened to it often enough at night, when sounds start leading a life of their own.

He runs towards the open door. His father seems taller in the moonlight. To the boy's surprise, he's not carrying a bundle of wood on his back, but a young tree. A lanky birch – he can tell from the bark – at least 3 metres high.

'Still up?' his father smiles.

The boy nods and points a questioning finger at the young tree.

'Come with me, son.'

He loves it when his father calls him 'son' and not by his first name. He follows him to the low stables.

Inside the stables, his father looks up at the roof. He points at two spots where some tiles are missing. Bundled moonlight forces its way inside. They don't have the money to buy new tiles. The stables have been empty since the beginning of the occupation. Not that it matters, the enemy requisitions everything anyway.

'All I need to do is remove a few more tiles, and we'll have two real holes,' his father says. He chooses a spot between the two bundles of light, kneels and feels the loam floor.

'Good soil, underneath that top layer,' he says. He positions the tree against a buttress and grabs a shovel. He starts digging without saying a word.

The boy looks on. This is an important moment and he wants to be part of it. 'Can I help you dig?' he asks. His father hands him the shovel. 'I'll do the holes,' he says.

While the boy digs and occasionally spits in his hands, his father carefully crawls across the cracking beams in the roof. The bundles of light grow bigger and the boy looks up. His father is waving at him. Fantastic, this feeling of togetherness, the boy reckons. Even though he doesn't have a clue what his father is up to.

The hole is deep enough now. He waits until his father is back by his side and leans on the handle.

'Could you fetch me a bucket of water, son?'
He runs and returns with a full bucket. The water sloshes over the rim.

His father carefully places the tree inside the hole.

'Hold it nice and straight son!' He fills up the hole, the boy looks at his father's slow and almost solemn gestures.

'Can I pour the water in?'

His father nods. Easy now, we don't want to wash away the soil, do we?' He does it carefully, in tiny splashes, and finds his own gestures solemn now.

When everything's ready, his father takes a few steps back and the boy follows him. His father's arm is resting on his shoulders. They look at the pale spots on the bark that light up in the moonlight.

'The freedom tree,' his father says, he finally says it. 'By the time its branches reach the holes in the roof, our country will be free.'

The boy nods, there is no reason to doubt this. How fast does a birch tree grow about a metre?

'I'll water it every day,' the boy says. 'And feed it horse dung. I'll mix in horse dung with the soil.'

His father points at the two gaps. 'It has a choice: grow crooked or opt for both holes at the same time. Even a tree is entitled to some freedom.'

The boy nods. Together they leave the stables, enter the house and wish each other good night.

For months the boy takes care of the birch tree. From a ladder against a ridge pole, he carefully checks its progress. It has chosen both openings. In summer its leaves look poorly, mainly the side branches in the shade. In the autumn they are strewn all over the stable floor. The boy does not rake them together, they give the empty space a festive air. He loves to walk barefoot across them. They rustle and whisper, as if in a silent pact.

When his father occasionally disappears late at night, the boy waits for him under the tree, with his back against the thin trunk. Thin but strong.

His father knows he will find him there, maybe this heartens him.

Sometimes they talk, sitting under the tree, watching the dawn creep up on them through the holes in the roof and the open door. Their shoulders touch.

Not long after the first leaves triumphantly pierce through the tiles, the war is over. The boy grows up in a free country and opts for a military career. Never again must the enemy overpower the nation.

His father dies and the son, a young man with a silver star on the lapel of his uniform, buries the urn with his ashes at the foot of the birch tree. His solemn gestures remind him of how it used to be.

Then come the years of revolt and unrest. Freedom means different things to different people, until a trio of generals seizes power. They tighten their grip on the population. All protest is nipped in the bud, yet the resistance grows, year upon year, with underground roots.

The commander has let his eyes glide over the row of shabby little houses. This is where they take shelter, the cornered resistance people. Men with ideals similar to his father's. Maybe one of them is crouching down behind the birch tree this very instant, and wondering how a tree ended up inside these stables. Maybe he is looking through the holes in the roof to catch one last glimpse of the firmament nobody owns.

The commander felt sweat tickle the hair at the nape of his neck.

'Not the house with the white windows and the stables, on no account,' he repeated falteringly. He took a deep breath.

'Fire,' he said, almost whispered.

The thundering echo and the noise of collapsing walls hit him and he arched his back. Something had left a nasty taste in his mouth.

From *From the Barrel of a Gun* by Ed Franck

LAST POST

The Flemish poet Herman de Coninck translated poems by the English war poet Edmund Blunden, which appeared posthumously in his Vingerafdrukken (Fingerprints). *This poem clearly shows Herman de Coninck's fascination with the Flanders Fields war poetry.*

This evening I was due in Ypres. It was getting on for six.
I drove toward the setting sun and three storeys
of Daliesque cloud being chased away
by gale force
winds, the sky was being blown away,
I had to let it go, I drove and drove, 100 mph,
and every minute saw me ten more behind. There goes
my horizon.

When I make it to Ypres it's 1917.
Germans have shot the sun
to pieces. The only light left is explosions.
I find myself in a poem by Edmund Blunden.

In the trenches he writes an ode to the poppy.
The earth's found time to grow a floral superego.
Blunden has set his sights on flowers.

Here for years it's always
your last second before dying.
Details are all there is.

Later by the Menin Gate I listen to the Last Post:
two bugles going back those eighty years
cutting to the bone that's lost.

From *Fingerprints* by Herman de Coninck

SAYING GOOD-BYE TO THE YOUNG ENGLISH SOLDIERS LEAVING TO FIGHT IN FLANDERS

In this short, illustrated novel Kath, a modern young girl, has gone to stay with her great aunt Kitty, just before Remembrance Sunday. At first Kath cannot understand why her aunt seems to be a cross and rather bitter old lady. But then, in a dream that takes place on Remembrance Sunday itself, Kath becomes her aunt as a young girl, seeing off her brothers who have joined the army to fight in Flanders. Through her dream Kath begins to understand why her aunt is so sad at this time of the year, and learns about the two brothers who never returned from the Great War.

She opened her eyes. The sun dazzled, shooting spears of light through the thick black-green lace of leaves. She leant forward and loosened the laces on her boots, which felt tight and hot. They were getting too small, she needed new ones. Her pinafore was hot too, over her dress. She stood up, brushing herself free of twigs and bits of grass.

The air was filled with a heady scent – musty, sweet. Beside her was a large bush, its branches weighed down with white plates of blossom. Flies everywhere. And the young fresh green of slender beech trees beyond.

There was somewhere she ought to be, something she should be doing. What was it? She had lost it, could not think what it was. A stick lay on the grass by her feet. She picked it up, tapping it against the open palm of her left hand, frowning with the effort of remembering.

From down beyond the cottage, she could hear the faint thump of drums and the thin sound of distant brass. The band. That was it. That was where she ought to be. She must hurry.

She ran down the path, past the back gardens behind the cottages, with their neat rows of green vegetables. A brown hen squawked away from her with a loud flurry of wings as she clattered by. She ran down, through the freshly mown churchyard, past the little yew, past the gravestones, down past the main side-door of the church and out under the lich-gate into the lane.

The band was louder now, she could hear it down the bottom of the dip.

She ran past the school and the school playground, rattling her stick across the railings as she went. No one in there today to tell her not to. Today was special.

Down the hill. Panting now. Music still playing. Not too late then. Past the tall oak tree next to the inn, and there they all were. Not yet gone. Crowds and crowds of soldiers, packed on to the platform of the station, with their kitbags and their rifles. She must have missed the march down there, they were all standing at ease now, some sitting on their bags, and the band was playing a tune she knew, Chalky was always whistling it, what was it? Oh yes, 'A Long Way to Tipperary'.

She scanned the faces under the caps for Tom, but there were so many, she could not find him. She could feel the tears coming, but she fought them back. 'No, Kitty,' he'd said, 'you mustn't cry, I'll be back, you'll see. But come and watch when we go, it'll be a grand sight, they'll have the regimental band playing an' all.'

And it was, it was a grand sight. She felt she could burst with pride. There was a small crowd of folk from the village gathered outside the inn to watch. All people she knew by name. She wanted to shout out loud to them all, our Tom, our Tom's down there. Vince had already gone, was already in France; Vince so much older, almost one of the grown-ups. But Tom. Tom was full of silly jokes, could always make her laugh.

She felt a touch on her shoulder and twisted round to see who it was. It was the landlord of the inn, with a tray of pewter mugs in his hands. He held it down towards her, beer frothing over the rims.

'Kitty, my dear, d'you think you can take this down to the platform, let 'em share it round? 'Tis the least I can do.'

Immediately she is anxious about the money. 'How much must I ask for?'

'No, no, tell 'em 'tis my pleasure, an' I wish 'em all luck. But hurry now, or the train'll be 'ere. I'll fetch more.'

Take the tray then, cross the path, careful now, down the grass bank, somebody has seen her coming; there is pointing, laughter, a cheer. Kitty feels herself go scarlet, falters. But Tom is down there somewhere, even if she can't see him, he will be watching, will be

proud of her. She steadies, keeps her eyes on the tray, feeling for the grass with her foot where it goes down. Safely on to the platform, the band louder now, beer slopping on to the tray, large hands reaching towards the tankards, tankards lifted, the tray lighter in her hands, the mugs being passed along after a couple of gulps, as many as can be getting a share. Hot hands on her shoulders, and 'Thanks', 'Thanks', all around her.

The distant whistle of a train, and a sudden jostling and stamping, everyone standing up, lifting packs and rifles, where is the tray? Someone has taken it. Then an arm round her shoulders and almost lifted off her feet, held, hard, against rough serge and a hard webbing belt, a kiss pressed down on her forehead, a voice saying 'Goodbye, darlin'.' Released, back on her feet, somebody shouting orders, escape, retreat back up the bank, the tray forgotten, everyone waving now, train doors opening, soldiers getting in, doors slamming, heads and shoulders coming out of carriage windows, arms waving, the station-master lowering his flag, the engine giving its first loud whoosh of steam.

Run now, just in time to get to the bridge to see the train go under it, past the oak tree, turn right up to the bridge, down the lane towards her a bicycle coming at breakneck speed, a delivery bike. It brakes, swerves wildly to miss her, skids on the gravelly lane and is down, on its side, and it's Chalky White on his butcher's round, hands and leg grazed, one trouser leg torn, scrambling to his feet and dashing to the wall with her to watch the carriage roofs go through below, then running to the other side to see the last of the carriages disappear round the bend. Chalky furious, 'I missed it, I missed seein' 'em go!' Hands clenched, face white, cursing 'that durn cook up the big 'ouse, made me go back fer more scrag-end, said I 'adn't brought enough.'

And then the two of them, walking back down to pick up Chalky's bike and the paper packages which have fallen out of the front basket, and the band marching past them, back up the lane, while Chalky is muttering half to himself, half to Kitty, 'I got six months to wait, then I'm going, I'm going too, jus' as soon as I'm old enough.'

From *The Echoing Green* by Mary Rayner
illustrated by Michael Foreman

FUTILITY

Wilfred Owen was the greatest of the English poets of the First World War and Futility *is one of his best known and best loved poems. Owen was killed on November 4th 1918, a few days before the Armistice that ended the Great War.*

Move him into the sun –
Gently its touch awoke him once,
At home, whispering of fields unsown.
Always it woke him, even in France,
Until this morning and this snow.
If anything might rouse him now
The kind old sun will know.

Think how it wakes the seeds, –
Woke, once, the clays of a cold star.
Are limbs, so dear-achieved, are sides,
Full-nerv'd – still warm – too hard to stir?
Was it for this the clay grew tall?
– O what made fatuous sunbeams toil
To break earth's sleep at all?

From *The Poems of Wilfred Owen* by Wilfred Owen

THAT'S HOW IT WAS

Hoofdbagage (Head Luggage) *is part four of an autobiographical cycle, in which the author tells us about her childhood years during and immediately after the Second World War. First-person narrator Rita was sent to Sweden after the Liberation to build up strength. Swedish Britt-Marie has come to pay a return visit. Rita has been instructed by her parents not to take her to places even vaguely reminiscent of the war, but the past weighs too heavy to be ignored. As it turns out, Britt-Marie also had war experiences, when as a*

Finnish child she was made to flee the advancing Russians to Sweden.

The wind is so strong on the Zeeweg that we occasionally have to throw our weight on the pedals. Britt-Marie needn't worry about my wanting to go into the sea today. Just looking at the waves will do, and kicking my toes in the blobs of spume. I hold my head down against the blowing sand.

'Hey, what's that?' Britt-Marie calls out and she points at the large wooden cross on the crest of a dune.

'That's a graveyard,' I say. 'A special one.'

'What's so special about it?'

'These are people who were shot in the war.'

'Soldiers?'

'No, ordinary people.'

'Mind if we go and have a look?' Britt-Marie asks.

I don't mind. I've decided not to pretend there never was a war anymore. Mother started it, going on about Sweden and that train business.

We take a twisting dune path and climb the last bit up to the graveyard. We take a pebbled path along the graves.

'So many of them!' Britt-Marie says. 'Why were they shot, in fact?'

'For being with the resistance and doing dangerous things.'

'What dangerous things?'

'Oh, distributing secret pamphlets and making fake ration coupons and passports and cutting German cables and hiding Jews and…'

'Is one of your uncles here by any chance?' Britt-Marie asks and she stops by a gravestone with the name Karel Roelof Verschuur on it.

'No, we're not related,' I say. 'There are many Verschuurs in Holland.'

'See the day he died?' Britt-Marie says. 'June 6 1944. My ninth birthday.'

'More men were killed that day,' I say and point at a few other graves. 'But most of them were shot at the end of the war. When the Swedes were already eating white bread.'

I close the door of the deep spare bedroom. There is a board in the back. 'Look,' I say to Britt-Marie and I remove the board.

We are staring into a black hole, some kind of mouse hole, but a big one.

'Can we go in?' Britt-Marie asks.

'This is where my father used to hide in the war, when the Germans came looking for him. And the last winter he was in there with another man,

'Two men together in that hole?'

'Yes, and then my mother put the board in front and piled the cupboard full of sheets and towels and opened the door for the Germans and said "Just linen, as you can see."'

'Did you ever go inside?'

'No, never. Want to try it?'

'Yes, but with a torch,' Britt-Marie says.

My father didn't have a torch in the war. Apart from the one you had to keep squeezing if you wanted any light. It was much too noisy. 'Zoòm, zoom'. I try to imitate the sound of a dyno torch.

Britt-Marie looks at me as if I've gone crazy or something. And then she crawls inside the hole ahead of me. Just like that, without a torch.

We stroll along past the graves. Britt-Marie says that at her gran's in Helsingfors there is this graveyard full of Finnish soldiers who were killed in the war against the Russians.

'It's a green hill full of white painted wooden crosses,' she says. 'And under each cross there lies a soldier. I went there once with my gran just after the war. It's very different from the familiar graveyard where my grandad lies. There they have high dark trees and large blue stones on the graves and heavy chains all around and gravel. It makes you all gloomy and sombre just walking around it. But the hill with the white crosses makes you feel happy and light. Because all those men died for their country. Their souls were taken to heaven by white doves.'

She says the bit about the white doves softly and fast. Then she stops talking. We climb on the wall and sit there for a while. Our legs are dangling high above the ground. The wind is blowing in our faces. There are dunes all around us. There is one huge brown cross on one hill. Gulls are shrieking in the sky.

Britt-Marie wants me to translate the sentences that are written under the names on the gravestones.

I tell her that most of them are too difficult to translate because they have been taken from the table. And that they're all about God and the mother country and faith and love and being brave and the good fight anyway.

Britt-Marie says I shouldn't lump everything together, she wants to hear what they really say. So I pick a few that aren't very biblical, that use kind of everyday language. 'It is better to die standing than to live on bended knees.' And 'I would give my life for freedom any day.' And then 'Rest peacefully dear boy' That's my favourite, because when you say it out loud, you're actually talking to the dead person in the grave. My translation is a bit clumsy, but Britt-Marie polishes my Swedish and then we both think of the boy who is lying there.

From *Head Luggage* by Rita Verschuur

CASUALTY – MENTAL WARD

Vernon Scannell's poem takes the violence and physical horror of war and makes it a psychic reality inside the mind of a survivor.

Something has gone wrong inside my head.
The sappers have left mines and wire behind;
I hold long conversations with the dead.

I do not always know what has been said;
The rhythms, not the words, stay in my mind;
Something has gone wrong inside my head.

Not just the sky but grass and trees are red,
The flares and tracers – or I'm colour-blind;
I hold long conversations with the dead.
Their presence comforts and sustains like bread;
When they don't come it's hard to be resigned;
Something has gone wrong inside my head.

They know about the snipers that I dread
And how the world is booby-trapped and mined;
I hold long conversations with the dead:

As all eyes close, they gather round my bed
And whisper consolation. When I find
Something has gone wrong inside my head
I hold long conversations with the dead.

From *Vernon Scannell Collected Poems 1950–1996*
by Vernon Scannell

MY GRANDAD AND THE BRASS BAND

*Mariana lives in a flat with her grandparents and her little sister
Rosa. Mariana wasn't too happy at first, when her sister was born.
She escaped into her own little world, where she found support
with her dolls and her goldfish. In this excerpt, she tells us of her
grandad, who used to play in the brass band on December 1st, a
national holiday in Portugal.*

Today is a public holiday.
This means: no school for me, no office for my parents, no fresh
bread in the morning, no letters in the mail box, no having to get
anywhere on time.

I let myself stay in bed a bit longer, while I listen to my sister
skipping about here and there as if all the hours of all the other days
weren't enough for her to play, sing, discover the wonders that only

her eyes can unearth from all the deepest corners of this house.

I roll myself up in the covers and the morning sounds of the house and the street drift towards me. The water which can be heard running from a tap, the hissing of the coffee percolator when the coffee is ready, the blinds someone is pulling up, the cars passing by outside, the dogs barking, the radio in the flat above, the neighbour on the ground floor who now and then shouts 'Louiiis!', calling her youngest son, who on Sundays and public holidays spends hours playing football among the stones, bricks, rusty wires and wooden poles of the little square.

What would a public holiday be like in Jorge's house?

But I soon stop thinking about this when I hear my father trilling away, under the shower:
'Oh Portuguese, the day of redemption has arrived.'

With a very long and trembling 'i', perhaps because by then the soap has slid out of his hands and he is searching for it around the slippery bathtub, as so often happens to me.

Still in bed, I hear the voice of my mother, laughing:
'You're very patriotic for so early in the morning!'
But my father doesn't seem to notice and there he goes again:
'...the chains fall from their wrists
and free, the nation rises...'.

Once again with another 'i' perhaps even more tremulous than the first one. It must definitely belong to the music.

I put on my clothes, slide into my slippers (which as usual are full of dolls belonging to Rosa, who uses every place she comes across to make beds for her many sons and daughters) and I go in to see my mother in her room.
'What are we going to do today?' I ask as I lay my head on her shoulder.
'I don't know. Anything as long as it's not queuing for the number 14, signing the entry book and typing' says she.
'Anything as long as it is not writing a summary, cleaning the blackboard and walking about with a satchel on my back' say I.
'Anything as long as it's not being subjected to the yoke of the

enemy!' shouted my father, his hair still dripping, raising his bath towel like a flag.

We all burst out laughing, with Rosa asking 'What is it, what is it?', not having understood anything, but also laughing.

'Are you all mad today! It seems that the 1st December has turned your brains' said my mother.

'A family weakness!' replied my father, trying to adjust the knot of his tie in the mirror. And turning towards me: 'Your grandfather, back home, whenever the 1st December came round, would carefully dress himself in his uniform, from top to toe, and go out with the band playing the Song of the Restoration all over the village. After two complete turns they would go up on to the bandstand and there would be music until nightfall. Then, when he came home he would make me sing "Oh Portuguese, the day of redemption has arrived," and then he would send me to bed. Once, when I was older, I asked him why he did it, why he was still so angry with the Spanish. He stood very straight and replied:

"I am angry with the enemy, son! It's not the Spanish. It's the enemy! The enemy who is no longer the Spanish, and who even speaks the same language as we do, but behaves the way they did: killing us with hunger, filling everything with misery, arresting people when they speak the truth. Don't ever forget, my son: the enemy is watching!" And it really was watching. Some time later the police came into the village and stopped the band from going out on the streets again on the 1st December. Only, they weren't able to stop my father from singing the song, the moment the sun came up...

My father went to fetch the coffee from the kitchen. When he came back into the room he smiled at us and said:

'I think that if your grandfather was alive, he would have sung the Song of the Restoration on the 25th April! And now will Dona Mariana please go and get ready as it's too nice a day to lose any sunshine, cooped up here at home.'

At that moment an enormous shout was heard coming from the little square.

'Goooooooaaaaal!'

Louis had become the champion of the world.

1   *1st December – a public holiday commemorating the*
     Portuguese restoration of independence in 1640
2   *25th April, 1974 – the date of the Portuguese Revolution*

From *Lote 12–2 Frente (Block 12–2F)* by Alice Vieira

1945

This short poem – barely one sentence – clearly shows how weird
sudden peace must have felt after the war.

We had heroes in for morning tea
they sat together on our settee
they weren't exactly
talkers, I looked and looked
until they squirmed
they were at a loss
with a peace like this.

From *Will this Do? A Few Poems* by Judith Herzberg

ETHEL AND ERNEST AT HOME DURING THE SECOND WORLD WAR

This full-length autobiographical comic-strip book tells the story of Raymond Briggs' parents, Ethel and Ernest. During the war their son Raymond is evacuated to the countryside with other children, but Ernest, who has always been a milkman, has to become a fire fighter while Ethel, too, is employed in a factory on work for the war. This extract shows what life was like for ordinary people then. Ethel and Ernest do not share the same political outlook. Ernest is rather left-wing but Ethel wants a refined lifestyle. They are always arguing very amusingly.

The battle for France is over...
the Battle of Britain is about to begin.
Upon this battle depends the survival
of Christian civilization.
The whole fury and might of the enemy
must, very soon, be turned on us.
Hitler knows that he will have to break us
in this island, or lose the war.

If we can stand up to him, all Europe
may be free and the life of the world
may move forward into broad sunlit uplands.

But, if we fail, the whole world
will sink into the abyss of a new dark age.
Let us, therefore, brace ourselves to our duty
and so bear ourselves that if the
British Empire last for a thousand years,
men will still say:

THIS was their finest hour.

Broad sunlit uplands!

Good old Winston!
Our finest hour!

I expect Jerry will
be coming over soon.

They're starting to
take away our nice
gate and railings.

I'll make a
wooden gate.

Shame.

They want
saucepans, too.
They make them
into Spitfires.

Funny to think
of our front gate
being a Spitfire.

From *Ethel and Ernest A True Story* by Raymond Briggs

SONG OF FIRE AND WAR

*During the dictatorial regime in Portugal it was virtually
impossible to voice a protest. Some poets and musicians, however,
such as José Afonso, Adriano de Oliveira and Sérgio Godinho, did
denounce Portugal's political situation in their songs. Most of them
were sent to prison several times. Some received political asylum
abroad. After the Carnation Revolution they went on following
events in their country with a critical eye.*

There's a huge fire in the garden of war
And men sow needles in the soil
Men walk by treading on coal
Lit by the gods with glowing embers.

To douse the flames ambassadors come
Bearing hoses and water in their breast
They extinguish the lives of those they save
And water the dead who no longer feel thirst.

The circus of war attracts eaters of fire
Who open their mouths when the pay is good
And blow out flames through rotting teeth
A fire that neither blazes nor burns at all.
The high and mighty hold picnics outside
Barbecue chicken over the heat of their spite
Swill sangria bled from the wounds of the dead
And wipe their lips on charred pieces of skin.

It's a war of the ragged, of the faint of breath
Of oil so tired it burns in a trice
Strong men dig their insides out
And fire sweeps in, makes straight for the heart.

From *Song Lyrics* by Sérgio Godinho

WHAT WERE THEY LIKE?

*This poem uses the question and answer format to give echoes of a
Vietnamese mode of speech, thought and expression. Its use of the
past tense to refer to the people of Vietnam is sad and chilling at
the same time.*

1. Did the people of Vietnam use lanterns of stone?
2. Did they hold ceremonies to reverence the opening of buds?
3. Were they inclined to quiet laughter?
4. Did they use bone and ivory, jade and silver, for ornament?
5. Had they an epic poem?
6. Did they distinguish between speech and singing?

1. Sir, their light hearts turned to stone. It is not remembered whether
in gardens stone lanterns illumined pleasant ways.
2. Perhaps they gathered once to delight in blossom, but after the
children were killed there were no more buds.
3. Sir, laughter is bitter to the burned mouth.
4. A dream ago, perhaps. Ornament is for joy. All the bones were
charred.
5. It is not remembered. Remember, most were peasants; their life
was in rice and bamboo. When peaceful clouds were reflected in the
paddies and the water buffalo stepped surely along terraces, maybe
fathers told their sons old tales. When bombs smashed those mirrors
there was time only to scream.
6. There is an echo yet of their speech which was like a song. It was
reported their singing resembled the flight of moths in moonlight.
Who can say? It is silent now.

by Denise Levertov

THEY MUST BE FOUND BEFORE IT IS TOO LATE

Silence blind faith inexplicable fear
life just the same as always the same business conversations
job expectations drug smuggling vehicle hire they are no
        longer enough
Sitting in front of an empty glass in the crowded café
or being a sailor on dry land drowning his solitude
in the tarnished familiar body of the nameless prostitute is no
        longer enough
Somewhere in the maze of the city a man and a woman
are in love watch the street through the blinds
hastily construct a world of love
And they must be found They must be found
It must be asked in which street they are hiding
in which unseen place they remain hold out
dream of future months potential new continents
Into which shadows they vanish in which gentle
conspiratorial
and loyal safe haven they while away the time
hiding their emotions at the sound of gunshots
Whose nameless hands clasp their own
in the ominous silence of the hostile city

Wherever they unfold their tranquil song
they open deep boundaries between day and night
And so we must go even further
destroy forever the sins of the child
erect prison walls with no way out
enforce violence tyranny hate

Meanwhile from the corners in huge letters pours out
the total condemnation of the man of the woman
who in halflight of the bar on a rainy afternoon
invented love as a matter of great urgency

From *The Creation of Love and Other Poems* by Daniele Filipe

Escape, Survival
and Rescue

ESCAPE FROM SARAJEVO

*Sarajevo is being bombed during the Civil war in the former
Yugoslavia. Asmir is a seven year-old Bosnian child whose family
escape from the besieged city just before the Bosnian borders close.
At this point in the story Asmir's family have to pack in a great
hurry to join the bus that will take them out of Bosnia. When
Asmir's father is captured the family do not know if and when they
will see him again. Meanwhile they have ahead of them a long and
very dangerous journey through several countries before they reach
Austria and safety.*

Asmir ran to his own room. His mother was sponging Eldar who
was still flushed and grizzly. She told Asmir to put on two of everything. He felt like a penguin waddling with its egg. 'Where's
Daddy?'

'He's gone to work.'

Asmir thought of the snipers hiding in the ruined buildings, picking off people as they passed. Not Muris. Not Muris. He had to reach
the office safely. Perhaps he would telephone in a few moments to let
them know he was there.

His mother was dressing Eldar. 'I can do that,' Asmir offered.
'You'll be late for work.'

'I'm not going,' she said. And Asmir remembered the bombed
chocolate factory. His mother was pulling two of everything on to
Eldar. He looked like a stuffed bear. But they couldn't put on two
pairs of shoes, so Asmir pushed their slippers into his rucksack with
the toys.

The telephone rang. 'I'll get it,' Asmir called and ran. He expected to hear Muris's voice. But it was Aunt Melita, ringing from
Belgrade. 'I must speak with your mother,' she said and her voice
sounded as tight as a guitar string.

Asmir stood close to his mother. He could hear Aunt Melita's
words bursting into the familiar room like bullets. 'My newspaper,
Oslo-bodjenje, is trying to evacuate women and children on a military plane today. I've put your name on the list. There are already

over two hundred people on that list. The plane can only take forty. If you want to be on it you'll have to be at the pick-up point in the city in thirty minutes.'

'But that's three kilometres away!' Mirsada sobbed. 'And Muris has gone to work. Our car's been bombed. There's no public transport and no taxis. And Eldar's sick.'

'It might be your last chance, Mirsada,' Melita urged. 'You've got to try, for the children's sake, and Mother's.'

Then the phone went dead.

Asmir looked at his mother. Her face was strained like a mask, tight and white. 'Tell Grandmother to get ready. We must leave in five minutes.'

Asmir ran to her room. But he didn't have to say anything. She was stuffing clothes into a bag. 'Now?' she asked. He nodded. And ran to the kitchen. Breakfast. He hadn't had breakfast. He gulped down a mug of water and stuffed two rolls into his pockets.

His mother was on the phone again. He leaned against her. He could hear his father saying, 'You can do it, Dada.' He loved the way his father called her Dada. 'You can do it. You must do it. For my sake.'

Then there was cracking and a crash. And the phone went dead again. Asmir hoped with all his heart that it was only the phone which was dead.

His mother was bundling up Eldar into a rug. She put him in Grandmother's arms and picked up the two suitcases. Asmir swung his rucksack on to his back and grabbed Grandmother's bag. The door banged behind them. Their footsteps clattered on the stairs. Asmir pushed open the front door. They hurried out into the scarred and rubble-strewn street.

'We've less than twenty-five minutes to get there,' Mirsada panted, 'before the bus leaves for the airport.'

'Follow me,' Grandmother said. 'There aren't any short cuts in Sarajevo that I don't know. And the alleys will be safer than the main roads.'

She took the lead, threading the way through lanes and courtyards and side streets, turning aside to avoid craters and debris, burned out cars and dead bodies. There wasn't time even to try and recognise friends. She shifted Eldar from hip to hip, and Asmir shifted her bag from hand to hand. His breath was coming in little panting panicky sobs. He felt sick and he wished he hadn't had the water which was sloshing round inside him, very close to the top.

His mother was flagging. Asmir grabbed a case from her with his free hand. The case had little wheels on it but they were no use, no use at all on the rough and broken roadway. Desperately he yanked and tugged. Desperately he wished he was taller, bigger, stronger, older. Daddy! How can I do your job, Daddy? I'm only seven and I feel sick.

The water came up in a sudden gout, splattering over the dark cobbles. Asmir did not even wipe his mouth. He didn't have a free hand now and it would have meant stopping. He was behind already. Behind, behind, behind. Further, further, further. Hurry, hurry, hurry. Faster, faster, faster. Oh Muris, why aren't you here?

His mother was waiting for him to catch up. 'Thank you for giving me a rest. I'll be able to manage now.'

'Are you sure, Dada?' he said.

She smiled at him over her shoulder, already hurrying on again with the two cases. Asmir stumbled on after her, feeling as if his arms were coming out of their sockets.

'We're more than halfway,' Grandmother called back to him. Asmir put on another spurt, though the horse and cart were digging in between his shoulder blades and he was sweating like a real horse under his extra layer and anorak. He changed hands again, noticing numbly that the bag straps had rubbed his fingers raw.

On and on. Coming to corners. Doubling back painfully when the way was blocked. Hearing the sound of mortars. Seeing the flash of gunfire. Hearing the crash of falling brickwork. Seeing blood and more blood on the road.

Asmir wondered when he would wake up in his own bed. Would the nightmare end soon? If only Muris would reach out and put his arms around him again. Then he heard Muris saying, 'War never does make sense.' And he knew he would not wake up in his own bed again. Ever.

And the tears made it even harder to go on, harder to see the holes, the humps, the hazards. He fell, struggled up, fell again. His breath was coming in choking gasps. He could hear Eldar crying. And Eldar almost never cried. Never.

'Nearly there,' his mother called back. 'One more spurt.'

Asmir didn't think he had another spurt left in him. Not even half a spurt. Then he saw Muris. Muris running towards him. Muris scooping him up, bag and all. Muris running with him in his arms across the finishing line. 'We won, Asmir said.

'Not yet,' his father said.

Lots of mothers were waiting with their children and piles of bags and bundles. Then a big bus came and everyone started to shove to get aboard. Asmir was glad their father was there. He helped other mothers and grandmothers too, squeezing their things in where it looked as if even a matchbox wouldn't fit.

The bus was almost ready to leave when suddenly soldiers appeared. They grabbed the men who had been helping. They grabbed Asmir's father by the arms. The driver revved the engine and the bus roared off.

Asmir gripped his mother's hand. 'Daddy!' he screamed.

So did thirty other children, and some began to cry. Even Eldar, always cheerful, always smiling until yesterday, began to bawl. There was no room to play peek-a-boo, so Asmir tickled him. Eldar loved being tickled. Even through a jacket, a jumper, a skivvy and a T-shirt he gave a little giggle. His mother smiled at Asmir over his head. 'Thank you, my brave son,' she whispered.

The bus rattled on. Crying subsided into sobbing. Sobbing became hiccups. The children fell asleep in the stuffy jolting capsule. Eldar snuggled up on his mother's lap. Asmir was sitting on Grandmother's knees and they were thin and bony. But she smelled good and he fell asleep too. He woke later to feel his hair damp and Grandmother's tears trickling slowly down his cheeks.

He patted her hands – the hands that made the best stuffed apples in the world – and wondered if the soldiers had let Muris go. He was glad he had put in two photos – one of Muris helping him to blow out the candles on his seventh birthday, and one of Muris holding Eldar on his first. Muris so handsome with his wavy hair and his eyes that laughed.

And every moment the bus took them further and further away from their father.

From *No Guns For Asmir* by Christobel Mattingley

THE SPRING OF '39

War looms large over Flanders. In his castle, the count is making preparations to flee to Switzerland, where it is safer than in his own country.

The orchard grows white, as if my mother is making it snow. She is spreading sheets and pillowcases on the grass. When she runs out of space, she hangs out washing in the apple trees. The blossoms too are white. My mother is standing in their midst. Tiny, with a little white lap. She works fast, oblivious to all else. I help and watch. Whenever my mother takes a step, I take one too. I wait until she has started hanging the last sheet between two branches, and quickly pull her skirt.

'Why are you angry with me, mum,' I say.

My mother produces a faint sound with her tongue and raises her eyes. 'I'll repeat it one more time, one more time, you hear?' she says. 'There is an Upstairs Cat and there is a Basement Cat. The Upstairs Cat belongs upstairs and the Basement Cat belongs with us. If I see our animal upstairs one more time, I'll kick it down those stairs.'

'You wouldn't dare.'

'Try me,' my mother says. She takes the two empty wicker baskets and ploughs through the high grass.

'The countess's cat gobbles down our cat's food!' I speak to her back. 'And that's allowed?'

'Yes, that's allowed,' my mother says. She turns around. 'What is it you want? Swap with the countess perhaps? What's got into you, child? You know your place and it's downstairs!' She closes the gate with a bang, and all I can do is watch her go.

I mutter between my teeth. Oh, if I catch that Upstairs Cat in the basement one more time, I'll kick it to kingdom come, or at least half-way there, and then I'll kick it all the way up those very same stairs.

The countess appears on the terrace. She calls me and waves. The Upstairs Cat is sitting on her arm. Fat as a toad, and shaggy and ugly.

I wave back. The tiny smile on my face turns sour. I open the gate and pretend to hop away cheerfully. I am boiling inside.

It is colder than outside downstairs, in the basement kitchen. My mother has wrapped a shawl around her and sits knitting another one. She's singing. 'Knit one, purl one, knit knit knit; knit one, purl one, make those garments fit.'

I stop and listen for a while. Mum's voice sounds warm and soft. I carefully close the door, so as not to interrupt the singing.

But she's seen me. She drops the knitting in her lap, and says: 'Go outside, Harriet, make the most of the sun now that it's out. Or else work on your school sampler. Your knitting's much too tight, you should practise if you want to learn.'

'Shall I darn the socks?'

'Outside or your sampler, I said.'

The bell rings. The countess wants tea. My mother is startled and gets up, throwing her knitting aside. She pours hot water from the kettle into the teapot on the worktop and disappears upstairs, carefully balancing the tray on her hands. The door is left ajar.

I pull mum's half-finished shawl towards me. The spot where mum's been sitting, is still warm. 'Knit, knit, knit with me,' I say to the cat on her cushion by the cupboard. She is lying there like a thick ball of wool. I look at her and she looks back at me.

'Knit, purl, knit,' I sing. I make one loop, two loops, finish an entire row. And another row. Soon the needles start squeaking. Mum's right, I'll never learn.

'Waaaatch youur moooother puuurl aaah roooow!' I sing. I press my lips in concentration. I try to make the loops looser, but can't

seem to manage. My hands are moist, I wipe them on my dress. As
if I've just touched something yucky. I look around. Surely nobody
has seen this? God's eye has, from its black frame over the door, but
that's the all-seeing eye. And the cat, perhaps.

The cat?

I gasp. The cushion by the cupboard is empty. I look at the door.
Wouldn't you know it! The cat must have escaped through the chink.

'Puss? I call out. I can hear cats' paws on the wooden stairs.
Softly trip trip trip upstairs. Up!'

'If I see our animal upstairs one more time, I'll kick it downstairs!' And she meant it too.

The narrow basement stairs creak as I sneak up them. The countess's stairs are wide and made of marble, covered with blue carpet.
However soft Pussy's landing may be, I still pray my mother does
not spot our cat.

The high drawing-room door is wide open. I hear voices through
the silence. Am I hearing correctly? Is that somebody crying or is it
the cat meowing? I tiptoe closer. Like I've become one huge ear,
that's how intently I listen.

'Germany,' the count says, like it's a curse. 'Hitler's not afraid of
war.'

I put my hand on my heart. War? Where? And with whom?

'Staying would be dangerous,' the countess says behind the door.
She's crying. Why cry, since we're not at war? All I see outside is
snow, and sunshine! Or hasn't the countess noticed?

'We're getting out of here. See this out in Switzerland. But we'll
be back. Oh yes, we'll be back,' the countess says in a creaky voice.

'We trust you. Take good care of the house. The entire house, as
if it were yours.' The count says it casually, as if he were reading
from the newspaper.

I feel rugged fur against my leg. The Upstairs Cat. The purring
Upstairs Cat. I slowly bend my knees, until I am able to touch his
head. I caress him.

'What's going on in there?' I whisper.

The countess is crying in the drawing room. The clock is ticking.
For an instant it seems the chimes are planning to sound the hour. But
the count says: 'These are the keys. All the keys to the castle, of all

the cupboards and doors, from attic to basement. Have them.'

I don't understand.

My mother appears in the corridor. She's not even surprised to find me there. I am, when I see her. I can feel my eyes bulging. My jaw drops.

Mother is holding our cat. A huge set of keys is dangling from her hand. She shakes her head wearily.

'Things change,' she says softly. 'Things change fast. Come, sweetheart. You take care of the Upstairs Cat.'

From *Fatso II* by Bart Moeyaert.

THE EVACUEE

During the second World War in Britain thousands of children from the towns and cities most vulnerable to enemy bombs were sent away to the safer countryside for the duration. This was called evacuation *and the children were called* evacuees. *Many of the children came from poor homes and industrial environments and were to experience living in the countryside for the first time. R S Thomas's poem is about one such evacuee and the extract which follows it is about another.*

She woke up under a loose quilt
Of leaf patterns, woven by the light
At the small window, busy with the boughs
Of a young cherry; but wearily she lay,
Waiting for the siren, slow to trust
Nature's deceptive peace, and then afraid
Of the long silence, she would have crept
Uneasily from the bedroom with its frieze
Of fresh sunlight, had not a cock crowed,
Shattering the surface of that limpid pool
Of stillness, and before the ripples died
One by one in the field's shallows,
The farm woke with uninhibited din.

And now the noise and not the silence drew her
Down the bare stairs at great speed.
The sounds and voices were a rough sheet
Waiting to catch her, as though she leaped
From a scorched storey of the charred past.

And there the table and the gallery
Of farm faces trying to be kind
Beckoned her nearer, and she sat down
Under an awning of salt hams.

And so she grew, a small bird in the nest
Of welcome that was built about her,
Home now after so long away
In the flowerless streets of the drab town.
The men watched her busy with the hens,
The soft flesh ripening warm as corn
On the sticks of limbs, the grey eyes clear,
Rinsed with dew of their long dread.
The men watched her, and, nodding, smiled
With earth's charity, patient and strong.

by R S Thomas

A TRIP ON A TRAIN

*Dot, a young girl, and her mother Gloria are living in London
during the blitz of the Second World War. Dot's father is apparently
away in the army, though we learn later that he had a nervous
breakdown early on in the war and was unable to take part in the
action. They are very poor and at the beginning of the story Dot's
baby brother dies in hospital. In this chapter they are travelling by
train to be evacuated to the country house of a rich lady. Dot has
been dressed in second-hand clothes, and because her mother
cannot afford her train fare Dot has to pretend to be her baby*

brother when the ticket inspector arrives. This novel shows what it must have been like for poor London children to leave their homes and families during war-time and taste the lives of people who were much better off. Although the rich old lady offers to look after Dot permanently, Dot really loves her mother and decides to return to her own family with all its problems as the war comes to an end.

The compartment was fitted out with everything they would need to live there for ever. It was like having a perfect home of their own. They had their own windows with dark blue oil-cloth roller-blinds through which Dot could see into the compartment of the train along-side just like looking over at a next-door house.

Beneath the window was a useful fold-out table. There were brass ashtrays, coat-hooks, a mirror where Gloria would be able to do her hair, an overhead net to store things. The two rows of upholstered seats facing each other were like a pair of matching beds, one for each so they would not again need to share except when they want-ed to.

'I like it here,' said Dot, stretching out along her bed while Gloria took off her hat and placed it carefully on the luggage rack. 'It's comfy.'

'We ain't there yet, pet. We ain't even started.'

Just as the train began to move, a soldier with a kit bag slung like a khaki corpse over his shoulder glanced into their compartment.

'Ooops-a-daisy,' he said. 'No smoker.'

Gloria pretended not to notice him. Usually she loved a good chat, specially with people from the services.

Overhead Dot noticed a row of shaded lamps each with its own switch. Gloria would be able to read her *Picturegoer* as late as she wanted without keeping Dot awake. Between the lamps, just as in a proper home, was a pair of framed photographs. Mrs Parvis had pho-tographs in her parlour. Hers hung on picture hooks. These ones were screwed to the wall.

'"*Brighton and Hove Southern Railway*",' Gloria read out. '"*The Royal Promenade, Eastbourne.*" That's at the seaside. I'll take you there. One day. Maybe. Other one's Brighton. I never been to

Brighton. Now sit still and stop hopping about, will you. Anyone'd
think you was a flea on the organ-grinder's monkey.'

The windows were streaky like at the basement.

'We'd clean them windows,' Dot said. 'If this was our home,
wouldn't we?'

First thing we'd do she thought, with a cloth and a big bucket of
soapy water. So they'd sparkle. So you could see out any time you
wanted.

Gloria closed the sliding door, pulled down the blinds, and
switched off the six lamps which Dot had just put on.

'Can't see!' said Dot. 'I need to look out my windows!' She lifted the bottom corner of one of the blinds.

'Oi, don't lean out or you'll get smuts in your eye! You don't
understand, it's better this way, love. You *will* behave proper when
we get there, won't you? You won't go letting me down. Oh, I do
hope you don't. Look at your face! You still got that hanky?'

It was in Dot's pocket, still scrumpled up, still waiting for its rinse
through. Gloria wrapped a corner of it round her index finger, spat to
make it wet, then dabbed at Dot's cheeks till they were sore.

'See, ducks, his Mrs Hollidaye what we're going to see, her
clothes are that shabby, but she's like a real lady. She has these pearls
round her neck. Wears them all the time, even when she's out digging. So I really want you to be like a proper sort of little girl. She's
ever so posh, but she's ever so kind too. I want her to think we're
nice people.'

'You *are* a nice person,' said Dot, though she was beginning to
feel unsure about it. Nothing in the world was ever certain or fixed,
things changed easily and when least expected. She thought she'd
found the perfect place to live, yet already it was slipping away and
this cosy compartment was only a stage on to something else. So
who were the nice people? Was the King a nice person and the
princesses?

''Course royalty is!' said Gloria, shocked. 'Goes without saying.
Now your socks.' She reached down to take off Dot's shoes, then her
socks, one long, one not so long, one greyish white, the other a different kind of fawnish white. She turned them inside out, returned
them to Dot to put on with the insides now on the outside. White

socks never stayed clean. It was all very well for the princesses. There probably hadn't been much dust lying around in a palace.

'Grey socks are better,' said Dot. They didn't show scuff marks at all.

'See, I don't want Mrs Hollidaye to go thinking you're riff-raff. I don't want her to go getting any wrong ideas about what's become of me.'

The train was moving fast. Gloria said, 'Come over here now. Lay in my lap. Suck your thumb, there's a love.'

Dot looked at it and was surprised to see how dirty it had become. She inspected the fingers and thumb on her other hand. These too had become smudged with dirt, and the velvet cuffs of her coat, and everything in the compartment was flecked with specks of greasy black which came off on to you the moment you touched them. She wondered if this coat had ever been on a train before, when it had belonged to the other child.

'Yes, *please* do,' said Gloria.

She pulled Dot onto her knee. Being cradled against her mother's soft warm body, Dot tried to feel like a baby, to remember what she had seen through the crack in the double doors as Gloria had cradled Baby against her while the nurses gathered round with protective outstretched arms.

Sometimes Gloria was so strange. First she wanted Dot to be nice, next she wanted her to put a filthy thumb in her mouth and suck it.

Obediently, Dot did as Gloria asked, gripping her thumb between her front teeth to prevent it slipping out.

'Where we going?' Dot asked, her thumb still lying firmly on her tongue like Gloria wanted it.

'And don't talk no more.'

So Dot whispered it.

'Sssh. You gotta be like my baby.'

Dot sat bolt upright. 'I can't be your baby! You said I was too big to be carried. I don't want to be no baby! I don't want to be blind and dead.'

'Please, ducky. Be a baby for Mum. Just on the train, till the man's been past. See, I didn't have the money to get no ticket for you.'

Gloria took from her bag a little blanket made of coloured squares that a long-ago lady in a shelter had knitted for Baby before he was born.

'Baby's blanket!' said Dot in surprise. 'You brought it!'

Gloria wrapped it gently around Dot's head and shoulders, pulling it well forward over her face.

'Now I can't even see,' said Dot.

'Just till after the bloke's been along. I told you, I haven't got no ticket for you.'

Although not exactly dark, nor scary because Gloria was holding her tenderly, it was stuffy under the blanket and irritating to be covered over when you wanted to look out. Dot sucked away on her thumb.

'Can I come out yet?'

'No, ssh. He's just coming.'

Dot heard the compartment door open. A draught of cold air blew in. Dot heard the man ask for Gloria's ticket, felt the movement as Gloria reached for her purse.

'Taking me little one down to the country to see her Nan,' she heard Gloria say, then the click-clack of the ticket-clipper before the man closed the door and they were alone again.

Dot said, 'Who's my Nan?'

'Your Nan died years ago.'

'But you said we're going to see my Nan.'

'Oh, that. That was to stop him asking nosy questions, like how old you was. But it's all right. I don't think he was that bothered. You look small enough.'

Dot pushed back the blanket, slid off Gloria's lap and moved back to sit by her window. She lifted the bottom of the blind.

'That's right. You take a peek. That's the real countryside out there. Ain't it lovely? Full of animals and that.'

'What kind of animals?'

'Aw, I dunno,' Gloria said vaguely. 'Cows and bulls. That sort of thing.'

The next-door train had been left far behind. The houses had all gone too. There was nothing out there now. No walls, no roads, no buildings. No red buses, no red letterboxes, no red telephone boxes. No iron railings. No pavements, no front doors, no streets, no nothing and it was growing dark as the black nothingness dashed past the window.

'I want to go back. I changed my mind. I don't like it no more.'

'Do stop that crying!' Gloria snapped. 'It makes your eyes all red. And now look at your face. All messed up again after I just cleaned you up! Take a look at it!'

She held Dot up to the mirror and Dot saw the greyish rivulets where tears had run down her cheeks and been smudged to grey by her hands.

She wondered how clean tears could make a person's skin go dirty.

'I told you you'd got to try and keep yourself looking nice for Mrs Hollidaye,' said Gloria. 'You wash clean and dry dirty, that's always been your trouble.'

From *Paper Faces* by Rachel Anderson

TANIA'S JOURNEY TO FIND FOOD FOR HER FAMILY

Tania and her family live outside Leningrad at the time of the German invasion of Russia in World War 2. There is no food and Tania's family is starving so she sets off to see if she can find food in a town a few kilometres away. However it is the Russian winter and Tania has to walk to the town in sub-zero temperatures. In this extract from the novel, in which Tania is eventually captured and sent to a Labour camp in Germany, Tania is at the beginning of her heroic journey to find food.

I knocked at the first house I came to, a large and beautiful building with smoke curling from its chimneys. I was looking forward to drinking some hot water to warm me up a little. Perhaps I could even sleep...

No chance of that. They didn't even open the door. I saw only a shadow flit across the curtains.

I knocked at the second house, and the third. But either they wouldn't open the door at all or they told me that there was nowhere for me to stay; all the houses were full to overflowing. And that was probably the truth. At first the villagers had taken in the refugees and tried to help them as best they could. But then more and more came, many dirty and covered in lice and bloated with hunger. And some of those to whom they gave shelter in the evening were found the next morning dead in their beds. But I only learned all this later on.

At the time, as I realized that I was gradually freezing to death as close to warmth and shelter, I became utterly frustrated. If I don't get some hot water to drink right now, I thought, I'll collapse and freeze in the middle of the village.

Then just as I had given up hope, somebody did let me into his house. It was the poorest and meanest little hut in the whole village. An old man lived there. He said that he had only recently buried his wife. She had died of hunger, but he would survive for a while longer.

'But it's bitterly cold, my little house,' he continued, as if he wanted to apologize. 'At night the cold comes straight in, so the water in the buckets turns to ice. Come to the hearth, little one, and thaw yourself out. You are quite stiff with cold already. It seems you can't even move your tongue any more.'

It was really true. My tongue was frozen stiff and my teeth chattered so much that I could only speak by making a big effort. I leant against the warm brick stove, and the old man continued, 'I'll just heat up some water for you, but don't expect anything else; there's nothing left. I am starving, too.'

Gradually I began to revive. I thought about my future. I would probably survive the next day, but then? How was I going to live through this cold without any food? And finding a place to stay was obviously almost impossible. But as I warmed up and drank the hot water, I pushed these dark thoughts aside. I was so exhausted I was ready to collapse.

The old man had other people staying with him too: a young

woman and her child. The old man had told them to crawl on top of the huge brick stove to sleep.

'And you – what's your name? Tatiana? Right, Tatiana, lie down on this bench. I don't even have a bed for you! Everything that we had saved before the war went long ago, swapped for a piece of bread while my wife was still alive. Now there is nothing left to swap.'

'Where are you going, little one?' he continued. 'You will die. The people in the villages are already cutting themselves off from refugees. They don't have anything left themselves, but you still keep coming.'

The old man's voice shook with fury. 'The devil take you, you cursed fascists!' he cried. 'Did you have to invade Russia? Things had improved before the war; we had some quite reasonable farms. Before that, after the last World War, there was no peace at all: first enemy troops, then civil war, then bad harvests. And now the damned fascists come visiting! Oh, Russia will never find peace.'

The old man grumbled on as he got himself ready for bed, but soon he fell silent.

I stretched myself out on the bench. It was long but narrow, and I didn't know where to put my arms, which hung down on either side. In the end I crossed them over my chest, like they do with dead people. My only blanket was my coat. It was a very uncomfortable bed, but tiredness overwhelmed me and I quickly fell asleep.

I woke up while it was still dark. I couldn't move. Had I been frozen to the bench, I wondered, horrified. But then I realized that only my clothes had frozen, and my back was numb from lying on the hard planks.

I stood up with difficulty. My whole body hurt; my legs had gone to sleep and wouldn't obey me any more. How could I continue my journey like this?

A thought flashed through my head: turn back! But where to? Starvation was waiting for me at home. I had to flee. I had to flee starvation as quickly as possible.

The child on top of the brick stove was crying. The old man threw chunks of ice into a copper kettle. Even the water in the buckets had frozen solid overnight.

While I rubbed my back and warmed myself with hot water, I made up my mind. If I was going to die, then it would be on my journey. There was no turning back.

The old man said, 'Another thirty, forty kilometres, Tatiana, then you might be able to get something to eat. Until then, don't count on it. The next thirty kilometres are tough. There are people dying every day. And finding shelter overnight will be hard. Here is a crust for your journey. It's only made of hay, but at least you'll have something to chew on. I would love to give you more, but there is really nothing left, not even the tiniest morsel.'

I thanked him for everything, and left the hut. I didn't walk – no, I flew onward. I would probably still last out for one more day. One more day of hunger, and then, according to the old man, rescue. If only I could travel more quickly. If only those dangerous kilometres were behind me.

After about two hours I came to the village of Nowinka in which I had intended to spend the previous night. It was strange: on the second day of my journey I was striding out much more strongly and quickly, as if I had found my rhythm.

But after I had walked for fifteen kilometres I began to feel dreadfully tired again, even though it was still light.

All this time I had been walking through a forest. The path was narrow and well used. Many people had obviously already taken it to the corn regions, but now there wasn't a soul to be seen.

The path wandered through the trees, between high, thickly planted firs whose branches met above it. It was dark, and suddenly I was afraid. What if a wolf appeared around the next corner? Where would I go? Up a tree? People said that many wolves still prowled here, carrying on their grisly business in the dense forest. And I was alone, completely alone.

I was afraid to stop, but hunger had been gnawing at me mercilessly for some time. Somehow I must make myself stronger. I fought back my fear, sat on the sledge and unpacked the crust which the old man had given me. It was frozen solid.

I had just bitten off a corner when I saw a man lying directly ahead of me. He was curled up against the cold, his glassy eyes staring at me.

The next minute it hit me: he was dead.

Horror gripped me. A man had fallen over here and had never got up again. That could happen to me. I must leave this brooding forest quickly, quickly!

I stuffed the rest of the crust into my mouth, jumped up – desperately trying not to look – and ran away as quickly as I could. I no longer felt hungry and tired. Panic drove me onwards. Where was the village, where was it? If only this terrible forest would come to an end.

At last, around a corner, I glimpsed a large village. It was only now that I realized just how tired I was. I was bathed in sweat and my legs were giving way. I had the feeling that I couldn't even manage the few steps separating me from the houses at the edge of the village.

But somehow I did manage it, and I was allowed to stay the night at the first house I knocked at. Only then did I realize that I had travelled thirty kilometres. How on earth had I done it?

This time the family who gave me shelter were cobblers. The master of the house was still a young man, but he had lost his legs. In the main room, beds had been pushed against the walls. The room smelt of newly cured leather. The cobbler obviously did his work in this room too.

The family gave me hot herb tea to drink and a few piping hot potatoes to eat. It was a real feast. I hadn't eaten so well for many months, ever since Wyritza was occupied.

After supper, the cobbler set to work. While he hammered a new heel on to a boot he said, 'As you can see, little sister, I was wounded on the third day of the war and sent home. Little did I know that the Germans were closing in here, too. Still, we're not beaten yet. Though, to be honest, the whole thing is a mess. The war, this awful war, has changed all our lives, and no one knows when it will end. It's going to be a while till it's over, as far as I can see. But there's one good thing: at least there are fewer Germans here now. They probably need all the help they can get for the fight at Leningrad.' That means the Germans weren't doing so well.

'Here,' he continued, 'take a few leather soles. You might be able to swap them for something on your journey. I can't give you anything more. I feel sorry for you, little sister. You may well die, but you're very brave – and angry, I know.'

They bedded me down on the floor and gave me a thick fur coverlet so that I was able to get warm in the night. As I fell asleep I thought, 'What friendly people I've met! I hope I meet many more good people on my travels.'

When I woke up, I was convinced that I could make it to the cornfields. My hosts, who had warmed me up and given me new hope, even gave me some food for my journey.

The cobbler also gave me some advice. 'Go quickly, Tania. The next forty kilometres will be hard, but then the corn regions begin. Mind you, they say the people there already have everything that can be bartered, from carpets to mirrors. However, perhaps you'll be lucky and find some good folk.'

That day I again walked many kilometres. Occasionally people gave me a piece of bread or a potato along the way. That gave me strength, and I strode out more energetically.

One village followed another, little ones and big ones. Tschastscha was far behind me; now I was passing Tscholowo. Should I stop here and sleep? Smoke drifted welcomingly from the chimneys. It would be lovely and warm in the farmhouses and the warmth was tempting, but my anxiety drove me on. Quickly, quickly. Bargain for corn and then turn back for home.

Would they still be alive? This thought worried me dreadfully. I tried to push it away by imagining how much corn I could get – I would take a whole sledgeful home – and by thinking what delicious bread Mama would make with it; just like it used to be, before the war.

I learnt a few things during those three days. For the first time I had to rely wholly upon myself, and I lived constantly with the feeling that dangers lurked around every corner. But now I knew I could work out my route quite accurately. I was not afraid of walking through the woods alone, and I had learned how to guess where one could ask for shelter at night and where there was no point in trying. But weakness, hunger and cold made it ever harder to cope, and I had to say to myself continually, 'You must, you must!'

How many kilometres did I put behind me on the third day of my journey? Thirty? More? Again my legs were failing me and my whole body was at the point of collapse. I found a large village and hoped I would be able to stay the night there. Then I could start on the last leg of my journey, refreshed, in the morning. Dog-tired and weak with hunger, I looked forward to my night's rest.

But what was that? Loud screams, dogs barking, women crying! Some men had surrounded the village and were shouting and cursing in German. It was strange: I was meeting German soldiers for the first time on my long journey. I had heard that they didn't show themselves much in the villages for fear of the partisans.

When the soldiers saw me they yelled, 'Get away from here! Scram!'

Then a woman shouted, 'Where do you want to go? You must make a detour round us. We are in quarantine. Typhus has come to our village! You see, they have cut us off. Perhaps they want to burn the lot of us!' She started to cry.

I was stunned. What was I to do now? I had forced myself to the limit already. The village was large; going round it would take at least an hour. And where then? It was twilight, and the frost was getting sharper.

I tried to force myself through the human chain of soldiers and others. 'Let me through! I don't care. I can't go any further.'

Typhus? Typhus? What was that anyway? I had never heard of it. The large village promised warmth and rest. I didn't have the strength to let this dream go. But one of the men grabbed me by the collar and said forcefully, 'Where d'you think you're going? Are you crazy? You heard – typhus. You'd be dead by morning. People are dying like flies here. Get out of here while it's not too late, or we won't let you go at all.'

He shoved me and my sledge far away from the crowds who stood there weeping and moaning.

'Go on, go! Get out!' he bellowed, as he saw that I didn't move.

I burst into tears and went. What business was it of theirs what happened to me anyway, I thought. How did they know that I would die of typhus? It was much more likely that I would collapse from tiredness and freeze to death here. Anyway, what did it matter what I died from. Dying of typhus might even be easier; at least I'd be in a house, in the warm.

With thoughts like this spinning through my head I wandered round the village, and with each step I sank deeper into the snow. The sound of the moaning and howling of women and children carried to me from the houses.

When I had bypassed the village, I couldn't find the road again. There was nobody there to ask. I was completely alone in that vast expanse.

It grew dark. The snow began to fall in drifts. Everything whirled and swirled around me. I couldn't even see my feet. Where to now? Where was the next village? Was it near? Far? And which direction should I take?

Fear and frustration gripped me. Eventually I couldn't take any more. I sat down on my sledge and began to cry. I thought of Mama's words: 'You will die, Tania.' Yes, I thought, that is what will happen. No one can help me, and you are far away, Mama. No one will find me here, in this snowbound field.

If only I knew in which direction I should go, I would march on with my remaining strength. But there was no path, only a thick snowy curtain surrounding me and cutting me off from the rest of the world. I couldn't stay sitting there all night; I would freeze. I hadn't died of hunger, but now I would die of cold – like the man I had stumbled upon yesterday by the path through the forest.

I buried my head in my hands, curled myself up as protection against the cold wind that whistled through my whole body, and waited to die. My arms and legs began to go numb. My face was covered with a light crust of ice. My mind became hazy. Soon, soon it would all be over. If only it would be quick.

Suddenly I thought of my family. Back home they would be waiting for me, hoping for corn, counting the minutes. I pulled myself together. While I had the tiniest spark of life left in me I had to carry on. I must walk on, walk on, never mind where…

I struggled to my feet and stumbled through the white veil of snow and icy wind. Snow and tears stuck my eyelids together. I battled my way forwards by guesswork, sometimes sinking up to my belt in a snowdrift, unable to see my hand in front of my eyes. All I could see was a thick wall of snow.

When I had fought my way out of the snowdrifts it was a struggle to pull the sledge behind me. I'll leave it behind, I said to myself. That will be easier. But how would I bring the corn home then? No, I had to take the sledge with me.

Gradually the snowstorm blew itself out. Far away in the darkness I made out a dim light. And then another next to it. A village!

I set out towards the lights, floundering and falling in the snow. Then, when I had nearly reached the first of the houses, I suddenly realized that I could not carry on – I couldn't go a single step further. I fell to the ground. Now I was on all fours, crawling. I reached the front steps of a house and heard a dog barking, but I couldn't make it to the door.

I heard voices nearby. 'It's another child. She's probably lost. Or the mother froze to death, like that other one recently.' It was a young woman's voice.

A different, slightly older voice asked, 'Aren't you afraid, Anjuta? Typhus has broken out round here. Where has the girl come from? After all, they gave orders that no one is allowed out.'

'But we must get her warm. We can't turn her away like a stray dog!' answered the first voice.

I wanted to scream, 'Please don't turn me away, please don't turn me away!' but instead I felt myself sinking into a deep sleep.

When I woke up, it was already light. I lay wrapped up in a warm fur by a stove. Sunbeams were crowding through the window. 'Sun!' I must have said it aloud, because a woman got up from the stove and came over.

'You're alive, my dear. Thank God! We worried about you all night. You were frozen through when we carried you into the house. We thought you were too far gone to live. But what were you doing, all alone at night? You should be glad that the dog started barking, otherwise you'd have died of cold on our doorstep. Now get up and have some hot soup. Then you'll forget all this.'

The young woman looked after me. I was happy and looked out

at the sunshine, telling myself, 'How wonderful it is to see the sun. I haven't seen it for so long. And I am alive!'

I no longer felt the terrible exhaustion of the previous night, and I didn't want to think about all the things I had endured. I ate the tasty barley soup and clung to the thought that the corn-growing regions were already very near.

'The villages with the cornfields aren't far from here,' said the older lady, guessing my thoughts. She too was fussing over me. 'We go there ourselves, and barter anything that we have in the house for corn. You can reach Oredesch town in an hour. But it's not worth staying there. By evening you'll find the villages where you can barter something for grain.'

'You have got something to trade?' she asked. 'Don't be too hopeful. They are very choosy. You might be lucky, but don't be too quick to give things away. Go from house to house and bargain with people. It could well be that one house will give you more than another. Before the war the farms were in good shape, and some still have food in plenty because they were able to finish the harvest – even if German bombs were dropping all around them. Corn is more expensive than gold, nowadays.'

I hurried on. By lunchtime I had gone past Oredesch and had reached a village where I was sure I could get some grain.

It struck me immediately that the people here were wealthy. The houses were new and solid and had obviously been built just before the start of the war. They were made of thick treetrunks and still smelt of pine.

I chose an attractive, large house and knocked at the door.

'Come in, come in,' said a man's voice.

I went in – and stood still with wonder. The whole room was covered in carpets from floor to ceiling, and it was full of mirrors. I had never seen so many beautiful things in one place before. All my courage left me. Who would be interested in my modest bits and pieces in a house like this?

'All right, what have you got? Come on, let's see,' said the man, without a word of greeting. In his white linen tunic, unbelted, he looked like a Russian folk-hero. Most impressive of all was his thick, well-cared-for beard.

'Well, I –' my tongue wouldn't obey me '– I have come to barter for some grain. I have walked a very long way…'

'Yes, I know,' the farmer interrupted. 'You want corn, that's obvious, but what have you got to bargain with? Show me.'

I opened up my sack.

'No, no, no,' he said, after he had cast an eye over my pathetic offerings. 'We don't need stuff like this. The place is already full to bursting. We can't fit any more in.'

'But please, sir,' I cried, terrified that he would throw me out at once. 'Look at these shoe-soles. Don't you want these? They are made of real leather and they are brand new.' I showed him the soles which the cobbler had given me.

'No, I don't need anything like that,' he said quickly. 'Hey, Wassili,' he shouted through the open door to the next room, 'do you need any soles? There's a girl here, trading.'

Wassili came into the room. He was another strong and healthy farmer, but younger. He looked at the soles and turned them over in his hands. 'Well, we could give you a loaf of bread for them. If you want a loaf we could do a deal.'

Only a loaf of bread? Was it possible? I had pinned my hopes on the leather soles. I had already realized that it would not be easy to trade my other things. But one loaf of bread! I would have to eat it on the way back, and then what would I have to bring home?

'No,' I said loudly. 'I won't give them to you for one loaf of bread. I need more. My family is waiting for me at home. They are starving.'

'More?' The farmer burst out laughing. 'You fool, I'm already offering you a good deal. Well, go on then, try and find yourself someone who'll give you more…'

I went from house to house. In every one they looked at my bits and pieces, felt the shoe-soles and offered me so little that I went away without trading anything.

I wondered if I should try to drive a harder bargain. But Mama had always said that a well-brought-up young lady shouldn't haggle. What was I to do? I couldn't leave the village without any corn.

I knocked on another door. This time I was determined – I would bargain more forcefully with these people.

An old lady greeted me. 'Come in, little one, come in. Oh, my dear, what a long way you've travelled,' she said, after I had told her my tearful story. 'And now you're to go home with nothing to show for it? Don't look so downcast. My sister and I, we'll help you. It's evening now. Stay the night with us and see what tomorrow brings. Things always look better in the morning.'

When I woke up the next day, the first thing I saw was my sack. It was full of corn.

The ladies said to me, 'Little Tania, we want to give you the grain as a present. We don't need your things. Try to swap them for something else. Perhaps some oilcakes and bran. You can use those to supplement the corn, so that it will last longer.'

'There are new rules in our village,' they explained. 'A new order. The Germans have set up a village leader, a very rich man. People are becoming grudging and mean-spirited. But we had put a little corn by and so we can share it with you.'

I ran joyfully through the village once more, and was able to trade my leather soles and other things for oilcakes and bran.

Now my sledge was packed full with corn, just as I had dreamed of. The kind ladies gave me something to eat, and slipped me some bread for my journey. They tried to persuade me to stay a little longer and rest, but the thought of home pulled me onwards. My anxiety about my family was growing by the hour. I knew they would be waiting for me, worrying and counting the hours and minutes. That very same day I turned for home.

It was the end of February. The sun was beginning to give some warmth. But the 120 kilometres I had only just travelled now lay ahead of me once more, and the sledge was heavily laden.

So what, I told myself. If I manage thirty to forty kilometres a day I'll be home in three or four days. I was no longer frightened of the journey. I only worried about my family. Were they still alive? Would I be in time?

Oredesch was soon behind me. The path now led through a field, the same field in which I had endured such torments two days before when I had lost my way. Now the sun was shining and the snow crystals glittered silver and gold like lights on a Christmas tree. It was painful to look at, but the shimmering crystals gave me a good feeling inside.

All at once I heard the snorting of horses and the swish of a sleigh behind me. I hardly had time to spring out of the way before the horses passed me at a wild gallop. They were harnessed to large transport sleighs which were piled high with sacks, and they were storming forward at such a pace that I couldn't make out the faces of the people on board. Nevertheless, my heart leapt with joy because I was seeing people in that vast expanse of snow-covered prairie, and I watched them go, wide-eyed.

Suddenly, one of the sleighs was pulled to an abrupt halt. A man wearing a motheaten fur cap jumped down, picked me up, baggage and all, and set me on top of the sleigh. Before I could gather my senses, he shouted, 'Go, Nicolaj! Get going! We'll be left behind!'

Then he turned to me. 'Well, little one? Don't you recognize me any more?'

I couldn't believe my eyes. 'Uncle Wanja?' I asked.

Iwan Samuilowitsch, as Mama called him, had been a tailor in Wyritza before the war. He had often stayed with us and had even made a stylish frock for my doll. He was always coughing, and Mama said Iwan Samuilowitsch was seriously ill.

'So, you've recognized me at last!' Uncle Wanja stroked my cheek tenderly. 'We are taking grain to the partisans, little Tania, and we have to make sure that we cross this open country as quickly as we can. Once we get to the woods we have the advantage again. But what on earth brings you here? Were you looking for food? How could your Mama let you go alone? Tell me, Tania, are you in a bad way at home?'

'Very bad. We are dying of hunger. That's why I came.'

'We must all fight and endure, Tania. Tell your Mama to hold on! We will come soon. We will definitely come.'

The driver stopped the horses. Iwan Samuilowitsch said, 'We can't take you any further, Tania. We're branching off here and your route goes straight on. Take care! Tell them to sit it out back home. We're coming. Be patient.'

He shouted the last words when the horses were already galloping. The sleigh drew away very quickly, and I could see it catching up with the line of other sleighs disappearing into the woods.

My own path now lay straight through open fields, but I didn't think of the danger. Home! I was going home. I didn't walk – I flew.

From *A Hostage To War* by Tatiana Vassilieva

NIGHT PATROL

Alan Ross's poem vividly describes the eerie feeling of the North Sea at night in the Second World War.

We sail at dusk. The red moon,
Rising in a paper lantern, sets fire
To the water; the black headland disappears
Into its own shadow, clenched like a paw.

The docks grow flat, rubbered with mist.
Cranes, like useless arms, hang
Over the railway. The unloading of coal
Continues under harsh arc-lights.

Turning south, the moon like a rouged face
Between masts, the knotted aerials swing
Taut against the horizon, the bag
Of sea crumpled in the spray-flecked blackness.

Towards midnight the cold stars, high
Over Europe, freeze on the sky,
Stigmata above the flickering lights
Of Holland. Flashes of gunfire

Lick out over meditative coastlines, betraying
The stillness. Taking up my position, night falls
Exhausted about us. The wakes
Of gunboats sew the green dark with speed.

From Dunkirk red flames open fanwise
In fingers of light; like the rising moon
Setting fire to the sky, the remote
Image of death burns on the water.

The slow tick of hours. Clouds grow visible.
Altering course the moon congeals on a new
Bearing. Northwards again, and Europe recedes
With the first sharp splinters of dawn.

The orange sky lies over the harbour,
Derricks and pylons like scarecrows
Black in the early light. And minesweepers
Pass us, moving out slowly to the North Sea.

by Alan Ross

THE RESCUE AT DUNKIRK

*This is a beautifully illustrated picture story book which tells, in
simple blank verse, the story of the evacuation of thousands of
Allied troops from the beaches of Dunkirk in France in the Second
World War. The story is told by a young girl, who with her father
crosses the Channel from Deal in Kent in a small boat, the* Lucy, *to
help ferry the men from the Dunkirk beaches to the warships that
can carry them back to safety in England. This part of the story
tells of the* Lucy's *arrival at Dunkirk. We never learn the young
girl's name, perhaps because so many of the people who took their
small boats across the Channel to Dunkirk remain anonymous and
unknown.*

Dad handed me a mug
of strong, sweet tea,
and a woolly thick jacket
to keep off the Channel chill.

And then the *Lucy* was there,
off Dunkirk's beaches,
in the night
and in the early morning,
and it was real.
We heard the Germans guns.
Other guns were answering back.
All the oily smoke that got in my eyes,
and all the terrible noise that got in my ears.
And all the men.
The sandy beaches at Dunkirk were black
with lines that curved like snakes.
And the lines were British soldiers.
And the French were there too.
There were even men standing shoulder to shoulder
along the length of the Mole,
the narrow wooden pier in Dunkirk's harbour.
Thousands of soldiers, waiting for ships.
We stayed close to a minesweeper,
then sailed into the shallows
to ferry our first load.
I called back the depth of the water
as Dad steered the *Lucy* toward the beach.
Not a beach like Deal's.
This beach was wide and flat,
its sand covered by men who were hungry and thirsty,
by horses running loose from their French riders,
by dozens of barking dogs,
by trucks and equipment,
by the wild mess of an army on the run.

And there were hundreds of other ships
that were little like ours –
English and French, Belgian and Dutch.
We were all there rowing
and carrying
and paddling
and ferrying –
from the sand beaches to the big ships
anchored out in deeper water
and back again.

From *The Little Ships* by Louise Borden illustrated
by Michael Foreman (see illustrations in the colour section)

SMUGGLING JEWISH REFUGEE CHILDREN INTO SPAIN

*This story, set in the village of Lescun in the Pyranees in the
Second World War, is told from the point of view of Jo, a young
boy. Jo has discovered that Benjamin, the son-in-law of old widow
Horcada, whom everybody likes to think is a witch, is hiding some
Jewish refugee children at her house, waiting to take them over the
mountains to Spain and safety from the occupying German soldiers.
As the story develops the villagers who know about the children
form a very daring plan. All the men of the village are about to go
off to the mountains to herd their animals during the Summer
months. On the first day the village children are to be allowed to
stay away from school to help them. The idea is that with all the
village children swarming over the mountain side and caves the
German soldiers will not notice the few extra Jewish children
among them and Benjamin will be able to get them away with the
help of Jo's father. The evening before the day of the escape the
village priest holds a long concert of German music in the church
which all the German soldiers will feel obliged to attend. This gets
them off the streets so that the Jewish children can be brought to*

different villagers' houses ready for the next day. In this way the
escape is carried out under the noses of the occupying forces.

Father Lasalle announced the concert during Mass. Everyone had
been told about it by now and was expecting it, except for the soldiers of course. Looking directly at Lieutenant Weissmann and the
dozen or so soldiers sitting with him Father Lasalle spoke with his
usual intoning drone but also with the authority of a man who was
used to commanding attention. 'For three months every summer,' he
said, 'our small community loses many of its men folk. As we all
know, on Monday next begins the great exodus, the transhumance,
the beginning of months of solitude and hard work. In Lescun it has
always been thus. Now I have lived here amongst you for most of my
life, long enough to know that some of these men might want to
spend their last evening in the café, and that is something I would not
wish to deny them even if I could. So by all means go to the café; but
I want everyone, and I do mean everyone, to come here to the church
afterwards.' Jo was looking along the pew towards the soldiers; he
wanted to watch their faces for any flicker of disbelief. The Corporal
leaned forward and winked at him and Jo looked away quickly.

'Vanity, vanity saith the preacher, all is vanity,' said Father Lasalle
smiling broadly and putting his hand on his heart, 'and I confess
freely to a great vanity. As you know, for many long hours I sit alone
at the organ here in the church and I practise. I have been practising
some of the greatest organ music ever written and it was written by
a German too, one Johann Sebastian Bach. But for a musician practise is not enough. I must perform. My music must be heard. From
time to time in the past I have given recitals and so tonight, to mark
the eve of the transhumance I will be giving you one of my short
concerts, and I want all of you here, a gathering of the entire community, every man, woman and child. No child is ever too young for
Bach.' He leaned forward over the pulpit, his eyes raking the pews,
his finger pointing. 'And you can be sure I shall know if you're not
here.' There was some laughter at that. And then he spoke directly to
Lieutenant Weissmann. 'The music, as I have said, will be German,
Lieutenant. I know how fond you are of Bach and since it was writ-

ten to glorify the God of both our peoples, you and your men will be most welcome. Catholic and Protestant, all will be welcome. Indeed, Lieutenant, I will be most disappointed if the entire German garrison is not here. Can I count on you, Lieutenant?' The Lieutenant nodded, smiling. 'That is kind of you, Lieutenant. I shall reserve seats for you. The concert will begin at eight o'clock and so it should be over well before curfew.' It was a masterly performance.

Father Lasalle's concerts were rarely well attended. That evening though the church was as full as Jo had ever seen it. But by five to eight the German soldiers had still not arrived. Jo sat next to Maman, her hand squeezing his. He squeezed back to reassure and be reassured. They would come, they had to come. Christine sat on the other side of her, thumb in her mouth, her legs swinging. The church was silent with expectation, not a murmur, not a cough. Jo turned and craned his neck. Still nothing. Maman pulled on his hand and he turned back again. The bells groaned in the tower and struck eight o'clock. Father Lasalle emerged from the vestry and looked at the empty pews where the soldiers should have been. He seemed uncertain what to do. At that moment the Lieutenant strode in, cap under his arm, the soldiers trooping in behind him. The sigh of relief was almost audible. Jo counted them in as Father Lasalle took his seat at the organ. Twenty-two. They were all there. Last to take their seats were the Mayor and Hubert. As they sat down in front of Jo he heard the doors close behind him.

The first piping notes sounded out through the church. Jo shivered, whether through pleasure or relief he did not know. From where he sat he could just see Father Lasalle's head rocking back and forth and the back of his heels stepping neatly across the foot pedals. Even the smallest children, Christine amongst them, were immediately absorbed in the music. Hubert was lost in it, his mouth open, his head nodding, but Jo found he could not keep his eye off the clock. He knew they needed at least an hour to be sure, an hour without soldiers in the streets, a clear hour to bring the children down from the cave and to hide them away in their allotted houses. Jo ventured a look at the Corporal. He was gazing up at the roof and his fingers were tapping out the rhythm on his knees.

At long last nine o'clock struck in horrible disharmony with the organ. Father Lasalle played on. There was a certain amount of shuffling and coughing now as people became more uncomfortable and the music too repetitive to hold their attention. Jo glanced across at Lieutenant Weissmann who was looking at his watch and whispering to the Corporal beside him. The Corporal shrugged his shoulders and smiled and then took out his handkerchief and blew his nose noisily. 'Keep going, Father,' Jo said to himself. 'Keep going, keep going.'

Hubert was fidgetting now and looking around the church through his binoculars until his father put a firm hand on his wrist and pulled his arm downwards. Hubert was not so easily deterred. Much to everyone's amusement he trained his binoculars on Father Lasalle and then on each of the soldiers in turn.

It was not far short of half past nine when the music built to a final crescendo leaving the church filled with a throbbing silence. The Mayor and Hubert led the enthusiastic applause and Father Lasalle came out to take his bows. He held up his hands and shrugged his shoulders. 'I'm afraid it lasted a little longer than I expected,' he said. 'Good night and God bless you.' Lieutenant Weissmann shook his hand and then came over to talk to the Mayor who nodded and turned to the audience. 'Ladies and gentlemen,' he announced. 'The Lieutenant has asked me to say that curfew is extended by half an hour tonight to allow us to get home at our ease. He asks us all to be home by ten o'clock.'

Jo danced his way through the crowd inside the porch and ran all the way home. He found Papa and Grandpère sitting at the kitchen table. Grandpère was pouring wine. 'Are they here?' he said.

'Up in the hayloft,' said Grandpètr, 'all three of them.'

'Did you get them all?' said Jo.

'All of them,' said Papa, 'and they're all where they should be. We did it in under the hour.'

Jo climbed the ladder at the back of the barn and pushed open the loft door. 'Jo?' It was Benjamin's voice whispering out of the darkness. 'Is that you, Jo?'

'It's me,' he said, and he hauled himself up into the loft.

'Léah's fast asleep,' said Benjamin, and in the darkness Jo could just make her out curled up tight against him, an arm thrown around his knee.

'I'm not.' It was Michael crawling towards them through the hay. 'Here,' he said. 'I brought you this.' He was trying to thrust something into Jo's hand. 'It's something you always wanted,' he said. 'Something you could never win. Squeeze it,' he said, 'and it'll bring you luck.' It was a chess piece, a white queen.

'I've told him, Jo,' said Benjamin. 'I've told him that for tomorrow he's your brother. And do you know what he told me, this horrible boy, he said if you were his brother he'd have taught you to play chess a lot better than you do.'

And then Jo saw Benjamin's face silhouetted for a moment against the window behind him. 'You cut your beard off,' said Jo.

'Your father's orders.' Benjamin stroked his chin. 'If you want to be taken for a native, he said, then you've got to look like one. It seems there's not many people round here with a red beard, so off it had to come. I feel a bit naked without it, a bit cold too. Still, it'll grow again. It had better do, hadn't it, or Anya won't recognise me when she sees me.'

'You're staying behind then,' said Jo.

'Yes,' said Benjamin. 'I'll see them safely over the border and then I'll come back.' He put his arm around him. 'Jo,' he said, 'I feel surer than ever that somehow Anya will find her way here. You remember what I said to you a while back when I hurt my ankle, when the snows came and it all looked hopeless? You remember what I said? I said 'Wait and pray'. Well we waited and we prayed and here we are. This time tomorrow, God willing, the children will be in Spain and they'll be safe at last. So I shall wait up in the cave for Anya, and I shall pray.'

When Jo went down to the kitchen they were all there and Papa was crouching down in front of Christine and holding her hands. There was an edge of impatience in his voice. 'Forget about the donkey, Christine, just remember – stay with Jo. You clap your hands when he does, and you chase the sheep like Rouf does, and if anyone asks you've got a big sister called Léah and a big brother called Michael. Do you understand now?'

'But I haven't got a big sister,' she said, 'and my big brother's called Jo.'

Papa gave up and Maman took his place. 'It's pretend, Christine,' she said. 'Just for tomorrow you've got a pretend sister and she's called Léah and you've got a pretend brother and he's called Michael and you've got to look after them, no squabbling.'

'But can I ride the donkey?' she said and everyone had to laugh.

When she'd gone up to bed Papa stretched out in his chair and Grandpère lit his last cigarette of the day – he always had a 'last one', usually several of them, before he went to bed. 'Some people,' he said, 'are so predictable. You know what Armand Jollet said when I told him? He said he ought to be compensated – compensated! You know what he said? He said, "if I go with you I'll have to close up the shop for a whole day and that'll cost me", and his chins shook like an agitated turkey. You should've seen him.'

'Money,' said Maman, 'it's all that man ever thinks of.'

'I've never really talked much to the schoolmaster, that Monsieur Audap,' said Papa. 'Always thought he was a strange fish. But he's not. He's a fine man. When I told him all about it and asked him about giving the children a day off school, he thought for a moment and I was sure he was going to refuse. He always looks such a miserable old so-and-so. Do you know what he said, Jo? He said the children would likely learn more in that one day than he could teach them in a lifetime. 'Nothing's important unless it stays with you,' that's what he said; 'and no matter what happens, none of us,' he said, 'none of us is ever likely to forget tomorrow'.

Jo did not even try to sleep that night, he knew it would be pointless. His mind went over the plan again and again. He tried to visualise it as the soldiers would see it. Would it all look normal to them? Would they notice all the extra children in amongst the animals? Would they catch a glimpse of Benjamin's face and know him for a stranger? He could almost convince himself that it was going to work, that the Germans would see only what they were supposed to see: but as the night wore on a terrible doubt kept recurring. It was something the Corporal had told him a long time ago. He'd come from a village in the mountains, in Bavaria, 'just like Lescun,' he'd said. Well, Jo thought, if it was a lot like Lescun then he'd know that you don't need dozens and dozens of children to drive the animals, he'd know you can do the job with a few men and a couple of dogs and he'd know too that the flocks and herds were moved out separately and not in one great, chaotic bunch. The more Jo saw it through the Corporal's eyes the more he worried, and by dawn a multitude of nagging doubts had eclipsed his hopes. He faced the day ahead with a deep dread welling inside him.

At breakfast he recognised the same anxiety in Maman's eyes. Papa and Grandpère were still arguing on and on about who would be best to stay with the children in the hut and guide them over the mountains. Grandpère said that he was fitter, that Papa's coughing could give them away. Papa said he was younger and that anyway he knew the mountains better. At one point they were going to do it together, but Maman would have none of that. She said it was silly for two of them to take the risk of getting caught. In the end it was Papa who had his way.

Léah and Michael looked awkward in their country clothes. They ate ravenously and in silence. Christine just stared at them and refused to eat her breakfast. 'Time to go, I think,' said Papa. Benjamin finished his coffee and stood up.

'Monsieur, Madame,' he said, 'I hardly know you, but before we leave I want to thank you and through you all the people of this village for what you have done and what you are about to do. What has happened here in this little place, whether it succeeds or whether it fails, is evidence enough, if any were needed, that no-one will ever suppress the power for good, for compassion is in the hearts of men and women. I have one regret though, that my little Anya is not yet here. But when she comes I shall tell her, I shall tell her often so that she can tell her children. Such things should not be forgotten. And now if you will allow me I will say a prayer. It is the last prayer we Jews say before we leave the Synagogue.' He closed his eyes. 'And the Lord shall be king over all the earth. In that day shall the Lord be one and His name be one.'

Rouf lay stretched out like a carpet by the stove with Léah crouched beside him stroking the top of his head. She leaned over and kissed him. ˙

'Jo,' said Papa. 'You'd better wake that dog up. We can't move those sheep without him.' Jo whistled and Rouf woke, a look of resignation on his face. He yawned noisily and Léah laughed and sat back on her haunches as he stretched, shook himself awake, and then led them outdoors into the yard.

The streets were already full of sheep noise, a cacophony of bells and bleating and, claiming a bass line in the raucous choir, the cows bellowed and the donkeys brayed. The first flock came past them, Laurent driving them with his stick. He was leading a heavily laden donkey that stepped daintily over the cobbles. He winked at Jo as he passed and grinned. He was enjoying every minute of it. He had two of the cave children with him. They looked for all the world just like the village children around them. Like them they carried switches and sticks, like them they whistled and shouted and clapped. Two more flocks and a herd of cows came by, and Jo counted at least another five children from the cave.

Now it was their turn. Hubert was sitting on the wall laughing and pointing as they gathered up the sheep in the yard. Jo shouted to him to open the gate and he began to flap his arms and whistle. Michael followed his example at once with uninhibited enthusiasm. When Benjamin too turned shepherd Léah seemed to warm to the idea and joined in as well. As he left the yard Jo turned and waved to Grandpère and Papa – they'd be coming on behind with the pigs and the donkey.

By the time they reached the Square Jo saw that the flocks had bunched together and every street leading into it was thick with sheep and cattle. The noise was deafening, an incessant chorus of animals punctuated with whooping and whistling and barking. Jo saw a sheep burst through the front door of Monsieur Sarthol's house, a dog went in after it. Jo never saw what happened for his eye was taken by something far more worrying. Three soldiers, one of them the Corporal, were standing on top of the wall by the war memorial and watching everything that passed through the Square below them. Jo looked away quickly and whooped even louder at the sheep. A cow was rubbing itself against the corner of the café and the soldiers were laughing. Benjamin was keeping his head down as

Papa had suggested he should, but to Jo his shepherding looked somehow forced and stiff. And then he felt Léah clutching his arm. She had seen the soldiers and was looking up at them, her eyes wide with terror. The Corporal was looking right at her and the sheep would not move on. There was nothing Jo could do. There were sheep behind him, sheep in front of him, sheep all about him. The Corporal had let himself down off the wall and was scrutinising them closely. He had noticed something – Jo was sure of it.

Why Hubert chose that moment to perform Jo never knew but he pushed his way through the sheep and began to leap up and down like a wild thing; and then raising his arms in the air he growled at the sheep like a bear. The Corporal pointed and laughed and the other soldiers laughed with him. Hubert saw it and performed his bear act again, but with redoubled vigour. All around him the sheep panicked. They pushed and shoved and jumped over each other and at last the great flock began to move again up past the baker's shop. Jo slipped around the back of Léah, ostensibly to chase a sheep, but this way he'd be between her and the soldiers so that she could not see them and they could not see her. He dared not venture another look at the soldiers until they'd left the Square behind them. When he did turn round the Corporal was looking straight at him. Jo turned away quickly and played shepherd again.

So the chaotic cavalcade wound its way slowly out of the village and up towards the hills beyond. They could see the circle of mountains ahead of them. All around him Jo could see and feel the exhilaration and relief. The ruse had surely worked. The cave children had passed undetected under the nose of the Germans. The worst must be over. Even Rouf seemed to sense the triumph. He was chasing his tail and he only did that these days when he was high with happiness. But Jo could not share in the general elation. He could think only of the patrols they might meet before they reached the high pastures and the hut; but worse he could not get out of his head that the Corporal had guessed what they were up to. There had been a look in his eye – he was certain of it – a knowing look. 'We must make it look like a fête, a holiday,' Papa had said. 'We don't hurry it, we enjoy it.' And so they did. They reached the plateau by lunchtime. They picnicked by the stream and the animals browsed hungrily in the lush grass. They did not wander far because they did not need to.

It was proving almost impossible to keep the cave children away from each other. Benjamin spent his time persuading them to stay with their newly adopted families, but in spite of all he could do they seemed always to gravitate to each other again. It wasn't that the language was a barrier between them and the village children – after all some of the cave children were French – but there seemed to be an instinctive reserve that kept them apart.

It was only when Hubert appeared lumbering across the stream, four children clinging to his back, that they all found a mutual source of fun that brought cave children and village children together. Hubert, the great giant, had to be hauled down and held down and it took almost all of them to do it. In the pile of children on top of him they were all allies in the one cause. Michael and Laurent clung to the same leg and were shaken off. They rolled away together giggling before returning once more to the fray.

The afternoon climb was slow. It was steep now, up along narrow, tortuous tracks, where the sheep could only move in single file. The pigs hated climbing and were forever trying to wander off, and the cows too had had enough of it now. For many of the children the adventure had lost its early magic. Their legs ached, their feet hurt, and many of them had to ride. Every donkey now – every horse – was carrying at least one child. Christine insisted on sharing a donkey with Léah. Michael's leg had lasted well until he stumbled and fell. He limped on for a bit until Hubert noticed him. He led Michael to a rock and crouched down in front of it. Michael climbed on and rode Hubert all the way up.

And so they came at long last to the high pastures, the horses first, then the sheep, the cows and last of all the reluctant pigs; and in amongst them all the hundred or so men, women and children who had brought them there. They lay down, man and beast, side by side, in silent exhaustion. They drank from the spring by the hut or from the stream that flowed from it. Michael and Jo cupped their hands in the spring and drank until they could drink no more. When Jo looked up the cave children were already being led towards the hut. 'Come on,' said Jo and they stood up.

'Is that Spain over there?' said Michael looking up at the peaks.

'That's Spain,' said Jo. They parted at the door of the hut.

'Don't lose my queen will you?' said Michael, and he went into the hut with the others.

When Jo turned round Benjamin was standing in front of him, Léah at his side. 'I'll be seeing you later then, Jo,' he said. Léah reached up and kissed him on the cheek. And then she was gone. He heard Papa's voice from inside the hut. 'Is that all of them? Have you counted them in?'

'That's all of them,' said Benjamin. 'All we've got to do now is wait until dark.'

Papa emerged from the hut and closed the door. 'You'd better get back down the mountain,' he said, and then his mouth fell open. He was looking over Jo's shoulder. Jo turned. Coming out of the trees were three soldiers. Everyone had seen them now. No-one moved. No-one said a word. There was no doubt about it, the one in front was the Corporal.

From *Waiting For Anya* by Michael Morpurgo

ESCAPE FROM KAZAKHSTAN

Old Mr Wassilewska (Stef) gradually narrates to young Richard the story of his family's capture by the Russians at the beginning of the Second World War, their exile to Kazakhstan, and their struggle to survive there in appalling conditions and very low temperatures. Stef's brother Josef becomes very ill and Stef knows that they cannot survive another winter on the steppe. In this part of the old man's story he tells how he loses his mother and brother while boarding a train to leave, never to see them ever again.

'We are starting out with almost no food. Many, who had arrived with us, will never be returning. Some who are leaving have buried their children on the steppe, whereas others who are returning have now received news of children who might be safe, back in Poland. It will be a difficult journey back. People will often tell you that suffering unites; now, I think that it divides us, one from another.

Then I notice that the doctor has come to see us off.

'Why have you come?' I ask him rudely.

'To give you this,' he replies gently, 'and to wish you a safe journey.' He hands me a parcel, something wrapped in cloth. I will not take it, so Josef does. For a moment he clings to the doctor's hand, then he skips off with the other children in the wagon. When I look again the doctor has walked away. He is standing by himself, shielding his eyes against the flat, white light of the steppe. He waves as the train moves and my mother is very quiet.'

'What was in the parcel?'

'Tea. Several pounds of good-quality tea. I cannot imagine what he had to do to get it for us.'

'But why should he give you tea?'

'In that land of nothing, tea was like gold. Better than gold. He knew that we could sell it along the way. That tea will save my life.

We are travelling for days on end and all the time more and more people are crowding on the train. It is very cold, although we are packed in tight. People are beginning to fall ill. Some say it is typhus, others that it is influenza. Maybe this journey back is even worse, for we are now all so weak. At first we do not notice that Josef is scrambling over the tops of everyone's luggage. He lies silently all day with his burning head resting in Mother's lap. Sometimes he tries a laugh, but his throat is so sore that he can barely swallow. At some stations guards are patrolling the trains taking off those who are sick. Mother is terrified that they will take Josef. We have heard stories of Russian hospitals, of sick people washed in cold water and left in unheated wards. We hide him, because we know that he is more likely to die in a hospital.

Then someone reports a sick boy in our carriage and the guards return. 'It is nothing,' Mother protests, 'just a bad cold, maybe pneumonia, and nobody else can catch that. He is no danger.' They will not listen. They make us get off, Mother, with Josef in her arms, and I with the bits of luggage. Once again we are stranded, cast like splintered driftwood upon an unfriendly shore.

For me, maybe that is my moment of greatest despair when I saw the train go on without me. Now I'm terrified that perhaps I will never, ever be able to leave the Soviet Union. I watch the carriages of single men go by. They are not tied down by their families; they are free to go and fight! Will I be trapped like the doctor, a forgotten man in a forgotten place? I cannot bear to think about it.

We discover that we are in a town in Uzbekistan and we stay there for·two weeks. All the time my mother is nursing Josef. The representatives of the Polish Army who are looking after the families en route find us a room with several other people who are also waiting to continue their journey of escape. My mother exchanges some tea for medicines and strengthening food for Josef. I spend all my time on the streets, queueing for everything that we need. I don't mind so much. For the first time I'm hearing news of the war and news of what is happening in Poland. It is not good news, but to me those streets in that town in Uzbekistan taste of freedom and the world beyond. In the evenings I must force myself to return to our cramped room that smells of women and sick children and old, dirty clothes.

For the first time I discover that the war is being fought all over Europe and that France is occupied. I cannot wait to join the army. I have spoken to men who have fought the Germans on Polish soil in 1939. Each day I ask Josef if he still is not better, and at last he says he is. He is still very weak, but well enough to travel. Now I am busy with permits and I queue for three days to get train tickets. We stand on the platform for most of the day. Soon I am feeling guilty, Josef has fainted. Maybe it was too soon: a few more days and he would have been much stronger.

'You *are* all right, aren't you?' I ask. I have him in my arms. He is very light for a big boy of ten. His blue eyes have faded. 'You're sure you're all right?' He nods. 'I'm fine,' he whispers. 'And I'm going to be a soldier too!' We smile at each other. He knew what would please me. More and more people are pushing their way on to the platform. We are all listening for the train.

Again, I hear the silence of a crowd as we all hold our breath. We have felt the distant rumble of the train. People start to push. The train which comes in is already very crowded. I have the tickets in my pocket but I know it will be a struggle. I put Josef down beside my mother. I have the bags in my hands. People are fighting their way forward. The guards cannot keep control. I feel behind me: the tea is safely there in my rucksack. If there is a problem with a guard at the last minute, it should help buy us our places. Somebody is screaming and has fallen. I'm not going to fall. I brace myself. I *will* get a place on the train. As it grinds to a halt there is a stampede. I'm so tightly packed against a door that I cannot open it, but I do, in the end. I have lost sight of Mother and Josef. I decide to climb aboard. Once on the train, I will surely be able to see them, and help them up too. Anyway, the crowd sweeps me on and I have no free hand because of the bags. It would be hard to turn back. I stumble over the iron step but strong hands from above grab me and haul me clear. Outside, the crowd roars. I hear his shrill voice, once more. 'Stefan! Wait for us! Stefan!'

I want to help them. When I manage to turn round Mother is at the door of the wagon. People have pulled her up too, but she is struggling against them. Josef is not with her. I'm trying to keep a small space free in the corner for the three of us. I cannot go back and help, because I might lose this place. Just then the train shunts the wagons and one crashes against another and the crowd howls like a beast disturbed. I watch in horror. Some people fall while others are still scrambling up. I watch my mother turn away from me and step back down into that crowd.'

He was breathing heavily, gasping in great gusts of breath as though he was suffocating.

I thought I understood why he had not wanted to tell me this.

'And... you never saw them again, did you, Mr Wassilewska?'

He shook his head. Tears were running down his cheeks. He leant back in his chair and looked away down the valley.

'All I do... all I did for them, was to push our bags out through the windows of the carriage. And I do not even know if they found them.'

We were quiet for a long time, he and I.

Finally he got up and fetched the old rug and held it in a bundle in his arms.

'It was on that train, which was travelling on to Krasnovodsk, that I got this rug...' His voice trailed away and I watched his shaking hands mechanically smoothing down the hairs on the rug, trying to lay them straight, again and again.

'Shall I go?' I asked.

'No,' he said, in a voice that was frail and fearful. It was the first time that I had heard him speak so hopelessly and so feebly and I couldn't bear to hear it.

I went down to the pool and stared into the water at the white clouds which were caught there between the reeds. I remembered how we had parted: that she hadn't turned back and that she had never even waved goodbye.

From *And the Stars Were Gold* by Anne Campling

ESCAPE ACROSS THE WATER

Fifteen-year-old Tan, a Vietnamese refugee, finds a home with a Flemish family. When his foster parents split up, his world collapses and memories of how life in Vietnam used to be, come back to haunt him. Tan goes on hunger strike. He has a hard time trying to voice his traumatic experiences and eventually does talk about his family, the war and the real reason why he ran away.

The sky turned mother-of-pearl and light pink. Every time Tan hit the crest of a wave he felt the sharp pre-sunrise wind. The sun eventually did rise, diagonally across from him. So that was the east! Don't swim to the east, he said to himself. Vietnam lies in the east. Now the red solar sphere was slowly rising above the waves and every time Tan reached the top of a wave, as if by magic he noticed something black inside it, tiny at first, then more clearly defined as the sun climbed higher. There was something out there, there was something out there, perhaps another boat. Each wave brought him closer to that sun, huge waves sucked him towards it. And each time the thing out there got bigger too. It was indeed a black shape, a mountain, a rock. An island perhaps? Tan knew the sun would be high in the sky before he reached it. He realised he had to keep heading in the right direction. Every time he reached a crest, he carefully studied the horizon, that black hill. He decided to give the swimming all he'd got. He felt strangely rested, but realised he shouldn't exhaust himself needlessly. Soon he'd be waging a battle with the surf. He came closer and, as he did, he gained self-confidence. He was not going to drown, the sharks would not get him! Two, three seabirds were flying overhead now, gulls. Maybe this was a huge island, maybe part of the mainland. Or it was covered in woods and he'd be able to live there, all alone. He swam and eventually felt the teeming surf under him. There was something in the movement of the waves that was less co-ordinated, no longer merely in one direction but movement and counter-movement at the same time. He knew he would be needing all his strength and decided to take it easy. He occasionally floated along and felt for the bottom with his toes. It was too early still. Suddenly he felt something glide past his leg. He also saw a black shape, it was underneath him now. A shark! His heart skipped a beat. But then he smiled. It was a rock under the water. Now he was really in the surf, and having to wrestle with forces that seemed to be pulling him all over the place, but whose real intention was to send him crashing against the rocks further up. He wisely offered no resistance, beating off the spume with his arms. He wanted to see where he was being taken. The water was quite shallow now; he tried to get up. He managed, but was so dizzy that he plopped back into the spume, smack on his face. Then he crawled back to his feet and laughed and laughed and laughed.

The island was an elongated rock formation in the ocean, barely a few kilometres large. It sloped up into the sky, an enormous rock like a watch tower, a mountain. Luckily the waves had eaten away the rock on the side where Tan got stranded. He stumbled onto the little beach and wondered what on earth those freakish shapes could be. Pieces of wood, branches and planks covered with grass and leaves. These were little houses, or rather huts, botched together between the rocks. Later Tan would find out that there used to be a layer of soil, stone flakes and grit on top of the rocks, and that a few years ago there had even been a wood of crooked, stone-like trees and shrubs there. None of it remained; the refugees, more than forty thousand of them, had uprooted the trees down to the last branch and built their 'dwellings' with them. What struck Tan the most, however, was the stench; he had washed ashore next to the 'crapping rock', as he called it! That crowd of forty thousand relieved itself on an almost flat piece of rock that was swept clean by the waves. It was less than twenty square metres large, and despite the breaking waves the cracks were full of excrement. The stench was unbearable. At first Tan felt embarrassed at having to crouch there with adults and children and he always swam into the sea. But after a while he did as thousands of others did, and barely even noticed what was going on around him. He shamelessly looked at the girls and stooped down to see the white, dirty cleft-peach that was their bum. But the girls were usually prudish, much more prudish than the older women. Of course the risk of epidemics was huge – in the last months of his stay on the island many diseases did in fact spread. Luckily by then the Red Cross was reasonably active.

At first all Tan had was a spot near the water, and twice in 24 hours he had to lug all his belongings up five metres – some wreckage which he had fished out of the sea himself. The Lang Van Fongs, whose land this was, had told him he was welcome to stay, but not for too long. That didn't bother him; all he had were his swimming trunks anyway. He tightened them with a piece of string he had exchanged for a chunk of wood, a half-petrified tree-trunk he had fished out of the swirling water near the rock wall. After a few weeks he was able to build himself with sticks and branches a little abode against a rock. The roof consisted of twigs he had plaited together and then covered with seaweed that provided shelter from the sun and the water.

Tan soon went and explored the other side of the island, where the rocks formed a steep wall, more than a hundred metres high, that vanished straight into the sea in a white whirl, with the odd piece of rock sticking out. It was dangerous to go there, but this was also where the best wreckage was found; planks, weed, but also bottles and plastic. Tan often went diving there and indeed found some wreckage, even once a real oil barrel. He bashed the front out with a sharp stone, which took him days, made holes in it and stuck diagonal sticks through them to make himself some kind of cupboard. It could be closed, sort of, in rough weather, by putting the piece of bashed-out metal back in front and securing it with stones. It was his larder. Not that he had much to store, mind. One day he gave the cupboard to Mr Fong's daughter. From that day on they more or less adopted him as theirs. He was given more room in front of his little hut, where he stacked his stuff, for he was gathering more and more wreckage. And now he had company too. Later on, Mr Fong, his eldest son and Tan formed a kind of alliance: together they went looking for the ocean's flotsam. Tan was a daredevil who went nearer the rock wall than anyone else and knew everything about the currents. This came in really handy and he was able, that way, to fish out a plank, a plastic bottle, a tree root, seaweed which, once dry, was incredibly tough and strong as rope, and the occasional dead fish that could still be eaten, grilled over a wreckage fire. It remained a dangerous thing to do, but Tan was an experienced swimmer. And when a seething mass of water approached to crash him against the rock wall, he ducked under a wave at exactly the right instant and resurfaced further up in the spume. He felt as agile as a dolphin. But he wasn't always lucky: a sprained ankle, skinned knees with bits of grit in them, an enormous bump on his head once, after a nasty mess of water had swung him against a piece of rock. He had escaped by the skin of his teeth and spent the rest of the day recovering on his mat of tough seaweed, while Sun waved cool air in his direction with a leafy branch. Sun smiled but he knew she had been crying just before, when her father and brother had assured her he had drowned. And she had cheered when, to everybody's surprise, Tan came out of the water a bit later.

From *A Piece of Fluff from the Sea* by Willy Spillebeen

Shoah

O WHAT IS THAT SOUND?

Auden's famous poem applies to all and any wars.

O what is that sound which so thrills the ear
Down in the valley, drumming, drumming?
Only the scarlet soldiers, dear,
The soldiers coming.

O what is that light I see flashing so clear
Over the distance brightly, brightly?
Only the sun on their weapons, dear,
As they step lightly.

O what are they doing with all that gear,
What are they doing this morning, this morning?
Only their usual manoeuvres, dear,
Or perhaps a warning.

O why have they left the road down there,
Why are they suddenly wheeling, wheeling?
Perhaps a change in their orders, dear.
Why are you kneeling?

O haven't they stopped for the doctor's care,
Haven't they reined their horses, their horses?
Why, they are none of them wounded, dear,
None of these forces.

O is it the parson they want, with white hair,
Is it the parson, is it, is it?
No, they are passing his gateway dear,
Without a visit.

O it must be the farmer who lives so near.
It must be the farmer so cunning, so cunning?
They have passed the farmyard already, dear,
And now they are running.

O where are you going? Stay with me here!
Were the vows you swore deceiving, deceiving?
No, I promised to love you, dear,
But I must be leaving.

O it's broken the lock and splintered the door,
O it's the gate where they're turning, turning;
Their boots are heavy on the floor
And their eyes are burning.

by W H Auden

REFUGEE GERMAN JEWISH CHILDREN IN SWITZERLAND IN THE LATE 1930S

Two Jewish children, Anna and Max used to live in Berlin in Germany, but when the Nazis came to power in 1933 and the persecution of Jewish citizens began, their family decided it would be safer to leave. In this extract they are living at an inn in Switzerland where Anna and Max have made friends with Vreneli and Franz, the children of the landlord and his wife. One day two German children appear at the inn, and all the children start to play together, but not for long. When Hitler Stole Pink Rabbit is the first book of Judith Kerr's autobiographical trilogy about growing up as a German Jewish refugee in Czechoslovakia, France and eventually England, where her family finally settled.

They all played chase together. It had never been much fun before because there had only been four of them – (Trudi did not count because she could not run fast enough and always cried when anyone caught her). But the German children were both very quick on their feet and for the first time the game was really exciting. Vreneli had just caught the German boy, and he caught Anna, so now it was Anna's turn to catch someone and she chased after the German girl. They raced round and round the courtyard of the inn, doubling back and forth and leaping over things until Anna thought she was just going to catch her – but all at once her path was blocked by a tall thin lady with a disagreeable expression. The lady appeared so suddenly, apparently from nowhere, that Anna was barely able to stop and almost collided with her.

'Sorry,' she said, but the lady did not reply.

'Siegfried!' she called shrilly. 'Gudrun! I told you you were not to play with these children!' She grabbed hold of the German girl and pulled her away. The boy followed, but when his mother was not looking he made a funny face at Anna and waved his hands apologetically. Then the three of them disappeared into the inn.

'What a cross woman,' said Vreneli.

'Perhaps she thinks we're badly brought up,' said Anna.

They tried to go on playing chase without the German children, but it was no good and ended in the usual shambles, with Trudi in tears because she had been caught.

Anna did not see the German children again until the late afternoon. They must have been shopping in Zurich for they were each carrying a parcel and their mother had several large ones. As they were about to go into the inn Anna thought this was her chance to show that she was not badly brought up. She leapt forward and opened the door for them. But the German lady did not seem at all pleased. 'Gudrun! Siegfried!' she said and pushed her children quickly inside. Then, with a sour expression and keeping as far way from Anna as possible, she squeezed past herself. It was difficult because of the parcels which nearly stuck in the doorway, but at last she was through and disappeared. With never a word of thanks, thought Anna – the German lady was badly brought up herself!

The next day she and Max had arranged to go up into the woods with the Zwirn children, and the day after that it rained, and the day

A small group of men from each side, unarmed, joined them. They all shook hands. One of the Germans spoke good English and said he hoped the war would end soon because he wanted to return to his job as a taxi driver in Birmingham.

Michael Foreman, WAR GAME

Then, from somewhere, a football bounced across the frozen mud. Will was on it in a flash. He trapped the ball with his left foot, flipped it up with his right, and headed it towards Freddie.

Freddie made a spectacular dive, caught the ball in both hands and threw it to a group of Germans.

Michael Foreman, WAR GAME

That afternoon we sailed for Dunkirk.
Dad didn't have much time for talk.
He kept his words in his hands,
stowing a rope ladder
and checking the engine gears.
And he kept his words in his eyes,
reading the Channel charts and maps,
scanning the sky, thick with clouds.

My father wasn't famous,
but he knew about the sea and the tides and currents
and how to steer clear of the Goodwin Sands.
He was the one who had taught me to read a compass.
And he could name all the stars at night
like explorers I had studied in school.

Louise Borden, THE LITTLE SHIPS
Illustrated by Michael Foreman

And then the Lucy *was there,*
off Dunkirk's beaches,
in the night
and in the early morning,
and it was real.
All the oily smoke that got in my eyes,
and all the terrible noise that got in my ears.
And all the men.
The sandy beaches at Dunkirk were black

with lines that curved like snakes.
And the lines were British soldiers.
And the French were there too.
There were even men standing shoulder to shoulder
along the length of the Mole,
the narrow wooden pier in Dunkirk's harbour.
Thousands of soldiers, waiting for ships.

Louise Borden, THE LITTLE SHIPS
Illustrated by Michael Foreman

And there were hundreds of other ships
that were little like ours—
English and French, Belgian and Dutch.
We were all there rowing
and carring
and paddling
and ferrying—
from the sand beaches to the big ships
anchored out in deeper water
and back again.

Louise Borden, THE LITTLE SHIPS
Illustrated by Michael Foreman

after that Mama took them to Zurich to buy them some socks – so they did not see the German children. But after breakfast on the following morning when Anna and Max went out into the yard, there they were again playing with the Zwirns. Anna rushed up to them.

'Shall we have a game of chase?' she said.

'No,' said Vreneli, looking rather pink. 'And any way you can't play.'

Anna was so surprised that for a moment she could think of nothing to say. Was Vreneli upset about the red-haired boy again? But she hadn't seen him for ages.

'Why can't Anna play?' asked Max.

Franz was as embarrassed as his sister.

'Neither of you can,' he said and indicated the German children. 'They say they're not allowed to play with you.'

The German children had clearly not only been forbidden to play but even to talk to them, for the boy looked as though he wanted to say something. But in the end he only made his funny apologetic face and shrugged.

Anna and Max looked at each other. They had never met such a situation before. Then Trudi who had been listening suddenly sang out, 'Anna and Max can't play! Anna and Max can't play!'

'Oh, shut up!' said Franz. 'Come on!' and he and Vreneli ran off towards the lake with the German children following. For a moment Trudi was taken aback. Then she sang out one last defiant 'Anna and Max can't play!' and scampered after them on her short legs.

Anna and Max were left standing.

'Why aren't they allowed to play with us?' asked Anna, but Max didn't know either. There seemed nothing to do but wander back to the dining-room where Mama and Papa were still finishing breakfast.

'I thought you were playing with Franz and Vreneli,' said Mama.

Max explained what had happened.

'That's very odd,' said Mama.

'Perhaps you could speak to the mother,' said Anna. She had just noticed the German lady and a man who must be her husband sitting at a table in the corner.

'I certainly will,' said Mama.

Just then the German lady and her husband got up to leave the dining-room and Mama went to intercept them. They met too far away for Anna to hear what they said, but Mama had only spoken a few words when the German lady answered something which caused Mama to flush with anger. The German lady said something more and made as though to move off. But Mama grabbed her arm.

"Oh no, it isn't!" shouted Mama in a voice which echoed right across the dining-room. "It's not the end of it all!" Then she turned on her heel and marched back to the table while the German lady and her husband went out looking down their noses.

'The whole room could hear you,' said Papa crossly as Mama sat down. He hated scenes.

'Good!' said Mama in such ringing tones that Papa whispered 'Ssssh!'and made calming motions with his hands. Trying to speak quietly made Mama angrier than ever and she could hardly get the words out.

'They're Nazis,' she said at last. 'They've forbidden their children to play with ours because our children are Jewish!' Her voice rose higher in indignation. 'And you want me to keep my voice down!' she shouted so that an old lady still finishing breakfast was startled into almost spilling her coffee.

Papa's mouth tightened. 'I would not dream of allowing Anna and Max to play with the children of Nazis,' he said, 'so there is no difficulty.'

'But what about Vreneli and Franz?' asked Max. 'It means that if they're playing with the German children they can't play with us.'

'I think Vreneli and Franz will have to decide who their friends are,' said Papa. 'Swiss neutrality is all very well, but it can be taken too far.' He got up from the table. 'I'll have a word with their father now.'

A little while later Papa returned. He had told Herr Zwirn that his children must choose whether they wished to play with Anna and Max or with the German visitors. They could not play with both. Papa has asked them not to decide in a hurry but to let him know that evening.

'I suppose they'll choose us,' said Max. 'After all we'll be here long after those other children have gone.'

But it was difficult to know what to do with the rest of the day. Max went down to the lake with his fishing rod and his worms and his bits of bread. Anna could not settle to anything. At last she decided to write a poem about an avalanche which engulfed an entire city, but it did not turn out very well. When she came to do the illustration she was so bored at the thought of making it all white that she gave up. Max, as usual caught no fish, and by mid-afternoon they were both so depressed that Mama gave them half a franc to buy themselves some chocolate – although she had previously said it was too expensive.

On their way back from the sweet-shop they caught a glimpse of Vreneli and Franz talking earnestly in the doorway of the inn and walked past self-consciously, looking straight ahead. This made them feel worse than ever.

Then Max went back to his fishing and Anna decided to go for a bathe, to try and salvage something from the day. She floated on her back which she had only just learned to do, but it did not cheer her up. It all seemed so silly. Why couldn't she and Max and the Zwirns and the German children all play together? Why did they have to have all this business of decisions and taking sides?

Suddenly there was a splash in the water beside her. It was Vreneli. Her long thin plaits were tied in a knot on top of her head so as not to get wet and her long thin face looked pinker and more worried than ever.

'I'm sorry about this morning,' said Vreneli breathlessly. 'We've decided we'd rather play with you even if it does mean that we can't play with Siegfried and Gudrun.'

Then Franz appeared on the bank. 'Hello, Max!' he shouted. 'Worms enjoying their swim?'

'I'd have caught a great big fish just then,' said Max, 'if you hadn't frightened it away.' But he was very pleased just the same.

At supper that evening Anna saw the German children for the last time. They were sitting stiffly in the dining-room with their parents. Their mother was talking to them quietly and insistently, and even the boy never turned round once to look at Anna and Max. At the end of the meal he walked right past their table as though he could not see them.

The whole family left the next morning.

'I'm afraid we've lost Herr Zwirn some customers,' said Papa.
Mama was triumphant.

'But it seems such a pity,' said Anna. 'I'm sure that boy really
liked us.'

Max shook his head. 'He didn't like us any more at the end,' he
said. 'Not by the time his mother had finished with him.'

It was true, thought Anna. She wondered what the German boy
was thinking now, what his mother had told him about her and Max,
and what he would be like when he grew up.

From *When Hitler Stole Pink Rabbit* by Judith Kerr

THE RED CROSS DELEGATION IS COMING

*Peter Ginz is staying in Terezin, a fortress town outside Prague
which the Nazis had designated a 'gift from the Führer', to the
Jews. The Terezin Jews have no idea that they are awaiting
deportation to Auschwitz. Life in the city is hell, but the educators
try to add colour to the boys' lives by organising theatre
performances and publishing a magazine. In June 1944 a Red
Cross delegation comes to visit. The boys decide to draw a realistic
portrait of Terezin life. Chaim is to sneak Peter Ginz' report to the
delegation.*

The Red Cross delegation is coming. This is to be a day like no
other. Already in the morning, there is music in town. Smiling little
string quartets make music on street corners. Girls in eighteenth-cen-
tury hoop skirts and with matching wigs on their heads, play short
pieces by Aryan composers on clavichords, violins and oboes. No
huge food distribution queues today. No hours of standing in line!
Everything works like clockwork, as if the Führer himself is about to
visit. And then a black Mercedes enters the town. SS men with click-
ing heels open the car doors. Three men get out and cast interested
looks at the people and buildings that look so crisp and clean.

Commander Rahm comes dashing forward, greets the men warm-ly, he is hospitability incarnate. He is so pleased they have taken the trouble to come to Terezin. That way they can see for themselves how good a life the Jews have here and that the stories Germany's enemies are spreading are untrue. The three gentlemen of the dele-gation fall for this and follow the commander, who introduces them to his officers and the gentlemen of the Jewish Board. How about a stroll through town? Any direction, any street, of course. The gentle-men are free to choose! The delegation just happens to take those streets that have recently been cleaned up and enters the very spaces that have only just been transformed into cosy flats.

The committee members happen to be strolling along when a bread cart stops in front of the bakery and a mountain of fresh loaves is carried inside by whistling baker's boys.

And when the delegation continues its stroll past the municipal park, cute toddlers in sweet little suits come running to shake Uncle Rahm's hand and give him a kiss. Girls in snow-white little dresses are busy decorating the Jewish monument with wild flowers.

On the sports field an exciting match is being played between two perfectly decked out boys' clubs, watched by 500-odd avid boy sup-porters. The gentlemen drink coffee in the renovated café, their hearts moved by the dancing couples around.

And at night they listen to Verdi's Requiem played by the musi-cians of Terezin, the *Brundibar* opera performed by the children, to our solemn music in four voices.

They actually brush away a tear of joy whilst getting into their black car and being waved out by a chuffed commander. It must be a happy people that dances in the streets, listens to folk songs at night, sees its children perform a moving play.

But now the gentlemen have gone and Chaim is still holding the tiny bundle under his arm. All day he has been running after the del-egation. Every time one of the gentlemen turned around to look at the people, he stood in the front row. But not one ordinary Jew even got near the committee members. A casual chat? Forget it. No time to raise objections and not a word was said about a transport to Switzerland.

These people have played their deceptive game, hoping today things might change. But they have been fobbed off. The next day the shops are emptied out again. Clothes must be handed back, the empty parcels are burned and the rations become possibly even more frugal.

The disappointment is deep. Even madrich Valtr Eisinger cannot find words to express his anger and disappointment. The train to Switzerland has been derailed, the arrival of the Russians or Americans is their only hope now.

The boys give vent to their pent-up feelings in their clubhouse the next day. No talk of a parliament now, a chairman or points on the agenda. Only anger and disappointment. No two ways about it: the Germans are a super nation if they can fool forty thousand people like that.

Now they realize they should never have taken part in this farce, *now* they realize the Germans were putting up a smoke screen to make sure the world never got to see the *real* Terezin.

But it's too late.

'Peter, you're getting your chronicle back,' Chaim says. 'Shame about the time and effort you invested in it.'

'Reckon you'll finish and publish it as a book after the war?' Jehuda asks.

Peter Ginz by Herman van Campenhout

A PARTY IN THE CONCENTRATION CAMP IN THE FORTRESS TOWN OF TEREZIN

This is a fictional story about a thirteen-year-old Jewish boy called Jan, who, with many other Jewish children, is imprisoned in Terezin near Prague. Although Jan is an invented character the children that he meets in the camp are based on the drawings and poems left by the real-life children who were imprisoned there. Their work can still be seen today at the Jewish Museum in Prague. The novel is written in a very original way. Jan is a time-traveller who can move between sixteenth century Prague and the present. In

*the sixteenth century Rabbi Loewe, the creator of the mud man
known as the Golem, is able to help Jan to cope with the appalling
tragedies around him. In this extract the children in the camp hold
a birthday party for a ninety-year-old lady who is living there.
Anna steals some flowers for the old lady from the guards' gardens,
with dreadful consequences.*

Old Mrs Kadarova lived in a musty little room leading off a narrow, stinking alley. Ivo had told Jan that the old people received the worst treatment in Terezin, and Jan now saw for himself that this was true. The tiny windows admitted only a glimmer of daylight; the walls were grimy, and there was no furniture of any kind. In place of a table, the blankets on which the old ladies normally slept had been spread over the floor to form a cloth, and on this the meagre party food had been carefully laid out on makeshift paper plates. Apart from the bread and jam saved from the children's rations, there were delicacies which Anna had stolen from the SS kitchens, including some currant buns, carefully divided into forty more or less equal pieces, and two bottles of lemonade which would allow the guests a sip each. Each guest was likewise allotted a half-biscuit and three raisins from Frantisek's food parcel, as well as a single lick of one of the sweets. The old ladies were allowed a whole biscuit and a sweet each, while the birthday girl had two biscuits and two sweets all to herself. In the middle of the tablecloth was the birthday cake, a plain sponge decorated by Ivana, the children's cook, with coloured sugar in the form of a figure 90. Nine matches stuck round the rim of the cake took the place of birthday candles. Jan did not know whether to laugh or cry.

And yet old Mrs Kadarova, a tiny wrinkled woman who reminded Jan of a sparrow, seemed overjoyed as she hugged Anna and greeted the rest of the children, smiling with delight as they handed her their cards and presents. The other old ladies seemed equally excited. They were all, Jan noticed, wearing what seemed to be their best clothes, and Mrs Kadarova had a flower clip tucked into her piled-up hair. Anna saw it, and suddenly clasped her hands together in dismay.

'Oh, I forgot!' she exclaimed.

'What did you forget, lovey?' asked Mrs Kadarova.

'Flowers. I forgot to bring you any flowers. How stupid of me! How can you have a ninetieth birthday party without flowers?'

'I don't need any flowers, dear... I've got everything I need already.'

But Anna insisted that Mrs Kadarova must have flowers. She would get some instantly from the gardens of the SS billets. Just one or two roses from each garden, she said. Nobody would even notice that they were missing.

And before the old lady could protest any further, Anna was gone, running like the wind, her heavy dark plait swinging behind her. Mrs Kadarova laughed and shook her head.

'Ah, if everyone was like our Anna, Terezin would be a better place,' she said. 'She's a wonderful girl. I only had to mention that I was going to be ninety today, and she insisted that I must have this party. I pray God will keep her safe and reward her with a good husband.'

Just then Friedl arrived with some party hats she had made for the old ladies out of scraps of coloured paper. She was pinning these to their scanty hair and apologizing for not having been able to make hats for the children as well, when Anna arrived back, flushed and joyful. In one hand she carried a bucket of water, and in the other a bunch of flowers – not just roses, but also petunias and marigolds and large silvery-white daisies. Their brilliant colour and perfume seemed to fill the dingy room with sunlight, and Mrs Kadarova clapped her hands in delight.

'There were so many to choose from,' Anna explained, as she arranged the flowers in the bucket and then placed it on the table-cloth next to the birthday cake. 'Why shouldn't they *spare* us these? After all, they have so much, and we have so little.'

'Didn't anyone see you?' asked one of the old ladies anxiously.

'Not they. I hid the flowers under my shirt.'

'When are we going to eat?' asked a little boy, eyeing the flowers without much enthusiasm.

'Soon, soon. After we've had the entertainments.'

'Can't we eat first? I'm starving.'

Before Anna could reply, the other children joined in, all insisting so vehemently that they would be able to act, sing, dance and recite better *after* they had eaten that she was forced to give way. Soon the guests were all squatting on the floor round the cloth, their eyes fixed eagerly on the food, waiting for the signal to begin.

'Before we start,' said Mrs Kadarova, 'I should like to recite a Hebrew blessing I'm sure you all know. I never thought ever to hear it again.' And to Jan's surprise, she began to speak the blessing with which his father had always inaugurated the Jewish festivals in the old days. 'Blessed art thou, O Lord our God, King of the Universe,' quavered Mrs Kadarova, 'who hast kept us in life, and hast preserved us, and enabled us to reach this season.'

After that there was a long silence. All eyes were fixed on Anna. Then she smiled.

'All right,' she said. 'You can start now.'

The children needed no second invitation. Within a few moments the bread and jam and fragments of bun and biscuit had been ravenously eaten and the lemonade drunk and the tell-tale bottles hidden, and the sweets were being passed round so that each guest could enjoy a long, luxurious lick.

'It's not fair,' cried one little girl. 'The boys are sucking the sweets, not licking them.'

'Now boys, no cheating,' said Anna sternly. 'Only one lick each, or there won't be enough to go round.' Then, hearing murmurs of discontent from the boys, she quickly added, 'I think Mrs Kadarova ought to cut her birthday cake now.'

The angry murmurs subsided, and someone handed Mrs Kadarova a knife.

'We must light the candles first,' said Anna, taking a box of matches from her pocket. The guests watched, fascinated, as she ignited the nine matches round the edge of the cake so that the sugar 90 seemed to glow in a ring of tiny flames. Smiling, Mrs Kadarova inclined her small head, which was now encased in a green paper crown, and blew them out. The children clapped and sang 'Happy birthday', and somebody called out, 'Speech, speech!'

'Ladies and gentlemen,' began Mrs Kadarova. 'This is the nicest party I've ever had.'

At that moment there came a thunderous knocking at the door.

It was the Commandant himself who stood in the open doorway, flanked by two grim henchmen. His eyes roamed round the room, and then came to rest on the flowers.

It seemed to Jan that everyone had stopped breathing. Then, after a few moments, the Commandant spoke.

'Aha, a party, I see,' he said.

Trembling, Mrs Kadarova raised her hand.

'If you please, Herr Commandant,' she said, 'today is my ninetieth birthday, and some of the children were good enough to give me this little celebration.'

'A ninetieth birthday party?' interrupted the Commandant with a smile. 'How touching. We don't have many of those. Why didn't you invite me?'

Jan felt himself relaxing. Was it possible, he thought, that the Commandant was going to be kind, just as he had been during the Red Cross visit? But the Commandant's next words shattered Jan's hopes.

'I recognize my prize petunias,' he said, and his face and voice were stern now. 'Am I to understand that they picked themselves and walked here?'

There was a long silence. Then the Commandant strode into the middle of the room, and brought his stick down on the shoulders of the nearest boy.

'I'm waiting for someone to own up!' he shouted. 'If no one admits to stealing these flowers, you'll all be severely punished. You all *deserve* to be punished, anyway. Where did this cake come from?'

'The children saved up their rations and baked it,' said Mrs Kadarova bravely.

'They stole the ingredients, more likely! However, I'm inclined to be lenient. If the thief who took my flowers owns up, I'll let the rest of you off.'

The room was as silent as if all its inhabitants were carved in stone. Jan felt his heart hammering. Then Anna suddenly jumped to her feet.

'It was me,' she cried. 'I took the flowers. And the party was my idea.'

A little moan came from the old ladies. Jan, to his own shame, felt himself sighing with relief. Then the Commandant smiled again.

'You've put me to a lot of trouble, young lady,' he said. 'I've had to knock on a great many doors to find you. I must tell you that we've had our eye on you for a long time. A lot of food seems to vanish from the kitchens where you work. I'm glad we've caught you red-handed at last. You won't be doing any more thieving.'

Some of the little girls began to cry, but Anna merely stared ahead defiantly as if she were not in the least frightened. The Commandant made a sign to his guards, and they seized Anna, tied her hands behind her back, and then frog-marched her out of the room. The Commandant picked up the flowers, and followed.

When the door had closed after them, pandemonium broke out. The old ladies and most of the girls were in tears, while the boys marvelled at how brave Anna had been. On the makeshift cloth the cake still stood uncut, its matches blackened and dead. They would never get to eat it now, Jan thought.

'That lovely young girl,' sobbed Mrs Kadarova. 'She's going to die for my sake!'

Jan felt his spine freeze. Surely, he thought, they were not going to do *that* to Anna, just for a few flowers!

Next day the children learned that Anna had been hanged in the Small Fortress.

From *Prisoner in Time: A Child of the Holocaust*
by Pamela Melnikoff

THE ORCHESTRA

*A year after his father's departure, Serge Goldberg and his mother
are sent to Auschwitz from the Dossin barracks in Mechelen. Serge
finds his father at the camp. His mother is killed in the gas
chamber. In this fragment, Serge is selected for the camp orchestra.
Thanks to the preferential treatment given to musicians, Serge and
his father survive the atrocities at the camp.*

The morning call.
'Achtung! Stillgestand!'
Serge meekly goes through the prescribed motions. stand to attention
in front of the bunk, straight as an arrow. His head is bursting, he
can't think anymore, has lost all feeling.
  'Du! Muzikant?'
Serge doesn't understand. The images of the selection flash through
his mind like a searchlight.
  'Du! Are you deaf or something? Violinist?'
'He wants to know whether you can play the violin,' Simon whispers.
Violin? Musician? Serge vaguely recognizes the soldier with the
rounded red cheeks. He is back on the platform. The train. Cartloads
full of skeletons. 'Can I take my violin?' Serge nods. 'Mitgehen!'
It's my turn, he thinks stoically. Finally. It barely affects him. On the
contrary. He wants out. Through the chimney, if he must.
  Serge stumbles behind the soldier. He can't keep up with him. His
feet keep sinking into the squelchy mud. One shoe gets stuck. The
soldier doesn't look back. Serge hobbles after him like a cripple. Past
the railway line, past the kitchen. Hundreds of frightened faces are
waiting at the entrance gate again. The reception committee has its
hands full. At twelve past six they reach barrack 24.
  Serge stands rooted to the spot.
  'Close that door,' somebody yells.
Serge obeys with large, uncomprehending eyes. Is he dreaming? This
is paradise. Abundant light. And heat. So much heat it makes him
uncomfortable. He unbuttons the top button of his suit, shaking, and
wipes the sweat off his forehead. The soldier pushes him on.

Two dozen men are sitting in a semi-circle behind their stands: well dressed, washed, smiling. One of them gets up, walks up to Serge and wipes his head dry. A second one takes off the other shoe and puts a pair of sandals on his feet. Leather sandals! Serge feels amazement, even gratitude, but is unable to utter a word. A few weeks have made him forget how to say 'thank you'.

His eyes stray through the room. If only Daddy could see this: mandolins, violins, guitars, flutes, trumpets, a big and a little drum, a grand piano even. Just like home, Daddy.

This has to be a dream. A wonderfully pleasant dream. So different from the nightmare of the selection. Any moment now it will come to an end. And daddy will walk in. Hey, wake up, he'll say.

'So you play the violin?'

Serge is startled. So it is real? The man in front of him is holding a baton. 'Yes,' Serge stutters.

'Is this one yours?'

God almighty, his violin! Where does that come from? His hands caress the sound box. He hesitantly places the bow on the strings and clasps the violin under his chin.

The conductor nods encouragingly.

Serge starts the introductory bars to the 'Allegro Vivace' of Felix Mendelsohn's 'Reformation' symphony. His stiff fingers cannot follow the tempo in his head.

'Stop!' the conductor shouts.

'The cold... my fingers,' Serge stutters.

'That's not it. Mendelsohn's forbidden.'

'Forbidden? Why?'

Serge doesn't understand. Mendelsohn is his favourite composer. His music is so lively, so full of feeling. And he has written so much: piano pieces, chamber music, solo works with orchestra, lieder, choir music.

'Play something else. Von Suppé, Mozart or Strauss. Anything. But no Mendelsohn. Mendelsohn is a Jew.'

'I'm sorry,' Serge stutters.

'Achtung! Commander Kramer's coming.'

The conductor turns pale. Everybody's suddenly busy: outfits are straightened, stands put in line, instruments given a quick polish.

The commander comes in, followed by two SS men. All the musicians jump to attention. Straight as arrows, eyes down. Look them straight in the eye, daddy said. Show them you're healthy and strong. Serge can feel his muscles tense up. That man. That face. The selection. Daddy. The blood is drained from his head. He feels dizzy, gropes for something, anything. A nagging pain nestles in his stomach. If only he could use the toilet now.

'Hang on in there,' somebody whispers.

Incredible. In front of him stands the man who barely a few hours ago condemned Daddy with one nonchalant flick. He's not tall, rather stocky in fact, head planted straight onto his torso. His uniform clings to his broad chest, like a harness. Supple as a predator, he walks up to the chair that has been put there for him. His crushing presence fills the entire space. He takes off his cap, crosses his legs and puts the kepi on his knee. His chestnut hair is cropped. The imposing head has the shape of a square.

'So that's the new one then?' Serge can hear him ask.

'Jawohl, Herr Kampleiter.'

The conductor is still standing bolt upright.

'Gut so. All work and no play. I reckon we've earned a rest, don't you? Play us something.'

A rest! Serge remembers the ditch. Jump or die. One false note could be the end of him here.

'What would the commander care to hear? Suppé? Mozart? Beethoven perhaps?'

'Hmm... Beethoven. Pa-pa-pa-pam. The Fifth Symphony. Seems rather difficult as a solo. No, make it Schumann. How about the 'Träumerei'?'

'At your service, commander'.

The conductor turns around nervously and looks at Serge with expectant eyes. 'Do you know Schumann's 'Rêverie'?'

Despite the tension and the threat Serge has to laugh inside. Does he know it? He must have played it dozens, no hundreds of times. Until he started cursing it. And now... Serge thinks of barrack 148 and compares. The difference! Day and night, heaven and earth. These are nicely groomed men, this is clean, warm. He has no desire to go back, no sir. He will play! He will overcome his aversion to Schumann and the murderer on the chair in front of him. How can anybody adore music and send thousands of innocent people to the gas chambers without the least remorse at the same time!

Serge takes his violin, passes the bow over the strings, tunes it with the ebony pegs and nods to the conductor. He's ready. The conductor raises his arms. The violins begin. Softly, distant and then swelling into the happy murmur of a mountain brook. After which they die down into rippling water again. Now it's Serge's turn. His fingers hesitate and try to find the right position. It's been so long. He's lost the rhythm. The conductor desperately tries to keep the pace. Kramer frowns. This doesn't look good! Suddenly a strange, unexpected warmth fills Serge. He is back in Isaac Jacobson's stately, slightly dark living room. Feeling, communication with the audience, emotion, that's what it's all about. Isaac smiles approvingly. Serge puts so much tenderness, so much expression into his play that Isaac closes his eyes and dreams away. Or is it Kramer?

After he has stopped and the orchestra's last tones linger, the commander stays put. His eyes closed. Then he takes his cap and gets up.

'Nice,' he says. 'Very moving indeed.'

His eyes glisten. Not a shred of terror in them now. Kramer is a human being again. 'I'm making you a member of the orchestra. Auf wiedersehen.'

'Thank you, commander,' Serge stammers.

The camp leader clicks his heels, abruptly turns around and walks towards the door.

'Herr Kramer, dare I ask you something?' Serge says on impulse.

The conductor drops his baton, shaking. He daren't pick it up. You never address an SS unless instructed to do so.

The camp leader stops for one second and turns around, exasperatingly slowly. His eyes have regained the coolness of the military man. The music lover has vanished.

'Na... und?' he barks.

Serge ignores the hostile look.

'My father... eh... daddy is an excellent musician too.'

'So? Where is he? What's his instrument?'

'In barrack 148, Herr Lagerführer. He was selected this morning and taken to the Sonderkommando. He's a great pianist.'

'Hmm... piano. We'll see.'

From *Sonata in Auschwitz* by Roger Vanhoeck

UNCLE GEORGE'S DEATH

Jutta, a Jewish girl from Germany, ends up in England in the late thirties. She finds out in a letter from her friend Johann that her uncle George has been killed. Jutta is devastated when she realises who's responsible for his death – but then Johann writes her a second letter. The Jewish author Ilse Losa ran away from the German oppressors herself as a little girl. She ended up in Portugal, where she became a famous children's author.

The fog enveloped London. Leaden and oppressive, it weighed on the city. Mounds of leaves covered the damp earth of the parks. There was no more foliage, only black, naked branches. And the flowers died. It was then that Esmé also died. Her dark, dissonant music was silenced. The books lay abandoned. And those sad eyes and white hands that searched awkwardly for the dinner plate were gone. They found her lying on her bed, her hands hanging loose and still, her enormous eyes staring into emptiness. Her thin, bony body had succumbed easily to the poison. And perhaps it was only Jutta who noticed the sardonic smile that distorted her mouth. Esmé had expired along with the notes of her violin, leaving behind a fleeting and painful echo.

The Trotters received visits of condolence.

'Still so young, poor little thing!'

'Always so quiet!'

'Who would imagine she was capable of such a thing?'

'So unassuming.'

Jutta thought that none of these people really knew Esmé. Esmé lived in her own isolated world, and suffered because of it. Winnie went about with a new expression, one might say of sorrowful bewilderment. Perhaps the sombre thoughts that had been present in Esme's mind at every moment, were present in her mind for the first time. It was because of this that her sister's escape into death terrified her. Jutta remembered the days when Tony was ill and the whole family had waited anxiously in the corridor for the crisis to pass. Then she had pleaded: 'Don't die, darling Tony! We are all waiting for you!' And the suffering and love they shared for the child had united them for several days. But Esmé had died. She had died alone and unhappy. And her death hadn't united the Trotter family and Jutta, not even for a brief moment. No-one had ever cared about what Esmé did or thought. There was nothing in common between her and the rest of the family. And that was why the tragedy of her death had left no indelible traces, for at no point had the troubled world she lived in ever touched upon the others. It was only for Jutta that she had left behind an emptiness. At the hour at which she used to climb the stairs, the hour they would read poems together, she felt a terrible abandonment. It happened that one day Emily observed, 'This business of dying isn't fair. There are so many people going about on their last legs...' Jutta looked at her with surprise. She knew that Emily felt sorry for her.

Jutta, my dearest love,

If I could only spare you the pain I am going to cause you! Everything would be easier if I could hold your dearest head in my hands so that you could cry. I would kiss away your tears. Oh why are we so far away from each other?

My Jutta: Uncle George has died. They killed him. They killed that wonderful man we owe so much to. I have nothing to comfort you with and any words would be meaningless. As do not I feel the same despair as you? It was he who brightened your childhood and it was he who helped me to understand so many things that had been all mixed up in my mind. And it was also he who helped me to bear your absence better. And now he has left us forever.

Someone saw him on the street. They reported him to the police and they came to our house to take him. My father, with tears in his eyes, begged them for mercy. They pushed him into a corner, and he shook his head almost like a child would. Oh my poor old man!

What more can I tell you? I was unable to say a single word to Uncle George. We squeezed each other's hands. That was all. But what a squeeze. My God! I will never forget it. This morning I learned that they had killed him.

I've already been to see your mother. She maintained her rigid posture, which is typical of her. But I know how she is suffering. She's been so brave during all this time that we've been helping her brother!

And now, Jutta darling, we have something to ask you. Come back! Come back, my love, never mind all the unhappiness that's going on here. At least we will be together, you, myself and your mother. Work can be found more easily, although it's seldom the kind that we'd enjoy. But, in the end, isn't it true that your dreams aren't being fulfilled over there either?

We no longer need your money, unfortunately. You can use it for your return. What do you say, my love? Our mountains are still there. And the flowers still bloom there in the spring. And we have our love. That's something that no-one can steal from us. Come quickly! Everything will be different and together we will be able to speak about our dead friend.

Whilst I am far away from you in person, I am near to you in my thoughts and trying to help you, as much as I can, to bear the great pain that I must have caused you with this letter. Jutta, my little Jutta, my dearest love.

I kiss you, I embrace you.

Always yours, Johann.

'What is it?' asked Emily.

Jutta was standing as if frozen by the kitchen table. 'Some bad news?'

Jutta merely moved her head.

Emily returned to stirring the pan with a wooden spoon but without taking her eyes off the girl. And when she saw her swaying towards the door, she let go of the spoon, and within an instant, was holding her in her arms.

'Come and sit down... For God's sake, sit down.'

Jutta obeyed, but still seemed as if she were unconscious. She couldn't connect her thoughts: 'Uncle George... Go back to Germany... They killed Uncle George... Esme... Johann...'

'There, there! It can't be as bad as that.' Emily's voice seemed to come from a long way off. There was something different about it. Jutta's eyes were dilated and fixed on some distant point. Emily looked at the letter lying open on the table.

'News of your mother?'

Jutta didn't reply, but the trembling in her body increased.

'There, there... What is it?' Her voice was almost tender.

Jutta raised her eyes towards her and, in a glance, remembered those dark, sad eyes that had met hers one summer afternoon. She felt a heavy hand on her shoulder. Plump and swollen. Emily at her side.

'Has someone died?'

'Yes, my uncle...'

'And did you love him so much?'

Jutta didn't reply. Only a dry sob tore at her throat.

'Poor child!'

Emily had said merely 'poor child' but as if by magic, Jutta's body was freed from the rigidity it had been protecting itself with. Like a child, she let her head drop on to Emily's bosom. A convulsive sob broke the silence.

After this day Emily came to learn many things about Jutta's life.

'They're bad people, them from your country!'

'Bad? Why Emily?'

'Where they can kill men like your uncle, just like that, there can't be any good people.'

'But there are good people too, believe me.'

'God willing, God willing...'

Jutta had so often dreamed of going back! Had embellished the moment of arrival with colours and brightness. But now everything would be different. Her uncle's death weighed on her heart and her arrival would be painfully distressing.

'Tell me, tell me everything! Who reported him?'

'Who was it?' This was the question she asked herself. But she drew away from the answer which, nevertheless, forced itself upon her relentlessly. No, No! How could she ever live at home again?

To Esmé, life had seemed absurd. But life wasn't absurd. Absurd was her uncle's death. And she saw him, very tall, with his arms swinging about his body as if they didn't know where to put themselves. She saw his shy smile and heard those grave words which she hadn't always been able to understand. And it was as if he was walking by her side, with his head thrown back, laughing with his mouth wide open. How different it was to laugh like that! 'Don't you feel a great joy in being alive, Jutta, in spite of all the difficult, complicated things?'

'I do, yes, that's exactly how I feel', she had replied.

'So we're alike, girl. And we mustn't give up hope.'

And she saw that her uncle had lived with the anguish of preserving his life, the life he loved, whereas Esmé had taken refuge in her little room of books with their covers embossed in gold. Now there was just one question: who had reported him? This question interposed itself between her and returning. Johann had perhaps not wanted to hurt her. In the letter he had merely said: someone saw him on the street. They reported him to the police

Someone...

For the first time, Emily invited Jutta to her room. It was at the top of the house, in the attic, whilst Jutta's room was on the floor shared by the family. There was a musty smell. On the dark chest of drawers, a vase, next to it an enormous trunk covered by a flowered shawl.

'My first mistress brought it back for me from Spain,'' explained Emily.

On the bedside table, in a fancy frame, Jutta noticed the photograph of a broad-faced man with startled eyes and a Kaiser moustache.

'Who is that Emily?'

'That was my fiancé.'

Jutta looked at her with surprise.

'Does it seems so impossible that I had a fiancé?'

'What happened to him?'

'He died in the war. It was them from your country that killed him.'

'Oh, Emily!'

Jutta understood why Emily had always been so hostile to her. Besides enjoying all the privileges of the Trotter family, she was German, and the two things couldn't have helped but to arouse her mistrust. Emily didn't add anything further, she wasn't used to talking about her problems nor to conveying her thoughts.

'Yes', she said. And she opened a drawer from which she took a wooden box. She exhibited the pretty things which she had collected during her life in service: a brooch with little violet stones, a bracelet with miniature gold roses, a bundle of hand-made lace, earrings, a silver thimble. She touched each object lovingly, in contrast to her coarse hands with their blackened lines. Then she carefully folded the shawl from Spain and opened the trunk: 'My wedding trousseau. Of course, I'm not going to get married now. But it's good to have some things, don't you think? A dozens sheets, see? And I have six of these towels.'

'Are your parents still alive, Emily?'

'My mother is still living.'

'Where?'

'In D. It's a village, it's near Wales.'

'Is it pretty?'

'Places where you can't earn a living aren't pretty.'

That night, when Jutta was lying in her bed she thought: so many different worlds! Esmé lived in her comfortable room; she spent the time playing sad music, reading poetry and feeding the ideas which led her to death. The Trotters, always burdened with work, dealing with a host of things for all kinds of people. Yet they didn't know anything about Esmé's intimate life, nor did they know anything about Emily's life, by the fire, or alone in her room, up there, in the attic, where there was an already fading photograph of a man with a Kaiser moustache. And herself, Jutta, with her anxiety to live, with so many broken illusions and with the fear of returning to her homeland, where the confirmation that her father was an informer awaited her.

Bern, 12th November, 1934.

Jutta darling, Everything has changed. I asked you: come back. Our mountains are still there, our flowers are still there. Yes, all this is still there in our homeland, but a long way from us, from you and also from me.

I arrived today in Switzerland and can hardly comprehend how everything happened so fast. I was warned by a friend that the police were going to arrest me because of my friendship with Uncle George, and for having helped to hide him. Then everything happened like a whirlwind. My father, Lammers and Martha helped me to escape. I would like to tell you everything, all the details, but it can't be just now, when there is only one problem that is on my mind: you. I gave you, for certain, great happiness when I proposed that you should come back. How can I ask you now: no, Jutta, don't come. I don't have this right. Hadn't you wanted to come back, after spending all this time in foreign places? Weren't you already comforted by the idea of returning? And what can I offer you? I haven't even finished my education. I would have difficulty in finding work and even in finding a country which would give me asylum. The money I have brought with me – with what sacrifice my poor old man managed to find it! It isn't going to last for long.

Jutta, Jutta, my love, in spite of all this, I ask you to tell me if you are able to give up your plans of returning so that we can live together. And listen, my love, listen well to what I have to say: the day will come when we will return to our land, the day when we can join in helping it to become free and worthy of the sacrifices of our dead friend and of so many others who are suffering and dying for its cause. We are young. Our spirit and strength aren't lacking in these bitter and difficult times. Do you agree, Jutta? I am waiting here for your reply. And if you decide to return, I won't stop loving you for it.

I will always, always be yours,

Johann.

The fog was everywhere. Paths covered in mud. You could hardly make out the naked branches which the trees lifted up to the sky. In her heart Jutta alternated tears with joy.

She would remain in foreign lands. She wouldn't see her mother. Nor the city, nor the mountains. But, within hours, Johann would be at her side. Johann who was her home and her return!

Nothing had been planned for certain. Perhaps they would stay here. Perhaps they would go to some other country. Perhaps. Perhaps. Courage, always courage, the words of Uncle George when he left his country. Walking among the tortured landscape, she thought of those who had been dear to her and who had left her forever. Uncle George, with his love for life and struggle for justice, and who they had mercilessly killed. Esmé, with her soul so troubled by her terrible loneliness and who hadn't been able to find the way to life and had sought refuge in death.

She thought of the others: her mother, Li, Bernhard Schuster, Martha, Lammers, Mamma, Emily.

She thought of Tony who had raised his little arm and asked with his small voice: tell me a story. Tell me.

'There was once a little poor girl who the stars felt sorry for and, so, they let themselves fall into her lap.'

From *Rio sem ponte* by Ilse Losa

TO THE GATES OF AUSCHWITZ

*Art Spiegelman's famous graphic masterpiece tells two
simultaneous stories. One is the story, told to Art by his father, of
his imprisonment in and survival of Auschwitz concentration camp.
The other story is the story of Art and his father now, many years
after the Second World War. This very powerful story shows not
only the horror of what the older Mr Spiegelman suffered in
Poland, but also how his experiences have scarred him
permanently, leaving him with habits and values that people who
were born later find it difficult to understand – so they need to hear
about what happened. This book was written not only for children.
In the scenes from Second World War Spiegelman depicts the Nazis
as cats, the Jews as mice, and those Poles who assisted or did
nothing about what was happening as pigs.*

From *Maus: A Survivor's Tale* by Art Spiegelman

EVERYONE CAME VERY NICE DRESSED. THEY TRIED SO THAT THEY WOULD LOOK YOUNG AND ABLE TO WORK, IN ORDER TO GET A GOOD STAMP ON THEIR PASSPORT.

WHEN WE WERE EVERYBODY INSIDE, GESTAPO WITH MACHINE GUNS SURROUNDED THE STADIUM.

LINE UP BY FAMILY AT THE TABLES TO REGISTER! QUICKLY!

THEN WAS A SELECTION, WITH PEOPLE SENT EITHER TO THE LEFT, EITHER TO THE RIGHT.

OLD PEOPLE, FAMILIES WITH LOTS OF KIDS, AND PEOPLE WITHOUT WORK CARDS ARE ALL GOING TO THE LEFT!

WE UNDERSTOOD THIS MUST BE VERY BAD.

ME AND ANJA CAME TO THE TABLE WHERE MY COUSIN WAS SITTING...

AH, YOU WORK AT THE CARPENTRY SHOP. GO TO THE RIGHT.

SO WE GOT STAMPED OUR PASSPORTS AND CAME QUICK TO THE GOOD SIDE OF THE STADIUM. THOSE THEY SENT LEFT, THEY DIDN'T GET ANY STAMP.

WE WERE SO HAPPY WE CAME THROUGH. BUT WE WORRIED NOW— WERE OUR FAMILIES SAFE?

LOOK! THERE'S POPPA, WITH LOLEK AND LONIA!

WE SAW WOLFE AND TOSHA. OUR FAMILY SEEMS TO BE OKAY.

DID YOU SEE MY FATHER?

I COULDN'T SEE ANYWHERE MY FATHER.

BUT LATER SOMEONE WHO SAW HIM TOLD ME... HE CAME THROUGH THIS SAME COUSIN OVER TO THE GOOD SIDE.

HER, THEY SENT TO THE LEFT. FOUR CHILDREN WAS TOO MANY.

SPIEGELMAN... TO THE RIGHT.

THEN CAME FELA TO REGISTER...

FELA!

MY DAUGHTER! HOW CAN SHE MANAGE ALONE - WITH FOUR CHILDREN TO TAKE CARE OF?

AND, WHAT DO YOU THINK? HE SNEAKED ON TO THE BAD SIDE!

AND THOSE ON THE BAD SIDE NEVER CAME ANYMORE HOME.

THOSE WITH A STAMP WERE LET TO GO HOME. BUT THERE WERE VERY FEW JEWS NOW LEFT IN SOSNOWIEC...

ONE FROM THREE THEY KEPT AT THE STADIUM.... MAYBE 10,000 PEOPLE— AND WITH THEM, MY FATHER.

WELL... IT'S ENOUGH FOR TODAY. YES, ARTIE?...

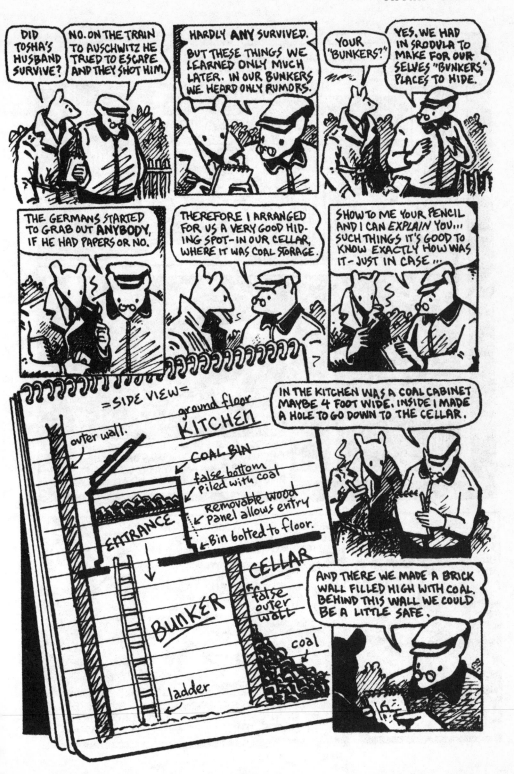

THEN, IN JUNE, THEY ARRESTED MONIEK MERIN AND ALL THE OTHER HIGHEST BIG SHOTS OF THE *JUDENRAT*, THE JEWISH COUNCIL.

false wall,
BUNKER
ATTIC
Entrance hidden by chandelier
UPSTAIRS BEDROOM

AROUND THIS TIME WE WERE PUT INTO A DIFFERENT HOUSE. HERE ALSO WE MADE A BUNKER.

BY THE END OF JULY THE NAZIS MADE TO LIQUIDATE COMPLETELY OUR GHETTO—IT WAS 10,000 JEWS TAKEN AWAY IN ONE WEEK.

EXCEPT TO SNEAK FOR FOOD, WE STAYED MOSTLY IN THE BUNKER.

LOLEK! THANK GOD YOU'RE SAFE!

IT'S LIKE A BATTLEFIELD OUTSIDE!

THERE'S HARDLY ANYONE LEFT IN SRODULA. EVERYONE HAS BEEN DEPORTED OR SHOT.

FROM ALL THE JEWS OF ALL SOSNOWIEC IT WAS LEFT MAYBE 1,000 IN THE GHETTO.

AT LEAST YOUR BAG IS FULL... YOU FOUND A LOT OF FOOD, YES?

JUST A FEW OLD TURNIPS... AND SOME BOOKS.

BOOKS!? WHAT'S THE MATTER WITH YOU? WE CAN'T EAT BOOKS!

SHH

ALL THE TIME WE WERE HUNGRY. WE JUST DIDN'T HAVE WHAT TO EAT.

ONE NIGHT WE WENT TO SNEAK FOR FOOD...

LOOK! A STRANGER!

WE DRAGGED HIM UP TO OUR BUNKER

WHAT ARE YOU DOING HERE?

I-I DIDN'T KNOW ANYONE LIVED HERE! I JUST STOPPED TO REST A MOMENT.

MY WIFE AND I HAVE A STARVING BABY. I WAS OUT HUNTING FOR SCRAPS!

HE'S LYING!

IN THE MORNING WE GAVE A LITTLE FOOD TO HIM AND LEFT HIM GO TO HIS FAMILY...

JUDEN RAUS!

...THE GESTAPO CAME THAT AFTERNOON.

HE MAY BE AN INFORMER. THE SAFEST THING WOULD BE TO KILL HIM!

WHAT HAD WE TO DO? WE TOOK ON HIM PITY.

THEY TOOK US TO A BUILDING IN A PART OF SRODULA SEPARATED BY WIRES— A GHETTO INSIDE THE GHETTO—AND THERE WE HAD TO SIT AND TO WAIT.

I HAD A SMALL BAG TO TRAVEL. WHEN THEY REGISTERED ME IN, THEY LOOKED OVER EVERYTHING.

WHAT'S THIS? SHOE POLISH??

YES. I LIKE TO KEEP MYSELF NEAT.

WITH A SPOON HE TOOK OUT, LITTLE BY LITTLE, ALL THE POLISH.

WELL, WELL... A GOLD WATCH. YOU JEWS ALWAYS HAVE GOLD!

WRAPPED IN FOIL, I KEPT IT HIDDEN THERE.... IT WAS MY LAST TREASURE.

IT WAS THIS WATCH I GOT FROM FATHER-IN-LAW WHEN FIRST I MARRIED TO ANJA.

WELL, NEVER MIND...THEY TOOK IT AND THREW ME WITH MANDELBAUM INTO A CELL...

WAIT A MINUTE! WHATEVER HAPPENED TO ABRAHAM?

WHO?

AH, MANDELBAUM'S NEPHEW! YES. HE FINISHED THE SAME AS US TO CONCENTRATION CAMP.

—BUT

YES. I'LL TELL YOU HOW IT WAS WITH HIM— BUT NOW I'M TELLING HERE IN THE PRISON...

HERE WE GOT VERY LITTLE TO EAT—MAYBE SOUP ONE TIME A DAY—AND WE SAT WITH NOTHING TO DO.

WHY DON'T THEY PUT US TO WORK LIKE THE REST OF YOU?

IT MEANS YOU WON'T BE HERE VERY LONG...

...EVERY WEEK OR SO A TRUCK TAKES SOME OF THE PRISONERS AWAY.

EXCUSE ME... DO ANY OF YOU KNOW GERMAN?

MY FAMILY JUST SENT ME A FOOD PARCEL. IF I WRITE BACK THEY'LL SEND ANOTHER, BUT WE'RE ONLY ALLOWED TO WRITE GERMAN.

I KNEW WELL TO WRITE GERMAN....SO I WROTE....

IN A SHORT TIME HE GOT AGAIN A PACKAGE...

YOU DID A GREAT JOB! TAKE ANYTHING YOU WANT FOR YOU AND YOUR FRIEND!

IT WAS EGGS THERE...IT WAS EVEN CHOCOLATES. ...I WAS VERY LUCKY TO GET SUCH GOODIES!

Hiding

A TIME OF KILLING

'A crime has occurred, accusing all'
W.H. Auden The Age of Anxiety

A time of killing
and the concealment of killing.
What's hidden behind that smokescreen,
behind those deliberately dirty windows?

A terrible landscape,
where my words won't adjust
nor my eyes: the burning man
stumbles bewildered out of the bunker
and stays there till I die
branded on my memory.

by Remco Campert

COURIER FOR THE RESISTANCE

Fourteen-year-old Polish Mosje Shuster ends up at the orphanage of the famous doctor/educationist Janus Korczak. It is 1939. When, a year later, the orphanage is moved to the Warsaw ghetto, Jewish Mosje joins the resistance as Marek. His sweetheart Reizele is unable to join him. She is devoted to Doctor Korczak and his children. More than fifty years later, Mosje and Reizele meet again during a Korczak commemoration in Tel Aviv. Old Mosje relives his painful past, such as the moment when he decided to leave the orphanage to carve out his own niche in life.

Zalewski is waiting for us, with Mrs Stefa, Judita, Jozef and the other caretakers who have returned from their holidays. They utter cries of admiration over our tanned faces and muscled arms, but their hearts aren't in it.

Jan has brought a cartload of apples, so we can have the tradi-
tional honeyed apples for New Year. Even that doesn't cheer them up.

After we've made our beds and admired the freshly painted walls,
we are told the news over dinner. The Germans have spent the entire
summer putting barbed wire fence around the Jewish quarter. Bits of
wall, built by teams of Jewish men, have been finished. Our stretch
along Krochmalna Street lies outside the ghetto.

The doctor tried to convince them to let us stay. No such luck.

We have to move. But where to? The quarter they've picked for
secluding hundreds of thousands of Jews, houses two hundred and
forty thousand of them as it is. Plus eighty thousand Poles, who are
being forced to vacate their houses. The Jews from Warsaw's 'Aryan
section' are swapping houses with Poles from the ghetto. The doctor
spends his every waking moment trying to find us a place.

Life goes on as usual at the boarding school. Classes are held all
over the building.

The onions and garlic we have harvested are woven into plaits in
the kitchen. The mushrooms we have picked in the forest, are thread-
ed on pieces of string to dry. The cabbage is chopped and pickled and
put in barrels.

Boruch cobbles the shoes that got worn out at camp and Sabina
uses bits of cloth from threadbare blouses and trousers to mend
clothes.

Zalewski simply carries on working. Repairing furniture, carrying
coal, taking care of the chickens. Whatever time is left, he uses to
make dolls' beds and wooden horses from bits of wood he's collected in a corner of the workshop.

'How about making more beds and wardrobes?' I say. 'The number of children is increasing and we'll never have enough if we move
to the ghetto.'

'I wouldn't be surprised if they only let us take a cartload of linen
and some cutlery, my boy. We'll be notified exactly one day in
advance and allowed one suitcase each. The rest will be confiscated.
As far as they're concerned, every poor Jew has a hidden treasure
stashed away somewhere.'

'Many Jews do have jewellery,' I say.

'That's because they're used to moving. Fleeing with a chest of drawers on your neck isn't exactly easy. So they take jewellery. The Germans snap it up at the ghetto entrance. They won't even look at the toys, I reckon.'

I'm not entirely convinced.

I sneak out the front door and walk down the street up to the ghetto. The barricade runs through Krochmalna Street. Barbed wire manufacturers must be having a field day. Or is this stuff handmade?

Kilometres and kilometres of it for one ghetto in one city in one country. How many kilometres for all the ghettoes in occupied Europe? New sums for German pupils.

I follow the droves of people and suddenly find myself at the gate in Grzybowska Street. SS men and policemen are mounting the guard, but they do not notice me in the throng and chaos. After I've passed through the gate I stop and watch for a bit. An SS man kicks over one family's cart. Too much junk, he yells. He hurls two suitcases at the man and the woman, which end up on the street, open. They hastily put their things back.

'My doll!' a little girl screams.

An agent chases her away.

The streets are so full of people it seems the houses themselves might get squashed.

I run north through Zelazna Street. The evicted Poles are walking against the flow with their handcarts and wheelbarrows.

In Karmelicka Street they can't even get past their own doorways. The new inhabitants' tiny loads are blocking the way.

I take Chlodna Street. Here, at number 33, stands the Polish commercial school that might want to swop with us. It's a dark, dilapidated building, much smaller than our modern boarding school. How can we ever get a hundred and fifty children in there? I carry on.

Crying children and shrieking people everywhere. A man is kicking his skinny horse, but the poor animal cannot move with all those people.

I worm my way through the crowd to Mila Street, by the graveyard. That must be the northernmost point of the ghetto. I go back south through Smocza Street and slip outside through the gate by the

Catholic church. I've seen enough. Close those gates and the Jews in this ghetto are trapped like rats.

Including myself. The boarding school is stuff enough as it is. We will be stacked like slaves in a ship's hold. I remember the fields in Goclawek. I could have been roaming, running through forests, swimming in the river. Instead, I stayed on the farm and milked cows like any country lad. And why? To be with Reizele. Because she's so sweet. But Reizele's sweet to everyone. I walk home slowly.

I go to the workshop, fetch Reizele's little cupboard that's almost finished, and put it with the firewood. Excess luggage.

I pack the things that are to go on the cart. Tools. Toys. Planks for the new house. I hear stumbling on the basement stairs. It can't be Zalewski. His pace is faster. It sounds like an old lady with a stick coming down the stairs.

But it is Zalewski.

His leg is stiff his hands are bleeding and his face is blue and swollen.

He sits down at the bench-screw and laughs at me with a strangely distorted face.

Boleslaw Screwface.

I'm so scared it makes me laugh.

'They just kept on going,' he says. He tries to wink with his half-closed eye.

'Where have you been?'

'I had to report to Head Quarters. I said I've been working here for twenty years and that I'm part of the furniture now. That I want to move to the ghetto with you. They said that working for Jews is not allowed. They beat me to a pulp like a discarded chair.'

'Mrs Stefa should dress your wounds.'

'She's far too busy. I've had black eyes before, you know. And I'm busy too.'

I point at the stuff around me.

'Everything's packed, boss.'

He lights a cigarette. A tear is running down his cheek.

'At least somebody will be able to hold the fort for you now,' he says. 'Until you're back.'

'You don't honestly expect these children to return, do you?'

'Don't say that. Why do you say "these children" anyway? You're one of them too, remember.'

'No I'm not,' I say. 'I'm not going.'

'You have to.'

'My uncle has lots of Polish friends. They'll help me.'

'They can't. If you hide a Jew and are found out, they kill you.'

He muses.

'You seem to have what it takes. I may have an address for you.'

I dash towards him and hug him, sort of put my arms around him. He's so big.

He winces and pushes me away.

'I'm sorry,' I say. 'I don't know what got into me.'

'It's the bruises, that's all. I'd wait and see where I'm being sent before getting too grateful.'

'The witch in Hänsel and Gretel?'

'The underground movement. They need couriers.'

I sit down on the edge of the table.

'Are you a resistance man?'

'That would be too dangerous for the children. But I do have contacts.'

He touches his leg. His face becomes distorted.

I lose courage.

'Reckon I'll make the grade?'

He looks at me.

'You must tell the doctor before going.'

'What if he doesn't agree?'

'Has it ever stopped you?'

From *Moshe and Reizele* by Karlijn Stoffels

MISHA TRIES TO OBTAIN MEDICINES FOR HIS PARTISAN GROUP IN THE POLISH FORESTS.

Misha in this novel is the step-father of Richard, a boy growing up in Britain long after the Second World War has finished. Richard hears from Misha the story of his boyhood experiences after Poland was invaded by the Germans. He hears how Misha, a Jew, escapes from the Warsaw ghetto and hides out in the forests with a group of partisans. In this extract Misha and his friend Berek try to obtain medicines from a nearby hospital. This is a very dangerous exploit, one that could get both partisans shot and put at risk the lives of the people who help them. Christa Laird's novel is full of excitement and adventure and is often tragic.

When we got back to the camp we found Henryk worried about Alexander's shoulder. He'd tried to remove the bullet but without success as he didn't have the right instruments. Alexander was very pale, but played down the pain.

'What hurts most is wasting good vodka – I think I'd almost rather have an infection!' He grinned valiantly, his teeth showing strikingly white against his dark complexion and curly black hair and beard. Alexander always reminded me of pictures I'd seen in children's books of pirates on the high seas. I obviously wasn't the only one – I once heard Berek suggesting to him that he ought to wear a gold earring to complete the image!

Before the raids, Berek had discovered from his widow that she had a cousin who worked as a nurse at a small Nazi-controlled medical post in the village of Jedlanka. The widow – Irena was her name – thought her cousin would probably be sympathetic to us and might let us have medical supplies should the need arise. Until then there had been no need to endanger either the nurse or any of ourselves in a raid on the clinic – now, however, the situation had changed. Quite apart from Alexander's injury, there were a lot of people in hiding who had been wounded during the raids and who required urgent medical attention. We also badly needed salve for the scabies which was reaching epidemic proportions amongst partisan fighters and refugees alike, because of the vitamin shortages.

So the next morning, at first light, Berek and I set off for Rudka. The idea was that we would ask Irena to alert her cousin to the imminent arrival of a boy with an 'injured arm,' which would then give me a pretext to visit the clinic. There had been a moderately heavy fall of snow in the night but fortunately a strong wind was blowing now, which meant that drifts would soon obliterate our tracks. All the same, the wind – or gale as it felt to us – was a mixed blessing, for it deafened us by howling around our ears, and blinded us by driving snow into our eyes. We couldn't talk on the way, as we needed all our energies to make progress, bent almost double against its force. That was the first time in the forest that I really felt the cold – it seemed to cut right through the several layers of dead men's clothing which we were wrapped in.

Irena's welcome seemed doubly warm because of the conditions outside her neat, cosy house. She made us sit down and drink hot milk and eat carrot cake while she went off, almost immediately, to see her cousin as we requested. I think that little meal still ranks among the most memorable of my life, like my first breakfast on the other side of the wall with Granny's home-made plum jam.

Berek and I took off our boots and luxuriously warmed our feet in front of the stove. Berek sighed. 'Maybe, Jan, maybe it's time to shut the truck door and let that train go to Sobibor at last.'

Poor Berek. He was still wrestling with what might have been, or should have been. I felt gratified that he should confide his feelings to me, who was at least ten years his junior. I even felt tempted to tell him about Eva. It would have been such a relief. But by then we'd already been sitting there companionably for an hour and a half, and before I could think of the right words, Irena had reappeared. 'Magda is expecting you. I must say she wasn't as willing as I thought she'd be, but she won't give you away, I'm sure of that.'

Berek and I exchanged glances; we hoped she was right. She didn't sound sure. Then Irena set to work. First, she took some old ashes from the bottom of the stove and rubbed them into my arm in several places to make it look bruised; then she folded a large white cloth and helped me bind it round my shoulder as a sling.

'You're to go to the front door like any patient. Tell whoever receives you that you fell off your bicycle and your mother has sent you to see a doctor or a nurse because your arm hurts badly and she wants to make sure it's not broken. If they ask where you're from just say you've recently moved near Rudka from Warsaw to get away from the city – that'll explain your accent. With any luck Magda will be the one to open the door. You must be out by four o'clock at all costs as that is when the Nazi doctor comes to check that everything is in order. You certainly don't want to get yourself examined by *him*!'

The clinic lay on the Rudka side of Jedlanka but it had started to snow again after a brief lull, and it took me an hour to get there even though I was now using the ordinary road. With my four o'clock deadline that was running things a little close. I kept my head down to avoid being spoken to, and arrived at the clinic without incident before half-past three.

The door was opened not, as I'd hoped, by Magda, but by a large severe-looking woman who took my name and asked in a bored way what was wrong with me. If I'd been a genuine patient I'd have felt I was imposing on her time; as it was, I was relieved by her obvious lack of interest! She made out a record sheet for me and then looked me up and down rather contemptuously.

'Well, if you want to see a doctor you'll have to wait until four. There's a nurse here who can see you now though – I should think that'll be good enough.'

'That's fine. I'll see the nurse.' Immediately I hoped I hadn't sounded too eager!

She called twice for Magda who eventually came into the hall to collect me. She led me into a small consulting room, closed the door and told me to sit down. There was one chair placed beside a table. She made no sign that I was expected, but before undoing my sling, she put my canvas shoulder-bag on the floor by her feet.

She was a conventionally pretty girl, very pale and slight, with hair drawn tightly back from her face, but I noticed the hardness of her eyes, and felt instinctively that she had no real sympathy for my predicament.

She examined my arm thoroughly, if a little roughly, and asked me one or two questions about the fall, and whether the arm hurt in certain positions. Anyone watching through the key-hole would have seen nothing untoward. Then, holding my arm up with her right hand, she bent down, opened a drawer in the table with her left, slid out a brown paper package and dropped it into my bag, all in one flowing and barely perceptible movement.

'It's not broken,' she said curtly. She made no attempt at small talk. I was worried by the size of the packet; it didn't look nearly big enough to contain all we needed.

'Well, I've also got some lacerations here,' I said, pointing to my leg in case anyone should be listening. 'Do you have some ointment? It's very painful.' I gestured with my eyes at the package.

'I think you have all you need,' she said coldly. 'They don't look serious.'

At that moment the telephone rang in the office next door, and Magda was called by the receptionist.

'You can go now,' she said.

'Well, I did just want...'

'Wait a moment, then, I'll have to see who's on the phone.' Her impatience to be rid of me was undisguised.

When Magda went out of the room she left the door ajar; I looked around quickly, wondering what I could take that would be of most use.

I looked at the clock on the wall. After half-past three. It was all too close to the time of the doctor's visit. There was no time to unpack the parcel to see what was already in it. I saw some jars in a glass-fronted cupboard, containing cotton wool. Useful but not essential. Surely I could do better than that. My heart was drumming right up in my throat, telling me that I mustn't on any account waste this opportunity. I got up and walked over to the window, my bag over my shoulder. I'd noticed a cabinet by the window with little narrow drawers. I opened the top one – a selection of boxes, presumably containing pills, with names that meant nothing. No good. Next drawer. More boxes. Third drawer. Miraculous! A set of gleaming surgical instruments – tweezers, a scalpel, curettes. I knew them from Henryk's descriptions. Even something called a 'kulociag' in

Polish, a special instrument for extracting bullets. I was really in luck. With panicky, grabbing movements I scooped them out of their felt-lined insets and dropped them into my bag. Seven or eight of them. Then I shut the drawer and listened. Magda was having a conversation with the receptionist so she must have finished with the phone. What else could I take in the few seconds left? Suddenly it occurred to me that Henryk would know what the pills were for – how stupid of me! I opened the top drawer again, scooped out as many of the boxes as I could and slammed it shut. Too loudly. They must have heard.

I didn't have time to sit down again before Magda came back into the room. She looked at me suspiciously.

'It's snowing again,' I said, pointing to the thick flakes whirling outside, almost obscuring the fir trees only about ten yards away.

'It is December,' she observed. 'What else did you want?' I caught sight of the clock. Nearly a quarter to four. All I wanted now was to be out of the building!

'Oh, it's all right. I won't take up any more of your time. Thanks very much.' Then, as I was leaving the room I said so that the receptionist could hear, 'Oh, Mother said to ask if I should carry on wearing the sling?'

'There's no need. It's only bruising. But try not to use the arm too much for the time being.' They were the friendliest words she had addressed to me.

'What's the charge?' the receptionist asked Magda.

'Waived. No treatment.'

'Hmm.' The big woman looked at me disapprovingly and I escaped, thankful and relieved, into the driving snow. But just as I walked down the little path a German army vehicle drew up; the driver jumped out and went to open the far back door for his passenger. The doctor was early!

I turned to stone. Supposing he asked me to go in for another examination; after all, there weren't any other patients to look at. There was an agonisingly long moment, while he sat in the back of the car pulling on his gloves. The driver's shoulders began to turn white.

Somehow I managed to move myself to the side of the path. The doctor was a big, tall man with a moustache. As he approached me, I just smiled and bowed. I was sure my bag must be bulging suspiciously.

But thanks to the snow, his own head was bowed and he took no notice of me at all. I just kept standing there, looking foolishly at the car. The driver brushed the snow off his shoulders and made a face at me which, if he hadn't been a Nazi, I could have sworn was of the conspiratorial eyes-to-heaven sort!

I was so pleased with myself, once the German car was finally behind me, that I scarcely noticed the weather. It didn't occur to me immediately that my theft might be quickly discovered and that they'd come straight after me. When it did, I veered off the road and took a small roughly parallel path through the trees. But as I got nearer Irena's house a thought struck me. Whenever it was discovered, how would Magda explain away the disappearance of so many boxes and instruments? Would she blame it on me and, if so, would she be punished for leaving me alone in the room? She had hardly been sympathetic but she *had* taken a considerable risk in agreeing to see me in the first place, and in giving me any supplies at all. Irena tried to reassure me, saying that Magda was well respected as a nurse and wouldn't be blamed. 'They'll think it was a break-in at night, or something.' But I could tell from the look in Irena's eyes that she was afraid for her cousin – and perhaps for herself too. She gave us the rest of the carrot cake to take back with us, and *real* coffee grounds which, she explained, had been used only once before and then mixed with a few fresh ones; but my pleasure in these things was now soured by a sense of unease, even guilt. Had I abused her generous hospitality? I'd quickly lost the sense of euphoria at having achieved what I'd set out to do. I hugged her when we left, wanting but unable to say I was sorry – for how *could* I be sorry? After all, I'd only done what was necessary to save Alexander's arm, maybe even his life.

On the way back Berek said, 'Jan, whatever happens back in Rudka now, it is not your fault. Your first loyalty was to us, where you belong. You understand that, don't you?'

The tears in my eyes were only partly induced by the wind which, contrarily, seemed to have changed direction since we'd set out. It was dark now and the snow made it very difficult to find the way back to the camp as many of the familiar landmarks were obscured. Once we were badly startled by a sound of crashing in the undergrowth. Berek put a hand on my arm and we stood absolutely still, hearts thumping. A couple of seconds later, a stag appeared on the track in front of us. He stared at us for a moment, his bulbous brown eyes registering in our torchlight the alarm we ourselves had felt. Another moment and he had disappeared into the brushwood on the other side of the track.

'I'm amazed there are any deer left after the uproar of those raids,' said Berek. And in fact, although I knew from Leon that elk and deer had been prolific in the area – the town crest of Parczew was actually a stag – that was the only one I ever saw in my year in the forests. Piotr always hoped to be able to cook venison for those of us prepared to eat it, but it never happened.

We got back to find that the others had lit a fire, after building a sort of three-sided igloo around it to hide the smoke. There was great relief at our return and Henryk's delight when he saw the instruments made me feel better about the circumstances of their theft. The parcel, as I'd suspected, did not contain a great deal – a few cotton bandages, some gauze and cotton wool, a yellow disinfectant power and two small tubes of ointment for treating scabies. It hadn't been worth risking my life for.

Alexander had his operation the following morning. We heard a single bellow from the 'hospital' bunker, presumably as the bullet was extracted, but afterwards he was dismissive about the whole thing. After that, whenever he saw me, he always had a special word or a smile for me.

The next Nazi raid took place on Christmas Eve, just as we were preparing to celebrate our own festival of Hanukkah. Very few of the Jews in our band were religious – some in fact were socialist or communist and actively anti-religious – but Hanukkah was an occasion of significance to religious and non-religious alike. The songs we would have sung might have united us in pride in a common ancestry, but the songs were never sung. For just as we were collecting together our eight bits of candle for the eight-day Festival of Lights, the guns announced the arrival yet again of the Forces of Darkness. We lost poor Leon in that raid, and one or two others I don't remember so well, but somehow that clash of dates was at the time a double cause for despair.

In the period of uneasy but relative calm in January, Berek and Alexander and a new member called Josef went to Rudka to try and replenish some of our supplies. When they eventually reappeared carrying only one sack, we could see from their faces that something was wrong. Berek made straight for me and put his hand on my shoulder, and I knew then what they were going to tell us.

'Irena's gone and her house has been burnt down.'

We were all quiet; we knew only too well why. Josef threw down the sack. It was full of carrots, good ones, Irena's legacy to us.

'We found them in an outhouse at the back. Everything else had been ransacked.' The thought of Irena's carrot cake made me feel sick. Berek looked at me and shook his head, his eyes – which despite everything often shone with laughter – now sad. 'Don't blame yourself,' they said. Yet how could I not? I'd experienced the deaths of many people by now, but Irena's was the first for which I was directly responsible.

From *But Can The Phoenix Sing?* also published as
Shadow of the Wall by Christa Laird

DEAR KITTY

This is an excellent non-fiction book about Anne Frank. It contains photographs of the secret annex, of Anne's family and of Amsterdam in wartime. It also presents facsimiles of pages from Anne's diaries.

On Wednesday, March 29, 1944, during the daily radio broadcast from London, Anne heard the Dutch minister, Bolkestein, say that after the war all the diaries and letters about the war would be collected. Anne fantasized:

Just imagine how interesting it would be if I were to publish a romance of the "Secret Annex." (March 29, 1944) She could not forget the idea. A week later she wrote:

Will I ever become a journalist or a writer? I hope so, oh, I hope so very much, for I can recapture everything when I write, my thoughts, my ideals and my fantasies. (April 5, 1944)

The Secret Annex

On May 11, 1944, she confided in her diary:

You've known for a long time that my greatest wish is to become a journalist somebody and later on a famous writer. In any case, I want to publish a book entitled het Achterhuis (The Secret Annex) *after the war, whether I shall succeed or not, I cannot say, but my diary will be a great help.*

On Sunday, April 9, 1944, there was yet another burglary. This was the most frightening thing yet. The front door onto the street had been destroyed, and it seemed that someone had warned the police, who came to search the building.

Then, a quarter past 11, a bustle and noise downstairs. Everyone's breath was audible, in other respects no one moved. Footsteps in the house, in the private office, kitchen, then... on our staircase, no one breathed audibly now, 8 hearts thumped, footsteps on our staircase, then a rattling of the swinging cupboard. This moment is indescribable:

'Now we are lost!' I said and could see all fifteen of us being carried off by the Gestapo that very night. (April 11, 1944)

Entrance to the Secret Annex

Twice they rattled the cupboard, then a tin can fell down, the foot-steps withdrew, we were saved thus far! A shiver seemed to pass from one to the other, I heard someone's teeth chattering, no one said a word.

They all spent that night together in the Van Pelses' room, though no one slept. They were all too terrified. The next morning they were delighted when the helpers arrived. Once again, everything had turned out right.

April 15, 1944, was an important day in Anne's life, the day of her first kiss. Peter and Anne were sitting close together on the divan in Peter's room.

How I suddenly made the right move, I don't know, but before we went downstairs he kissed me, through my hair, half on my left cheek, half on my ear; I tore downstairs without looking round, and am simply longing for today. (April 16, 1944)

In the days that followed, Anne thought again and again about that first kiss and how things might now be different. In her diary she wrote:

Dear Kitty, Do you think that Daddy and Mummy would approve of my sitting and kissing a boy on a divan – a boy of seventeen and a half and a girl of just under fifteen? I don't really think they would, but I must rely on myself over this. It is so quiet and peaceful to lie in his arms and to dream, it is so thrilling to feel his cheek against mine, it is lovely to know that there is someone waiting for me. (April 17, 1944)

When Anne had filled her first diary, she continued writing in exercise and accounting books. She kept everything in a leather briefcase which had belonged to her father. A few weeks after Anne heard that diaries would be collected after the war, she decided to rewrite her own diary so that it could be published. While copying the diary, she also edited it, adding some things and taking out others. The fresh copy was made on thin sheets of tracing paper which she got from the office. Sometimes she doubted the point of doing all this. On April 14, 1944, she wrote:

I really believe Kits, that I'm slightly bats today, and yet I don't know why. Everything here is so mixed up, nothing's connected any more, and sometimes I very much doubt whether in the future anyone will be interested in all my tosh.

"The unbosomings of an ugly duckling," will be the title of all this nonsense.

Anne decided to talk to her father about her feelings for Peter. When they were alone one day, she asked: *"Daddy I expect you've gathered that when we are together, Peter and I don't sit miles apart. Do you think it's wrong?"* (May 2, 1944)

Her father warned Anne to be careful. The next day he told her that it would be better if she did not go to Peter's room so often. But Anne did not want to obey her father.

Not only because I like being with Peter; but I have told him that I trust him, I do trust him and I want to show him that I do, which can't happen if I stay downstairs through lack of trust.

No, I'm going! (May 2, 1944)

Anne wrote a long letter to her father to explain why she would continue to visit Peter. At the end of it she wrote:

You can't and mustn't regard me as fourteen, for all these troubles have made me older; I shall not be sorry for what I have done but shall act as I think I can! (May 5, 1944)

She asked her father to trust her through thick and thin, but Otto was angry and disappointed with her. Later Anne was sorry about her angry and passionate letter, but not about her feelings for Peter. *I am not alone any more; he loves me. I love him.* (May 7, 1944)

Yet more than love was on Anne's mind that spring of 1944. The everlasting war was never far from her thoughts.

What, oh, what is the use of the war, why can't people live peacefully together, why all this destruction? Oh why are people so crazy? (May 3, 1944) Anne also wrote: *I am young and I possess many buried qualities. I have been given a lot, a happy nature, a great deal of cheerfulness and strength. Every day I feel that I am developing inwardly, that the liberation is drawing nearer and how beautiful nature is, how good the people about me, how interesting and amusing this adventure! Why, then, should I be in despair?* (May 3, 1944)

On June 6, 1944, the news of the Normandy invasion in France was on the radio! Anne was ecstatic.

Great commotion in the "Secret Annex." Would the long-awaited liberation about which so much has been said, but which still seems too wonderful, too much like a fairy tale, ever come true. (June 6, 1944)

Could we be granted victory this year, this 1944? We don't know yet, but hope lives on; it gives us fresh courage, it makes us strong again. Since we must put up bravely with all the fears, privations, and sufferings, the great thing now is to remain calm and steadfast, now we must clench our teeth rather than cry out!

Oh, Kitty, the best part of the invasion is that I have the feeling that friends are approaching. (June 6, 1944)

From *Anne Frank: Beyond the Diary* by Ruud van der Rol
and Rian Verhoeven

FOR ANNE F

In *Het geluid van de vrede (The Sound of Peace)*, Theo Olthuis'
poems talk of small and big wars and moments of peace. *For Anne
F.* reverses the roles. Kitty, the imaginary friend to whom Anne
Frank writes her diary, pens her own reply.

Dear Anne,
What you write is true.
Adults just haven't got a clue.
They drop bombs,
steal a country,
Pollute the air,
the sea and the beach.
Drive too fast
and drink too much.
They split up
or pretend.
But I have this wonderful vision:
One day we'll do things differently!

Your friend
Kitty

From *The Sound of Peace* by Theo Olthuis

ANTONIA

*Aida and four other young Bosnians have escaped the mad war in
their country. They find temporary food and lodging with Antonia,
a widow and the only survivor in a small village. After Antonia's
death, they anxiously meander their way to the Croat coast. In this
fragment, Aida meets Antonia and Josip, her nephew, who is to join
the group of refugees later on. They are all on their guard.*

Antonia could see that Aida was completely confused. She was as jumpy as an animal, ready to spring off at any moment. She was even bolting her food, and her reaction to Josip was strange.

When Antonia had recognized her nephew on the mountain path she had thought of telling him about her new house-guest, but she had kept quiet. To protect the girl, to keep him away, and the others too, of course. She had to be careful to keep her own life and theirs strictly apart, except for the days when Josip came to fetch food. For months, like a stout guardian angel, she had toiled and slaved to keep four other people alive besides herself. Not that she ever complained. She had in fact often thanked God for the weight on her shoulders, which had arrived at the very moment when she thought her life was pointless.

And now there was someone else stranded in Brodiste, even younger than the others. Antonia kicked off her house-slippers and put on a comfortable pair of shoes.

'Shall we take a little walk?' she suggested innocently. 'I'll show you my goat.'

Aida glanced at her wrist-watch, which had stopped.

'Five o'clock,' said Antonia. 'My battery has run out too, but I know the position of the sun. Come on, or it will get dark. You've slept for such a long time.'

Aida stood up. It worried her that the old dog waddled out after them. She would have preferred him not to be there.

'Why is he called Napoleon?' she asked, to have something to say.

'A joke of my husband's. He gave all the animals names: the dog, the goat, our hens. But we ate them, they were not laying any more, and we were hungry. Did you know it was difficult to eat an animal with a name? Chicken and rice sounds different from Irina and rice, in my opinion.'

'Where is your husband?'

Antonia pointed with outstretched arm to an open space on the edge of the village. 'I buried his body, up there in the cemetery, and his soul – oh, I hope it's at peace. I hope it doesn't matter to God if someone was Catholic or Serbian Orthodox.' She glanced sidelong at the girl, with her aristocratic profile. The rising wind blew back her hair, showing her fine features to still greater advantage.

Uncomfortable under the woman's gaze, Aida scratched her forehead, hiding her face behind her hand.

'Who did this to the village?'

Antonia sighed. 'The Serbs came first,' she said. 'They searched Brodiste for Muslims and set their houses on fire. They took on Croats as well. My husband shot into the house like a rocket, got rid of all traces of Catholicism and hung up an icon. That was how he cheated that trash. He was a Serb, you see. Was that right? Was it wrong?'

Aida shivered but did not speak.

'The neighbours, the few who were left, thought what my husband did was vile. The Croats called us arse-lickers, who only wanted to save our house, and the fourteen Serbs, the only ones living here, called us degenerates because we had a mixed marriage. There were three Muslims here as well, who were saved by a miracle, and they stopped talking to us.'

Aida's silence disturbed Antonia. Aida was a Muslim name. She did not want to hurt the child.

'My husband,' she went on quickly, 'took eggs, fruit and tobacco to the Muslims, but they simply turned their backs. "I'm a Bosnian," he said. "I've never done anything to you. I am a dentist, a doctor, it's my calling to help people!" But they never answered and that made the Croats laugh. In the end that was what broke him. He had a weak heart which could not stand up to his guilt feelings. I buried him up there, beside the church that lay in dust and ashes. And do you know the maddest thing? When I was burrowing a hole in the ground with my spade, the Muslims came and helped me. They bared their heads and said they were sorry. Jovo had always taken good care of their teeth. He had always been friendly, never superior or cold. They began to dig and asked if I would allow them to say their own prayers. They too were suffering from remorse. We covered up the grave together, and never have I been so happy and sad at the same time.'

'What became of the Muslims?' asked Aida. 'You're all alone here, aren't you?'

While they were talking Antonia had sat herself down on a low wall. She rubbed her thighs and stared into the distance. 'Soon after the Serbs, the Croat soldiers arrived, and this time the Serbian farms were set on fire – and two Muslim houses. The chaos was so great that the last people moved away. I stayed, but not because I'm brave: I simply had not the will to start again somewhere else. I thought, with the goat, the vegetable garden and the orchard, I'll get by.'

She stood up slowly, wondering as she walked on if it had been a good idea to talk about all those things. She looked searchingly at Aida, hesitated, and then said, 'It went well at first. I used to talk to Napoleon or Svetlana, the goat, but gradually I began talking to anything that had paws or wings. I was well on the way to going completely mad. That was when Josip came. He had escaped from Sarajevo in order to hide here in Brodiste with a friend. He had meant to ask for my help, but in reality he helped me.'

Embarrassed by what she had heard, Aida did not ask about Josip. Why had he gone away again? Just as she was nerving herself to ask, Antonia touched her arm and cried, 'Look, there's Svetlana!'

In a meadow beside the orchard stood a little white goat which suddenly stopped grazing and ran towards them until the cord that tethered her was taut. Antonia stroked the animal and playfully tugged her beard. 'Hallo, my girl. Got enough water?' She checked the water-trough, a bathtub hauled up from the village. 'I'll fill it up for you tonight, all right?'

She turned a laughing face to Aida. 'If anyone had prophesied when I was young that I would one day be milking a goat every day like a farmer, I would have laughed aloud. I went to university in Sarajevo. Do you know Sarajevo?'

'A bit.'

'A beautiful town,' said Antonia. 'I came from a village originally and I had nice parents, but they never agreed, and then they would quarrel. My student years were a release! In Sarajevo everyone has a mind of his own, too, but they don't fight about it. That would be pointless, with all those religions and nationalities.'

Aida looked across at the mountain behind which the sun had vanished. Only its reflection in the clouds above the peak sent a little light over the top, outlining the village before it melted into the background of the mountain. It was too late to go any further. She had slept the day away.

'Where are you heading?' asked Antonia.

'South-west, to the coast.'

'Over the frontier, you mean, and alone?'

Aida nodded.

'Dangerous,' said Antonia, catching her breath. 'The boys don't dare to do it, though there are two of them. There are smugglers, madmen and muggers everywhere. Wait until you get a lift.'

'But who from?'

Antonia waved towards the road. 'Sometimes UN convoys come along here with Blue Helmets. Brodiste is on a back road which they take when the main road is too risky or not passable. They know me, they always stop. Next time I'll ask if they will take you along. All right?'

'How long would that be?'

'I'm expecting one any moment, but that one will be travelling north and you need one that will take you to the coast. You will have to wait for that.'

From *No Roof in Bosnia* by Els de Groen

HIDING THE LITTLE RIDERS FROM THE GERMAN SOLDIERS

This short novel is set in Holland during the German occupation of the Second World War. Johanna is staying with her grandparents in a house where a German soldier, Captain Braun, has taken a room in the attic. The Germans need all metal for arms and munitions and are threatening to take away the set of twelve beautiful and very valuable figurines, the little riders, that have adorned the church tower for hundreds of years. In this extract the German soldiers arrive at Johanna's house to collect the church key from

*her grandfather so that they can steal the little riders from the
church. Unknown to them, the little riders are already hidden in the
house and when the soldiers march Johanna's grandparents away
she very quickly has to find a new hiding place for the statues. In
this she is very unexpectedly helped by Captain Braun. When
reading this story it is easy to imagine what it must have been like
for people (like Anne Frank's family) who were hiding from the
Germans too.*

For that one night the riders were hidden in Grandfather's den
under the couch that was now Johanna's bed. The next morning
Grandfather would try to find a place where they could stay hidden
until the war was over, some place far away where no German would
think of looking.

Johanna went to bed exhausted but happier than she had been in
many weeks. The little riders would be safe. If she reached under her
bed, she could feel the curly mane of one of the horses. Outside, the
night cleared, the rain stopped and the wind died down. A few stars
appeared and with them, like more stars, came the lights of aeroplanes overhead. Their buzzing sound gave Johanna a safe feeling
and made her drowsy. Just before she fell asleep she thought again of
her father. He walked towards her, taking long, impatient steps. He
lifted her high in the air and said, 'Give my very special love to the
little riders and help Grandfather take care of them.'

The next morning after breakfast Grandfather went to a nearby
village where he had a friend who was a farmer. Dirk was one of the
few farmers who had been allowed to keep his horse and wagon.
Because he delivered eggs and fresh milk several times a week to the
house of the German town commander, the German sentries who
stood guard at the entrances of the town never searched his wagon.
Many times young men who were hiding from the Germans had left
town in Dirk's wagon, hidden underneath the tarpaulin between the
empty egg boxes and the rattling milk containers. Grandfather and
Dirk had often worked together to take such young men to safer
places in the country and Grandfather was sure Dirk would help hide
the little riders.

Grandfather was gone most of the day. He came back around tea-time. Grandmother and Johanna had just started to worry about what might have delayed him, when Grandfather entered the house. He was happy and pleased. Everything was going to work out beautiful-ly. Dirk had given him twenty-four heavy burlap sacks. In the course of the evening Grandfather's friends would come, unseen through the dark, and each would take home a sack with a rider or horse in it. The next morning they would take the sacks to the small café near the edge of town where Dirk always stopped on his way home for a cup of coffee and a game of billiards with his friends. In the small room behind the bar many people had waited to be taken to safety by Dirk's horse and wagon. The little riders and their horses would wait there now. And they would stay hidden on Dirk's farm until they could return to the church steeple.

It was still a few hours before dark. Grandfather and Johanna went upstairs to put the riders and their horses in the burlap sacks so that they could be taken away without delay when the men came. Johanna looked for the last time at the riders' faces. With her hands she covered their small hands that so many times had lifted the swords in proud salutes to each other. The Germans will not get them, she thought. They will always ride over the town. Even a hun-dred years from now.

It was still light when Johanna and Grandfather finished and went downstairs. Grandmother picked up her knitting at the round table in the living room. Grandfather sucked on an empty pipe and Johanna leafed through an old magazine. The curfew would start soon and, except for the bark of a dog and the cooing of the doves that nested under the eaves of the church tower, it was quiet outside.

Then, from the side street that led to the marketplace, came the sound of marching soldiers. It was unusual for a group of soldiers to be exercising at this late hour. Now that they came nearer, they sounded not so much like a group of soldiers exercising, but more like eight or ten soldiers who, by force of habit, marched instead of walking. They came out of the side street into the marketplace.

' God knows what they are up to,' Grandmother said, 'but it's never good if they come by night.'

'And there are quite a number of them.' Grandfather looked out of the window. 'They never use so many for a simple arrest.'

'But they do if they search' A house, Johanna was going to say, but she didn't complete her sentence.

One of the soldiers shouted a command and the group stopped still. They were in front of the house. Grandfather quickly stepped back from the window into the dark room.

'They may have come for something else.' He tried to reassure Grandmother and Johanna.

The doorbell rang loudly and insistently and Grandfather went to open the door. Grandmother and Johanna followed him into the hall. Nine soldiers were standing on the doorstep and one of them was the spokesman. Johanna was so frightened that for the first time since the beginning of the war, she forgot all about her promise and looked the soldier straight in the face. She saw a large man with a big, red face and two small shiny eyes under shaggy eyebrows. He spoke to Grandfather in heavily accented but otherwise good Dutch that Johanna could easily understand.

'We are sent by the town commander to requisition from you the key to the church tower.' As he spoke he looked around with his shiny little eyes. 'We will take the statues of the riders with us tonight and you can get the key back afterwards at Headquarters. Hurry, we don't have all night,' he concluded.

Grandfather reached up slowly for the big iron key that always hung on a peg near the stairs. He handed the key to the soldier. When they had gone, he closed the door and for a moment leaned heavily against it. Johanna saw small drops of perspiration under his nose and on his forehead.

'They will be back as soon as they have seen the riders are gone,' Grandmother said. 'We will have to hide them better.'

'There is no time,' Grandfather said. 'They will be back in a few minutes, and where can we hide the riders? No, our only chance is somehow to keep them from going upstairs. If we can tell them something that will make them go away, even if it's only for a short time...' Grandfather straightened his shoulders and gave Grandmother and Johanna a sly look.

'There is only one thing for us to do. We must try to fool them. We'll act very surprised when we hear the riders are gone and we can even suggest that because they are so old and therefore valuable they must have been stolen.'

'They will never believe us,' Grandmother said.

'They will certainly be back to investigate, but they might believe us long enough to give us a chance to hide the riders.'

Grandmother still looked doubtful, Johanna thought, but Grandfather couldn't talk about it further. The soldiers were back. This time they didn't ring the doorbell. Instead they pounded the stocks of their rifles on the door. The spokesman was hot and red and so angry that he could hardly speak Dutch any more. He kept lapsing into heavy German shouts that Johanna couldn't understand.

'The riders may have been stolen.' Grandfather's deep, quiet voice tried to interrupt the angry flow of words. 'We all know that they are very valuable.'

The big red soldier made so much noise that Johanna didn't think he had heard one word of what Grandfather had said. But now he started to laugh loudly. Sneering, he turned to the other soldiers and mimicked Grandfather. 'He thinks they may have been stolen because they are so valuable.' And all the soldiers roared with laughter. Suddenly the big soldier turned again towards Grandfather, and he was not laughing now.

'You old liar!' he barked. For a moment Johanna thought that he was going to hit Grandfather. But Grandfather went on talking as if he had not heard him.

'Take me with you to the church tower and I will show you where I left the riders when I last saw them. I never saw them again after I closed the little doors the night the town commander gave us the order to do so.'

Grandfather spoke so convincingly that Johanna was almost ready to believe that the riders were now in the possession of some clever thief instead of upstairs in the den under her own bed. But the big soldier didn't care what Grandfather said. He turned his back to him and gave his orders to the other soldiers.

'The old man and the old woman will come with us to

Headquarters. The town commander can conduct the hearing himself. If he orders so, we will search the house later. We will not leave
a thing unturned, and if those riders are hidden here,' he said, shrug-
ging his shoulders in disgust, 'we will find them. And these people
will learn what happens to those who dare defy an order given by a
German officer.'

He looked at Johanna. 'The child can stay,' he said. But he didn't
let Johanna kiss Grandfather and Grandmother good-bye. Johanna
was standing near the hall cupboard and quickly she slipped down a
coat for Grandmother, but she couldn't get Grandfather's coat off the
hook. The coat was heavy and the hook too high and now they were
leaving. She could give Grandfather only his hat and his woollen
scarf, which weren't enough for the chilly September night.
Grandfather and Grandmother walked arm in arm out of the door and
the soldiers followed them.

When the last soldier slammed the door behind him, Johanna
found that her knees were shaking. She had to sit down on the bottom step of the staircase. The clock in the hall ticked and the minutes
passed by.

'If those riders are hidden here, these people will learn what happens to those who dare defy an order given by a German officer,' the
soldier had said.

They must be hidden more safely, Johanna knew, and she would
have to do it. The men would certainly not come now. The neighbours must have seen what happened and they would have warned
the men to stay far away from the house. Johanna looked out of the
peep-hole in the door. One soldier was left standing on guard.

'We will not leave a thing unturned, and if those riders are hidden
here, we will find them,' the German had also said.

The riders were big and there were twelve of them and the horses, too. What hiding place would be big enough? As she sat on the
bottom step of the stairs, Johanna's mind wandered through the
whole house, thinking of all the different cupboards, but not one was
big enough to hide the riders safely. At last she thought of her attic
room. Of course, her own secret hiding place was there. It was certainly big enough, but it was right in Captain Braun's room. But the

more she thought about it now, the more she became convinced that it would also be the safest place to hide the riders. The Germans would certainly not think that the riders might be hidden in the room of a German officer and they would probably not search his room. Captain Braun apparently had not discovered the cubbyhole and perhaps never would discover it. Anyhow, it was the only place in the house where she could hide the riders. She would leave them in the burlap sacks and push them all the way deep in.

Tonight was Friday night and Captain Braun was not home. If she worked fast the riders would be hidden before he came back. Johanna ran upstairs and started to carry the sacks to the attic room. She didn't put on a light for fear the soldier on guard would see it and come to investigate; instead, she took Grandfather's torch. She decided to do the heavy work first and carry everything upstairs. Putting the riders in the cubbyhole would be easier. She also decided to take the radio from behind the books and put it in the cubbyhole, too.

It wasn't easy. By the time the last horse and rider were in the attic room Johanna was out of breath. Her hair was mussed up and her skirt was torn in several places. It had also taken her much longer than she had expected, but if she worked fast there was still time enough before Captain Braun came home. In the cupboard she pushed Captain Braun's uniforms aside and reached to open the bolt of the little door, but it had become stiff and rusty. She got down on her knees and tried again. The bolt didn't yield. Johanna felt warm and her hands started to tremble. Surely she would be able to open the bolt, it had never given her trouble before. But no matter how hard she tried, she could not open the bolt on the little door. She forgot everything around her, even the riders and Grandfather and Grandmother and the danger they were in at this moment. She thought only of one thing. The door must open. It must.

She was so busy she didn't hear the footsteps on the stairs or the door of the attic room opening. She first saw Captain Braun when he was standing in the door of the big cupboard. He had to bend down a little, not to hit his head against the low ceiling.

'What are you doing in the dark in my cupboard?' he asked.

He switched the light on so that Johanna's eyes were blinded by it and she turned her head away. Around her on the floor were the sacks with the riders. The radio was right beside her and Johanna pushed it behind her back, but she couldn't hide the riders. Captain Braun kneeled down and opened one of the bags. There was nothing Johanna could do or say. He took out a white horse with gentle black eyes and a fierce curly mane. Then he opened the other bags. The little riders and their horses were lying helpless on their backs on the floor of the cupboard. The legs of the horses were bent as if they wanted to get up and gallop away. The riders looked more brave and proud than ever, but Johanna knew that no matter how brave and proud they looked, they were forever lost and she could not save them any more.

A feeling of reckless despair came over Johanna. Nothing that she would do or say now could make the situation any worse than it was already. She had tried hard but she had failed; she had failed Grandfather and Grandmother and also the little riders and even her father, whom she had promised to take care of the little riders. If it had not been for Captain Braun she could have saved them. If he hadn't come home early, the riders would have been hidden and Grandfather and Grandmother would have come back. Now she didn't know what the Germans might do to them. Everything she had ever felt against the Germans welled up suddenly in her.

'I hate you and I despise you,' she burst out, 'and so does every decent person, and you'll never win the war. Grandfather says that you have already lost it.' She talked so fast that she had to take a deep breath before she could continue. 'And in a few months there will be nothing left of Germany, Grandmother says. You only have to listen every night to the aeroplanes that fly over.'

Then Johanna raised her eyes and looked at Captain Braun for the first time. With his boots and his uniform he looked like all the other Germans. He looked the same as the soldiers who had taken away Grandfather and Grandmother, but his face was different. Captain Braun did not have a soldier's face. He had the face of a flute player. His face was unmoved and, except for a little heightened colour, he appeared not even to have heard what Johanna had said to him.

'So these are the famous little riders,' he said quietly. He took one into the room and held it under the light. 'They are much more beautiful than I was ever told.' He looked again and hesitated for a little while. 'I would like to look at them much longer, but it would be safer for them and for you to put them back in the sacks and hide them where they will not be found.'

'But I can't,' Johanna said. She wasn't feeling angry any more, only very frightened. 'The bolt of the door is rusty. I can't open it.' She was surprised to hear that she was crying. 'And they took Grandfather and Grandmother. They said, 'If we find the riders in this house, you will see what happens to people who disobey an order given by a German officer.'

Captain Braun kneeled beside Johanna. His hands were strong and quick as he slipped aside the stiff bolt. He took the sacks and started to put the riders back in.

'What will you do to them?' Johanna asked. 'The little riders will be my guests for as long as they want to be,' Captain Braun said. 'I owe that to them. They are the first Dutchmen who looked at me in a friendly way and did not turn their faces away when I spoke to them.'

Johanna felt her face grow hot and red as he spoke. She bent down and started to help him put the riders and the horses back into the sacks.

'There may not be much time,' he said. 'Crawl through the door and I will hand you the sacks.'

Johanna still hesitated. Was he really going to help her?

'Come,' he said. 'Do as I tell you.' There was a faint smile around his mouth, but the rest of his face looked grave. 'This is an order given by a German officer.' He gave her a gentle push.

In a few minutes the riders were hidden and the radio, too. At a moment when Captain Braun had his back turned, Johanna pushed it deep into the cupboard. One day when he was out she would come and get it. Grandfather couldn't be without his radio.

'Go down now,' Captain Braun said. 'It's better for all of us if no one sees us together.'

Johanna went downstairs and alone she waited in the dark living room. Outside, the soldier was still standing guard. She pushed

Grandfather's big chair near the window and sat down, her tired arms leaning on the windowsill. From there she saw them come across the marketplace.

Grandfather had his arm around Grandmother's shoulders as if to protect her from the soldiers who were all around them. This time there were more than nine. As soon as Grandfather opened the door with his key the soldiers swarmed over the room. The big red-faced soldier was again in charge. At his command the others pushed aside the furniture and looked behind it. They stuck their bayonets into the upholstery and ripped it open, although Johanna couldn't understand why. The riders and the horses were much too big to be hidden in the upholstery of a chair. With their rifles they knocked on the walls, and when Grandmother's Delft-blue plates tumbled from the wall and broke into pieces some of the soldiers laughed. When they left to search the upstairs, the room looked as if a tornado had passed through.

Grandfather and Grandmother went upstairs, too, but they were always surrounded by soldiers so that Johanna could not speak one word to them. All she could do was follow. The big red-faced soldier told Grandfather to turn on the light, and while he fumbled clumsily to find the switch, the soldier pushed Grandfather aside and turned the switch himself. In the soft glow of the lamp the den looked immaculate. Johanna could hear Grandmother give a little gasp of surprise.

The soldiers began with the desk, taking out the drawers and dumping the contents in a heap on the floor. They went through all the papers. Now and then one of the soldiers went over to the red-faced man to let him read something. He always shook his head and shrugged his shoulders.

At last they went to the bookcase and began to take out the books. Johanna saw Grandfather's face grow tight. She wished she could show him somehow that there was nothing to worry about, but there was always at least one soldier standing next to him and Grandmother. The soldiers reached the shelf where the radio was always hidden, but there were only the books they kept dumping on the floor. Now they went down on their knees and looked under the bed and knocked on the wooden floor. Over their bent heads Grandfather looked at Johanna with more pride than she had ever before seen in his eyes. Grandmother gave Johanna a little wink.

The soldiers finally gave up. They realised that there was nothing hidden in these rooms. Only the attic room was left. They climbed the last stairs. Johanna felt weak and shaky again. Even when they found Captain Braun, they might still decide to search the room. She was glad now that Grandfather and Grandmother had no idea where the riders were hidden. They walked confidently up the stairs, Grandmother winking again at Johanna behind the soldiers' backs.

The soldiers could not have been informed that this room was occupied by one of their own officers, because they were taken aback when they found Captain Braun with his legs on the table, writing in his music book. He rose from his chair. The soldiers apologised profusely and the red-faced man especially seemed extremely upset at having intruded so unceremoniously into the room of a German officer. Captain Braun put all of them at ease with a few friendly words, and he must have made a joke, for they laughed. For one terrible moment Johanna thought that, after all, Captain Braun's face looked no different from all the other soldiers. What he had done tonight could be a trap and he could betray them. But the soldiers now made ready to go, and they went without searching the room. Captain Braun swung his legs back onto the table and took up his pencil and music book.

The attitude of the soldiers changed during their walk downstairs. When they came they had been sure they would find the riders. Now they seemed uncertain. The big red-faced soldier seemed to take it very much to heart that he had failed to find the riders or even to find any evidence that Grandfather had anything to do with their disappearance. He and the other soldiers seemed suddenly to be in a terrible hurry and they left the house without saying a word, except for one young man with a pale complexion and fair hair whom Johanna had hardly noticed before. He stopped on the doorstep to talk to Grandfather.

'We hope you understand, sir, that we only did our duty. Our duty is more important than the little inconvenience we caused you.' His pale face started to glow now with enthusiasm and he raised his right hand. 'Heil Hitler,' he shouted as Grandfather closed the door behind him.

Grandfather picked up Johanna and swung her high in the air, as he had done when she was still a little girl.

'Oh, Johanna, we are so proud of you, but where in this house did you hide the little riders?'

Grandmother hugged Johanna, but she wouldn't let her tell the secret until they were all sitting quietly with a warm drink. 'We will clean up the rooms tomorrow,' Grandmother said and she didn't even look at her Delft-blue plates. She could look only at Johanna. They talked till deep into the night and both Grandfather and Grandmother went upstairs with Johanna to tuck her in and kiss her good night.

'Will they ever come back?' Johanna asked Grandfather.

'I don't think so,' he said as he sat down on the edge of her bed. 'They are convinced that the riders are not hidden here and they can't prove that I ever had anything to do with their disappearance.' He turned off the light and left the room.

As Johanna lay thinking about everything that had happened during the long day, she could hear the aeroplanes flying over the house. The night was almost gone and, with the daylight, the planes were returning from their mission. Every night it sounded as if there were more planes than the night before. This time Johanna didn't think of her father; instead she thought of Captain Braun. She put on her slippers and walked upstairs. The door of the room stood ajar. Johanna pushed it open. Captain Braun was sitting at the table with his face buried in his hands. He looked up when he heard Johanna.

'I cannot sleep,' Johanna said. 'If I leave my door open, would you please play the flute for me?'

From *The Little Riders* by Margaretha Shemin

WHY I CAME TO HATE WAR

In Mijn botjes zijn bekleed met deftig vel (My Bones Are Covered
with Decent Skin), *the poet Ted van Lieshout published a number
of poems based on relatives' war memories. He looks at what
happened through the incredulous eyes of a boy who has never
been through a war before.*

Uncle Han the colonel, bristling with pride,
showed me inside the secret command bunker.
Descending stairs beneath a concrete slab
with camouflage-coloured grass on top:
all whitewashed walls and not an ounce of flab.

This is where the troops will sleep, and this side
is for officers. Here we'll watch TV, maybe…
When war breaks out and everything's burnt black,
he said, we'll be down here in this fortress
leading the brave Dutch army and fighting back.

I watched a massive, reinforced steel door
slide shut behind us, sealing off the floor.
You were safe here. Safe from your worst nightmares.
And Aunty Miep, I asked relieved, where
does she sleep? I must have missed something.
Uncle Han just laughed. Miep stays upstairs.

From *My Bones Are Covered with Decent Skin*
by Ted van Lieshout

Friend or Foe

THE MAN HE KILLED

In this poem Hardy shows in a simple but powerful way the
meaninglessness of terms like 'foe' and 'enemy'.

'Had he and I but met
By some old ancient inn,
We should have sat us down to wet
Right many a nipperkin!

'But ranged as infantry,
And staring face to face,
I shot at him as he at me,
And killed him in his place.

'I shot him dead because –
Because he was my foe,
Just so: my foe of course he was;
That's clear enough; although

'He thought he'd 'list, perhaps,
Off-hand like – just as I –
Was out of work – had sold his traps –
No other reason why.

'Yes; quaint and curious war is!
You shoot a fellow down
You'd treat if met where any bar is,
Or help to half-a-crown.'

by Thomas Hardy

THE INTERNMENT OF ITALIAN NATIONALS IN BRITAIN IN THE SECOND WORLD WAR

This story is set in the Clyde shipyard area of Glasgow during the Second World War. Kezzie, a teenage girl, is visiting Scotland from Canada and she has a job with a group of Italians who run a cafe. Kezzie becomes very fond of her Italian friends, the Biagis and the Casellas. In this chapter of the novel Kezzie and her friend Peg, who is in love with Ricardo, the Casellas son, discover that all male Italians living in Britain have been rounded up and interned (imprisoned) for the duration of the war. Suddenly people who have lived in Britain for many years and who have nothing to do with Italian politics are to be regarded as 'enemies'.

When the two girls reached the café it was shut and in complete darkness. They knocked on the door and rattled the window but no one answered. Kezzie went through the pen at the side and round to the back entrance. She banged on the service door.

'Signora Casella! Signora Biagi!' she called loudly. 'It's Kezzie and Peg. Let us in!'

Several minutes elapsed and then the door was cautiously pulled open a crack. Such fear on their faces made Kezzie shiver. Alec was squirming in their arms as they clutched him desperately. They had expected men with guns, thought Kezzie, as she followed them upstairs into the house.

The two women were beyond tears.

'The *combattenti*,' Signora Biagi told Kezzie. They took my son away.' She kept repeating, more to herself than anyone else, 'We have done nothing wrong. We have done nothing wrong.'

Kezzie and Peg looked at each other helplessly. They sat down round the big circular table. Signora Casella twisted the hem of the embroidered cloth over and over in her fingers. She turned her large brown eyes on Kezzie. 'My sister and I, we are scared to go out on the street. What can we do? What will happen now?' she asked.

Kezzie shook her head. 'I don't know. First of all we have to find out what is going on.' She stood up. 'I'll go to the police station and see if I can get any information. I'm sure it's all a terrible mistake.'

Half an hour later Kezzie discovered that it was not.

'Sending them away?' She repeated the words the desk sergeant had just said. 'All the Italian men living in Britain? Where are they being sent?'

The sergeant shrugged his shoulders. 'I don't know. They're setting up camps in different places.'

'Camps?' said Kezzie sharply. 'What kind of camps?'

He hesitated before replying. 'Like detention camps, sort of,' he said. 'They'll be all right,' he went on. 'It's just a precaution.'

'You mean camps such as they have in Europe?' demanded Kezzie. 'The same as the Nazis have done. Those people that we are fighting against.' She heard her own voice rising higher and higher. 'One of the reasons we are at war, in fact?'

The policemen fidgeted under her gaze. 'Don't take on so, hen. It's not as bad as you think. They'll get treated quite well.'

Kezzie took a deep breath. 'Where are these places?' she asked quietly. 'And where are the Biagis just now?'

The sergeant consulted some papers. 'I can't give you exact information,' he said. 'They could be on their way to one of the islands. There's also been talk of shipping them out to Canada or Australia for the duration. Come back tomorrow and ask again.'

As Kezzie hurried back to the café her thoughts were swarming in confusion. The policeman had said 'the duration'. Did he mean the whole of the war? How long would that be? And what could she tell Signoras Casella and Biagi? Or for that matter Peg, who was completely distraught about Ricardo.

She felt desperately sorry as she gave them her news.

Peg was stunned. 'I didn't know they could do things like that in Britain,' she said.

'When there is a war, they can do anything they please,' said Signora Casella.

Despite the restrictions on reporting, the newspapers carried the story over the next days. The entire Italian male population of Britain between the ages of seventeen and sixty had been rounded up. There was a large Italian community in the west of Scotland and many of Signora Casella's friends and relatives were involved. Eventually they discovered that Ricardo and his father were part of a group who had been kept at Maryhill Barracks and then sent on to the Isle of Man. Their cases would be reviewed in time, meanwhile the family could apply for permission to visit, though it would not be for many weeks.

'This is awful,' cried Peg. 'How can we afford to travel all that way to see them? How can we take the time away from the shop?'

'The shop,' said Signora Casella. 'How are we going to manage the shop? How are we going to survive?'

Her complaint was echoed in a thousand other households. The internment had struck a blow into the very hearts of the Italian families. Worse was to follow.

One of the ships transporting some of the men to detention in Canada was torpedoed and sunk. Only hours after its departure from Liverpool the *Arandora Star* was attacked by a German U-Boat and over four hundred Italian men were drowned.

A great gloom settled over the shop. No cooking was done or food prepared. Kezzie found that she missed the smells of the frying oil, and the baking dough, the constant flow of the Italian conversation. She and Peg stacked the café chairs and tables to one side, and only sold the grocery goods. Custom began to fall off. It was a sad place to be, and even Lucy, coming in from school, swinging her legs from one of the high bar stools commented on it.

'There's no happy noises in this café any more.'

Kezzie realised it was true. The wireless was only switched on for the news bulletins, and Peg and herself hardly spoke as they served behind the counter in the deli. Occasionally Kezzie could hear one or other of the older women breaking out in a heart-rending lamentation. Peg wasn't much better, wandering around listlessly, beginning a task and not complaining it. Baby Alec quickly picked up the mood of the place and became grizzly and fractious. Their supplies were running low. Kezzie saw that if they did not reorder soon the shop would have to close. She called them all together one morning and told them that she had made a decision.

'We are reopening the café tomorrow,' she announced.

Signora Biagi shook her head sadly. 'Not without the men,' she said.

'Yes,' said Kezzie firmly. 'Lots of other women are doing it, working in factories and on the land while their men are away. They can manage, so can we. Also I hear that there are tribunals we can appeal to. There is a very good chance that they might be released early, particularly Ricardo. His citizenships papers were almost cleared.'

'I cannot cope with it any more,' said Signora Casella.

'Do you want your own son to come home from the war to no business?' demanded Kezzie. 'If we don't begin our sandwiches and lunchtime snacks again soon then we will lose all our customers.' She appealed to Peg for help. 'We can run the front, can't we?' she asked.

'Yes, probably,' said Peg. 'I suppose we owe it to them to keep going.'

'We've got to try, at least,' said Kezzie. 'It's not doing us any good moping all the time. Look at you,' she spoke to Signora Biagi. 'You who were always so neatly dressed, with your hair so beautifully arranged. What a welcome for your husband should he return just at this moment.'

Signora Biagi glanced in the mirror hanging on the wall. She sighed and fixed one or two hair grips in place.

'Kezzie is right,' she said. 'We must at least try.'

'So.' Kezzie rubbed her hands together. 'Tonight you make some pasta. We will share all our ration coupons and make some chocolate cake and pies. And then we will begin again.'

From *A Homecoming For Kezzie* by Theresa Breslin

TIGER MAN IS LEAVING

After the Second World War, Germans on the Dutch island of Texel
were still hunting for Georgian deserters who had turned against
them. In this poetic story, Imme Dros recounts the Georgian battle
on Texel. Through her own eyes as a little girl, we are introduced to
her world and Tiger man, the handsome, jolly Georgian soldier
whom she met every day on the dyke. When the Russian army unit
finally does leave the island, she is unable to wave her hero
goodbye.

And then, on my father's birthday, the war was over.

Flags rose above the Krauts' heads, one flag from each garret window, and my mother's best girlfriend said: 'I never thought I'd live to see the day and watch this scurrilous lot parading under those flags!'

The Krauts swore, but they also kept their guns and continued to hunt Russians; another two hundred were shot after May 5th.

So what difference did it make, that the war was over?

We saw plenty of English aeroplanes, mind. They grazed over the island, but never touched ground. The Germans ran the roost. What kept those liberators, what on earth was keeping them?

We ran to the harbour at least once a day.

'The Canadians are coming! The Canadians are coming!'

The boat appeared in the harbour entrance, but no Canadians to be seen.

I gave up on them after a week, and when they finally did turn up, I wasn't there.

They had actually made it, and the Germans were finally forced to hand in their weapons, two weeks after the liberation.

The Russians crawled out of their hide-aways, basements, wardrobes, haystacks, holes in the ground, barns. They ran in the streets, danced, tried to find each other, embraced, sang like larks.

I could not find the soldier I was looking for. So many had died, 476 of the eight hundred Georgians to be exact. They stayed on the island and were given their own graveyard, next to ours.

The others went home. One Sunday morning in June.

I had woken up because I thought the war had started all over again.

The Georgians came driving along the New Road in lorries and fired shots in the air to celebrate their return home.

My parents refused to let me go to the harbour and watch.

'Are you out of your mind! It's only six o'clock.'

'I want to see it!'

'You'll find out soon enough what happened.'

But what I wanted to know, I was never told.

I ranted and raved, kicked my mother, scratched her, bit her. I yelled that I would run away from home, that she would regret this. I had never done anything like it before. My father was furious and sent me off to bed.

'You're grounded for the rest of the day. That'll teach you!'

I sat in front of the open window of my little room, crying.

The sun rose above the sea, the entire world was red and golden like a fairground booth. Not a boat in sight. They were still in the harbour and maybe, just maybe, Tiger Man was on one of them and now I would never see him again.

My girlfriend came to fetch me to go to the harbour around half past eight.

My parents wouldn't hear of it. She waved at me from the dyke and ran off.

My father and mother also went, with my little brother. I was alone. The boat left the harbour at nine and slowly steamed up the smooth sea. Not a leaf stirred, it was so quiet that I could hear voices over the water. People were standing on the dyke near the harbour, shouting in the direction of the boat and waving their arms above their heads.

I craned my neck as far as I could, found support in the gutter with one hand and waved the little sheet from the doll's cradle.

'Bon voyage!' the people on the dyke shouted. 'See you!'

'Bon voyage!' I went. 'See you!'

Then followed a song, in their wonderful, velvety language, about farewells or reunions or some such thing, and one voice on the boat rose above the strange, sad, dark others, one single male voice, clear, light, distant, high and then low again, warm and sharp, soft and hard.

'Soldier!' I shouted. 'Soldier! Tarzan! Tiger Man!'

I climbed into the gutter, which was definitely out of bounds and waved, waved that sheet.

'Come back! Come back! Please come back!'

But that day the westerly winds refused to blow, my words never even reached the dyke.

The boat glided on and the sea was empty.

From *Hi Soldier, Hi Handsome Soldier* by Imme Dros

TWO MEN WHO JUST COULDN'T TALK

After a pilgrimage to the Holy Land, a Danish knight wants to return to his country. He has promised his wife and children to be back by Christmas Eve. On his homeward journey he visits Venice, Florence, Genoa and later Antwerp, Bruges and Gent, where he meets a motley variety of people and listens to their gripping stories. After many adventures he makes it home just in time, on Christmas Night.

Then, at the merchant's request, the Captain began to talk of his travels. He recounted how from an early age he had chosen the life of a sailor, passing through all the ports of Europe, from the Baltic Sea to the Mediterranean. But it was between Flanders and the ports of the Iberian Peninsula that he had done most of his travelling. One day, however, he had a desire to go further afield, to go as far as those unknown lands that rose up out of the sea. He decided, therefore, to enlist with a Portuguese expedition that was sailing south in search of new countries. He came to Lisbon and from there boarded a caravel that was setting sail to survey and explore the coasts of Africa. They followed the banks of the Tagus towards the Canary Islands, where they stopped for some days. Then they continued their voyage, approaching the lands of Africa, rounding the Cape of Bojador and journeying onwards within sight of the scorched and deserted coast, with neither trees nor people. They dropped anchor by the White Cape, in the shelter of some high cliffs. There, dark-skinned men, wearing flowing capes and mounted on camels, came to the edge of the shore to trade with the Portuguese. The caravels continued sailing southwards, far towards the south. A steady breeze swelled the great sails and the masts and ropes creaked gently. Then, from the endless bare and empty coasts, with neither tree nor shade, the first palm trees came into view. Thick, green forests began to appear covering all the land, from the white beaches to the blue-tinted mountains. And out of these forests black, naked men appeared who climbed into their canoes and circled the ships. The Portuguese mariners had orders to strike up a relationship with them. But this was difficult. In most cases, the canoes never came within reach of the ships, and at other times, the natives disappeared into the forest the moment the caravels dropped anchor. Then, those sailors who came ashore would be greeted by the poisoned arrows of the hidden men.

Yet, in some of these stopping-places, the Africans and the Portuguese were already acquainted, and traded with one another. And sometimes, in parts of the coast where no ship had ever stopped before, they were greeted with great festivities and excitement. Then, dancing and singing, the natives would come out to meet the Portuguese and they, responding to the warm welcome, would also dance and sing in the manner of their own country.

But often, they would have a hard time communicating with each other, for each of the sides would be unable to understand the language being spoken by the other, and even the Berber interpreters were unfamiliar with the speech used in such far-off places. These differences in language were the cause of many deaths and battles. Thus it was one day, when the caravel dropped anchor before a wide and beautiful bay surrounded by wondrous trees. On the long, white sandy beach a small group of natives was watching the ship. The captain decided, therefore, to send two boats ashore with some men who were to try to make contact with the Africans. However, as soon as the boats touched shore the natives ran away and disappeared into the forest. 'Perhaps they were frightened at seeing that we are many and they are so few', said a Portuguese sailor called Pero Dias. And he asked his companions to leave him a boat and for them to board the other boat, taking it well away from the shore. But his companions were unwilling to accept this plan, thinking it too risky. However, such was Pero Dias' insistence that they ended up by doing as he had requested and rowing out into the bay.

As soon as the Portuguese sailor found himself alone, he walked to the middle of the beach, where he placed some coloured pieces of cloth which had been brought along as gifts. Then he withdrew to the edge of the shore and, leaning against the boat which had been left behind, he waited. After some time, a man came out of the forest carrying a long thin spear in his hand, advancing black and naked against the paleness of the sand. He advanced slowly, one step at a time, carefully watching the movements of the white man, who remained motionless by the boat.

When he reached the pieces of cloth, he stopped and excitedly examined the gifts. Then he lifted his head, looked straight at the Portuguese mariner and smiled. The other returned the smile and took a few steps forward. There was a short pause. Then, by mutual consent, the two men, smiling, walked to meet each other. When there were just six steps between them, they halted. 'I want peace with you', said the white man, in his language.
The black man smiled and replied with three unknown words.
'I want peace with you', said the white man in Arabic.

The black man smiled again and repeated the unintelligible words.

'I want peace with you', said the white man in Berber.

The black man smiled again and once more replied with the three exotic words.

Then Pero Dias began to talk in signs. He made the sign of drinking and the black man pointed to the forest. He made the sign of eating and the black man pointed to the forest. Making a sign of invitation, the mariner pointed to the boat. However, the black man shook his head and took a step backwards. On seeing him withdraw, the

Portuguese sailor, so as to re-establish trust, began to sing and dance. The other, with great jumps and laughter, followed suit. One in front of the other, they danced for some time. But in the excitement of the dance and the mime, Pero Dias raised his sword in the air, causing it to flash in the sunlight. The bright light startled the native who leaped back, trembling. Pero Dias made a sign to calm him. But the other began to run away and the sailor, too hasty in his pursuit, laid hold of him by the arm. Finding himself caught, the black man began to struggle, first out of fear, then in fury. With hoarse cries and grunts, he responded to the words and gestures that were meant to pacify him. Far out to sea Pero Dias' companions had seen the signs of the fight and began rowing ashore.

The black man seeing them approach, believed himself trapped and that all was lost. He aimed his spear. Pero Dias tried to parry the blow with his sword, but both of them were struck and fell to the ground. The Portuguese sailors jumped out of the boat and ran towards the bodies lying stretched out on the sand. Two lines of blood ran from the black man's breast and the white man's breast.

'Look', said a boy, 'their blood is exactly the same colour'.
The captain came from the ship with more men, and for an hour they all cried over the sad battle.

The Sun was rising in the sky and the mid-day heat was approaching. Not knowing when they would next be setting ashore, the captain decided not to carry the body of Pero Dias back to the ship. The two bodies were buried right there, on the beach. And with the Gentile's spear and the Christian's sword, the sailors made a cross, which they placed in the sand between the graves of the two men who had died because they were unable to speak to each other.

From *The Knight from Denmark*
by Sophia de Mello Breyner Andresen

LUCAS MEETS BENOIT

Lucas and his mother are spending their summer holidays in the house of his dead grandfather, in a town somewhere in the south of France. Lucas gradually finds out how during the war his grandfather gave away a group of Jewish children to the Germans, as well as the nuns with whom they were hiding. In his confusion, Lucas becomes entangled in a neo-Nazi movement. In this excerpt, he meets self-confident Benoît, one of the leaders of this extreme right-wing group. Lucas is fascinated by his way of acting.

The shopkeeper, with a fatherly look, came to my rescue.

'A pistol,' I said hoarsely. None of the three showed any reaction to the word. Only when I added apologetically, 'for my mother,' did they smile again. The shopkeeper showed with a wave of his arm that I should be on the other side of the shop, near the locked cases. He went to open one. He showed me things I hadn't even suspected existed. He talked about blank rounds and self-loading actions. While he explained the differences, the advantages and the possibilities of the five or six different types he had in stock, I peered at the price tags. Every single one was more expensive than I had expected, and I sidled away from the man, telling him I had to think about it. As soon as I said anything, the men in the corner became silent again. They looked at me, obviously interrupted in their discussion, but also interested.

'My mother is just like that,' the taller one said. He was obviously the elder, too; I guessed he was maybe ten years older than me. Because he'd spoken to me, I couldn't avoid looking at him. The shop was dimly lit. The only daylight came through the glass door at the front, but because it was an elongated space, artificial light was needed in the middle and the back. A few fluorescent tubes hanging from the ceiling gave a weak, flickering light. It was difficult to discern the man's face. He was wearing a bright blue Armani jacket with a lighter coloured, well-ironed shirt. He was fair, and had smooth features.

'She doesn't dare go out by herself any more. Sixty-three, she is.

Fit and healthy. But what can she do when four or five of them crowd around her like a wolf pack? You hand over. There is no other choice.' The shopkeeper and the other man nodded, although it was clear he had been mainly speaking to me.

'It only has to happen to you once. Once, and you live in fear. She's not so much worried about what actually happened – what does she care about that bit of money? She's worried about what could happen. The worst things happen in her dreams.'

As he spoke, he had come closer. I could now see his intensely blue eyes, looking at me fixedly. He smelled of musk and mild soap. His friend nodded as if his head was coming loose. For a moment I thought It was my turn to say something, but the man continued: 'She never feels safe now. She would only feel safe if she had some weapon herself, like a small pistol in her handbag. Just in case. Not a real one, of course, just something to scare those men. Sons have to see to it that their mothers get something like that. I like sons who protect their mothers.' Both hands loosely on the counter, the shopkeeper stood listening to the man. A fan was revolving slowly above his head, making his thin hair stand upright at intervals.
'How old are you?' asked the blond man.
'Seventeen,' I lied. He threw a quick glance at his friend. The latter's face brightened. He seemed to be the more restless of the two, smaller and darker, and his clothes didn't look as new.

'Do you hear that?' said the blond man. 'Seventeen! Really young, a minor still, but already with such a sense of responsibility.' The shopkeeper scraped his gold ring along the glass of the counter. Immediately, the blond man turned to him.

'Come on, René, we're not going to be difficult, are we?' he said. The shopkeeper looked away quietly and shook his head. He smoothed his hair, but as soon as he removed his hand, the hair sprang up again.

'I can't do it, Benoît,' he said. 'If I sell to a minor, I've had it!'

'But, René, this isn't a weapon! It's safety equipment! And it's for his mother, anyway.'

'Can't she come and get it then?'

'René, I thought we'd agreed we weren't going to be difficult!'

The exclamation hung in the air for a while, as if it had been a question.

'Yes, well,' the shopkeeper said eventually. 'I just hope I won't get caught. He looks so young, nothing like seventeen.'

'The boy does look seventeen,' said Benoît quietly. 'He appears young because of his haircut. But have a good look at him.' The three heads turned towards me. 'Imagine him with an ordinary short haircut. Then what do you see?' The shopkeeper kept looking at me intently. 'Yes, exactly,' Benoît said emphatically. 'A boy of seventeen.' He came and stood next to me. With a movement of his head he indicated the starting pistols the shopkeeper had been showing me and said: 'Expensive, eh?'

'Too expensive,' I agreed quickly.

'How much have you got?' asked his dark haired friend, who had been listening all this time.

'Not enough.'

'Not enough, Alex,' said Benoît over his shoulder.

'Too bad,' said Alex. Again he made that grating noise in his nose. The fan above the counter squeaked and didn't help a bit against the heat which hung in the air like fog. The carpet felt spongy and the air smelled of melting fat. The only thing I wanted was to get outside.

'Terrible,' said Benoît while I was getting ready to leave the shop. I slowed my step, out of politeness, because he spoke to me again. 'For your mother, I mean. Did they threaten her?'

'No,' I said hurriedly. I thought of the night before, and felt engulfed by remorse. 'They only come inside when we're not there. In the shed, too. They went off with my chain saw.' He clenched his fist, and the muscles in his jaw tightened.

'They're...' said Alex, backing him.

'So which one do you think you'll get?'

'I'll have to discuss it with my mother,' I said.

'Shouldn't you have a look at the other ones?' he asked. 'The real ones?' The shopkeeper started getting agitated.

'Just have a look,' Benoît said to him emphatically.

I shook my head and repeated that there was no need. I picked up the painting, muttered a greeting and moved towards the door.

'Hang on,' said Benoît, 'Alex will hold the door for you.' As he heard his name, Alex stretched his back. He moved past Benoît who whispered a few words to him, and walked ahead of me to the glass door.

'Is that a painting?' he asked once I was on the footpath.

'Yes.'

'Do you paint?' He peered through the gaps in the wrapping. The glass door closed soundlessly behind us.

'No, I don't. My grandfather did.'

'Really? Was he famous?'

'Felix Stockx,' I said. His mouth fell open when he heard the name.

'Felix? You're Felix's grandson?' His reaction surprised me. My grandfather painted landscapes which weren't up to much. And Alex didn't seem the sort of person who would spend money on paintings. He pushed the door open, stuck his head in and called out: 'He's Felix Stockx's grandson!'

'I didn't know he was a painter,' said Benoît a few moments later, after he had come outside and I had unwrapped the painting to show them. Out here in the sun, his hair had a reddish sheen which I had-n't noticed inside. It was quite short, but longer than Alex's. His was so short I could see the skin of his head through it. 'A man of many talents, obviously,' he said. 'Your grandfather was a great man. They've dragged his name through the mud, but for us he remains a shining example.' They both stood facing me, slightly bent towards me as if they were about to shake my hand. They must have expect-ed me to square my shoulders and say something memorable about my grandfather. But I did the opposite. I didn't know what they were talking about, got all confused, looked away from them and started stuttering. They must have assumed it was because I felt ashamed, because Alex nudged me and said: 'Hey, you're not one of those, are you?' He made a gesture I could not read.

'One of which?' I said squawking like a turkey.

'Someone who pretends the past does not exist? Who shrouds everything in a cloak of silence?' Fortunately, Benoît, who was obvi-ously more sensitive and noticed my confusion, intervened and said:

'Of course not, Alex. This boy is simply careful. He doesn't know who we are, so he doesn't let on. Can you blame him? God knows how often he has been abused when he said who he was.' I nodded, without knowing what I was confirming.

'I can put your mind at rest,' he continued. 'Our ideals are the same as your grandfather's. We want to act the way he acted, for the good of our country. People like him have taught us about obedience and loyalty. So remember: if anything is wrong, you can always come to us. I'll do anything I can to help you.'

I saw Benoît many times during the summer. He never wore that blue Armani jacket again, probably it was too hot even for him, but whenever I think of him, I think of that jacket. Somehow or other it went with his eyes, which were incredibly bright, and blue like the flame of a gas burner.

From *Falling* by Anne Provoost

A MODERN-DAY ROMEO AND JULIET

This playscript is based on one of the novels in Joan Lingard's trilogy about a Catholic boy (Kevin) and a Protestant girl (Sadie) who try to go out together in spite of the huge prejudice and opposition to such a relationship in both their communities. This scene shows just how dangerous such a relationship could be during the Troubles. Kevin has been beaten up by some Protestant boys and is in hospital. Sadie has to think about whether she can see him again.

SCENE 10

A cafe, Belfast city centre, Monday 6.00 p.m. Sadie enters and places two chairs at a table. She sits with her head in her hands. Brede comes on with two cups of coffee. She sits at the table. She places one of the cups near Sadie, then touches Sadie gently on the arm. Sadie looks up at Brede.

SADIE: Was he badly hurt, Brede?

BREDE: A lot of bruises, cuts on his head and leg. He got three stitches in his head.

SADIE: Oh God...

BREDE: Mr Kelly found him lying unconscious outside the yard late last night. He called an ambulance and Kevin got carted off to hospital.

SADIE: Which hospital is he in?

BREDE: They let him out this morning.

SADIE: It happened because of me, didn't it?

BREDE: (*Quietly*) Yes, I think so.

SADIE: D'you know who did it?

BREDE: There were a couple of them. One of them was Brian Rafferty.

SADIE: I thought he was Kevin's friend.

BREDE: It just shows you, doesn't it.

SADIE: Did Kevin ask you to come and tell me?

BREDE: He doesn't know I'm here. He's going to meet you tonight as planned. He'll not let you down. But... I've come to ask you not to meet him.

SADIE: You want me to let him down?

BREDE: It might be best. He's too proud to try and see you again if you don't see him. I know it's hard, but it would be easier if he thought you'd given in.

Pause. Sadie is fighting back her tears.

SADIE:... I'm sorry.

SADIE: I don't know, Brede, I don't know... I don't know anything at all. I want to see Kevin and he wants to see me and all these people are getting between us... Is it right for me to give in to Brian Rafferty and his friends? Is it?

BREDE: You don't want Kevin to be hurt again, do you?

SADIE: You know it's funny, people say I'm my own worst enemy. I make trouble for myself. They say you should go out with one of your own kind, it's easier less aggravation... Well for goodness sake you're all missing the point, aren't you... I'm not going out with

Kevin because he's a Catholic, or a Mick or whatever you want to call him... I'm going out with him because he's Kevin... We like being with each other, we don't want to be with anyone else. I mean I could have met a Protestant and felt the same way about him as I do about Kevin, but it didn't happen like that, did it? If I meet Kevin he might get beaten up again, if I don't he'll hate me ... What sort of choice is that for anyone? I just want a laugh, I want a bit of fun...I just want us to be walking out together, just the two of us, sharing things, spending time together... Why can't we do that?

BREDE: There's times when it might be all right for a Catholic boy to be walking out with a Protestant girl, but now's not one of them.

SADIE: It's not much to ask to want to walk by the river with some-one you like... I'm not sure. I can't promise, Brede. How can I prom-ise never to see Kevin again? I have to think about it.

BREDE: Think carefully then. There's enough blood, Sadie, without any more getting shed.

Brede exits, leaving Sadie alone on stage. Sadie starts to drink her coffee, then puts it down and pushes the cup away.

SADIE: *(Almost to herself)* I'm sorry, Kevin, you've got to believe me, I'm really sorry.

She rushes off in tears.

From *Across the Barricades* adapted by David Ian Neville
from the novel by Joan Lingard

THE DECISION

*This story, set during the Second World War, deals with the
confrontation between Flemings and Walloons. The twins Bavo and
Lode have different opinions on who is right in this war. Lode
hopes that Hitler will help emancipate the oppressed Flemish
people. He volunteers to join the Germans in their fight against the
Russian army. Bavo becomes a resistance courier.*

Lode sneaked into the kitchen while the others were busy working
in the stables. 'Bavo, can I have a word? You didn't say a thing just
now.'

'You know exactly how I feel.'

'You're my twin brother. I...'

Lode swallowed, pulled his shoulders back decisively and blurted
out: 'I know you're with the resistance, Bavo.'

How did you...'

'So does mother. I had this hunch. So I followed you a few times.'

'You sneaky bastard. You...'

'Listen, Bavo. I respect your opinion. But all this resistance, this
secret army, partisan, or whatever-you-want-to-call-it stuff, it's ille-
gal. Forbidden by the The Hague Convention. Join an organized
army if you must fight, but don't become a freeshooter.

'Easier said than done, Lode. It's like father said: it's not as if the
Germans didn't violate that convention of what's-its-name when
they invaded Belgium either. We were supposed to be neutral,
weren't we? Lode shrugged his shoulders.

'I know, I know. I've told you a hundred times.'

'Your answer's useless, that's why.'

'No, all it means is that you don't like it.'

He flung his arm over Bavo's shoulder, but the latter slipped away
almost unnoticed.

'Ah, Bavo, what on earth's come over us, that we should end up
at loggerheads?'

'You should talk, Lode. You, who are about to don the enemy's
uniform?'

They fixed each other's gaze and it was Lode who looked away first. He spoke softly: 'We're brothers, Bavo. We grew up together, we played, laughed together, were sad together. And now we're enemies.'

'You're not my enemy, Lode.'

'I'm about to join the SS. I'm going to fight in the German army. And you...'

'Me? I'm not fighting you, I'm fighting injustice, inhumanity,...'

But Lode interrupted him, fiercely.

'And I'm fighting bolshevism, godlessness. I'm fighting for our religion.'

He could hear himself talk and wondered: why can't I say: I'm fighting for Flanders? But he knew the answer to that one. Bavo too would say: I'm fighting for Flanders. This is madness, he thought. Two brothers who think they are fighting for the same ideal yet are at loggerheads.

'I'm fighting for freedom, Bavo said, just as fiercely. 'The freedom to say what you think, what you feel. I'm no bookworm, like you bro', you know that, but the other day I read this sentence by some author on the calendar and it stuck. *I beg to differ*, is what it said, *But until my dying day I will fight for your right to state your opinion.*'

Lode laughed sadly. 'My, my, Bavo! Been reading Multatuli, have we?'

Lode left early the next morning, even though he wasn't expected in Brussels until the evening. He somehow assumed parting like this would be easier on him and the others.

The stove had been lit and the water in the kettle was boiling when he came downstairs, washed and dressed. Mother was busy preparing sandwiches and father had both elbows on the table, his head resting on his hands.

'You can still change your mind,' he said.

But when Lode answered resolutely: 'I've signed, father', he shrugged his shoulders and yielded. Silke was busy drawing flowers on the steamed up panes. She turned around and said: 'I don't care what they say at school, Lode, you're still my brother.'

From *Country at War* by Paul Kustermans

LET'S FIGHT, MY LOVE

*Under the fascist regime in Portugal, and the censorship that came
with it, Daniel Filipe wrote a long poem about the invention of
love. A man and a woman have secret meetings in the city because
they are wanted by the police. The poet uses some kind of city
jargon to describe their sad lives. The famous Portuguese poet
Fernando Pessoa once said: 'All love letters are ridiculous, but
only he who never writes a love letter is truly ridiculous'*

If a man suddenly interrupts your enquiries
and demands to know your name and what you are doing
there gun at the ready
you already know your sworn duty Kill him Be he friend or
kins man
kill him Even if he has eaten at your table grown up at
your side
kill him It may be that when you have him in your sights
he may stare at you with overpowering loathing in his eyes
which by the end of the night look away
full of watery sadness Ignore the plea for a last request
a single compassionate but fatal blow is enough
to put a silence both secret and steadfast into effect

Seek the woman the man who in a hotel bar
met one rainy afternoon
If needs be erect blockades
arrange passes safe conduct a curfew
a Press blackout kangaroo courts
For the good of the city the country society
They must be found the runaway couple
who invented the notion of love as a matter of great urgency
The morning papers publish the news
that they have been seen walking hand in hand smiling
down a quiet street bordered by acacias

A lonely old man the witness states
that all at once he felt a strange sensation of peace within
a sense of freedom a smell of spring
a gentle warm breeze evoking the memory of adolescence
At the official inquiry amazed he confirmed
that the man and the woman bore stars on their foreheads
and strolled along with unfamiliar yet natural movement
enveloped in a swathe of music The view is that
the situation will reach its climax
and the police will be able to fulfil their duty

A man a woman a wanted poster
The voice of the broadcaster resolute and unambiguous
Blood-red headlines on the front page of the newspapers

From *The Creation of Love and Other Poems* by Daniel Filipe

Acknowledgements

In Times of War is published as a result of collaboration in the Comenius Project *War and Peace in Children's Literature*, funded by the Socrates programme of the EU 1997-2000.

The institutions in the partnership are:

Katholieke Hogeschool, Leuven, Belgium (Annemie Leysen, Annemie DeWynck)

University of Brighton, Faculty of Education and Sport, UK (Dr Carol Fox, John Clay)

University College, Chichester, UK (Dr Rob Batho)

Escola Superior de Educação, Setubal, Portugal (Manuela Fonseca)

Translators:

Nadine Malfait, David Colmer (Dutch and Flemish extracts)

Irène Koenders, Amanda Booth (Portuguese extracts)

Further assistance was given by: Pam Blackman, Julia Colclough, Roland Matthews, Josh Hook (UK) Rachel Gutterrez, Jane Beswick and David Brookshaw (Portugal).

Acknowledgements (in order of the anthology)

Robert Westall *Gulf*

pp 46-53 from the novel *Gulf* by Robert Westall (Methuen 1992) printed and translated by permission of Laura Cecil, Literary Agent, London

Michael Foreman *War Game*

The extract from *War Game* is printed by permission of the author Michael Foreman and the publisher Pavilion Books Ltd.

Edward Blunden *Vlamertinghe: Passing the Chateau, July 1917*

Reprinted by permission of Peters Fraser & Dunlop Group Ltd

Peter Dickinson *AK*

pp 161-173 of *"AK"* a novel by Peter Dickinson (Corgi 1992) is printed by permission of A P Watt on behalf of the Hon. Peter Dickinson

Andrew Davies *Conrad's War*

Chapter 7: *The Nuremberg Raid* (pp 48-63) from *Conrad's War* by Andrew Davies (Blackie 1978) Copyright © 1978 by Andrew Davies

Colin Rowbotham *Relative Sadness*

Relative Sadness is reprinted by permission of the author Colin Rowbotham and the publisher Harper Collins Publishers Ltd

John McCrae *In Flanders Fields*

Reprinted from Punch 8 December 1915 p 468 reproduced with permission of Punch Ltd

Linda Granfield *In Flanders Fields*

Text and illustrations (pp12-15) from *In Flanders Fields* by Linda Granfield, illustrated by Janet Wilson (Victor Gollancz/Hamish Hamilton 1995) Text copyright © 1995 by Linda Granfield. Illustrations copyright © 1995 by Janet Wilson

Michael Morpurgo *War Horse*

pp 26-31 of the novel *War Horse* by Michael Morpurgo translated and printed by permission of the author and Egmont Children's Books Ltd

Mary Rayner *The Echoing Green*

pp 58-67 of *The Echoing Green* by Mary Rayner (Penguin Books 1994) is translated and printed by permission of the author, Mary Rayner

Wilfred Owen *Futility*

From *Collected Poems* Chatto and Windus Ltd 1963

Vernon Scannell *Casualty – Mental Ward*

Casualty – Mental Ward is reprinted from *Collected Poems 1950-1996* Robson Books London ISBN 0582 058112 by permission of the author Vernon Scannell

Raymond Briggs *Ethel and Ernest: A True Story*

The extract from *Ethel and Ernest: a true story* is reprinted by permission of the author Raymond Briggs and the publisher Jonathon Cape

D Levertov *What Were They like?*

Reprinted from *Stay Alive* published by New Directions Publishing Corporation

Christobel Mattingley *No Guns For Asmir*

pp 8-15 from the novel *No Guns For Asmir* by Chistobel Mattingley, illustrated by Elizabeth Honey (Penguin Books Australia 1993) is printed by permission of the author, Christobel Mattingley, the illustrator, Elizabeth Honey and the publisher, Penguin Books Australia

R S Thomas *The Evacuee*

From *War Poems* (Ed. Christopher Martin) printed by permission of the publisher HarperCollins Publishers Ltd and of the author R. S. Thomas

Rachel Anderson *Paper Faces*

pp 24-28 from the novel *Paper Faces* by Rachel Anderson, published by Oxford University Press 1991, is printed and translated by permission of the author, Rachel Anderson

Tatiana Vassilieva *A Hostage To War*

pp 19-36 from *A Hostage To War* by Tatiana Vassilieva, translated by Anna Trenter (Hamish Hamilton 1996) Copyright ©1994 by Beltz Verlag, Weinheim and Basel. Translation copyright ©1996 by Anna Trenter

Alan Ross *Night Patrol*

Printed by permission of Alan Ross

Louise Borden *The Little Ships*

The extract from *The Little Ships* by Louise Borden, illustrated by Michael Foreman, is printed by permission of the author, the illustrator and Pavilion Books Ltd and Margaret McElderry Books

Michael Morpurgo *Waiting For Anya*

pp 138-153 translated from the novel *Waiting For Anya* by Michael Morpurgo is printed by permission of David Higham Associate on behalf of the author and the publishers Mammoth, Reed Consumer Books 1990

Anne Campling *And the Stars Were Gold*

pp 80-85 from *And the Stars Were Gold* by Anne Campling is translated and printed by permission of the author, Anne Campling, and the publisher, Orion Children's books

WH Auden *O What is that Sound?*

Reprinted from Collected Poems by W H Auden by permission of the publisher Faber & Faber

Judith Kerr *When Hitler Stole Pink Rabbit*

The extract from *When Hitler Stole Pink Rabbit* is printed by permission of the author Judith Kerr and the publisher HarperCollins Publishers Ltd

Pamela Melnikoff *Prisoner In Time: A Child of the Holocaust*

Extract from *Prisoner In Time: A Child of the Holocaust* by Pamela Melnikoff (Blackie 1992) Copyright © 1992 by Pamela Melnikoff

Art Spiegelman *Maus: A Survivor's Tale*

pp 108-115 from *Maus 1 A Survivor's Tale: My Father Bleeds History* by Art Spiegelman (Penguin Books, 1987) copyright © Art Spiegelman, 1973, 1980, 1981, 1982, 1983, 1984, 1985, 1986 reproduced by permission of Penguin Books Ltd.

Christa Laird *Beyond the Wall* (Original: *But Can The Pheonix Sing?*)

The extract from *But Can The Phoenix Sing?* (Reissued under the title *Beyond the Wall*) re-printed by permission of Christa Laird and the publisher Random House Children's Books Ltd

Margaretha Shemin *The Little Riders*

Extract from *The Little Riders* text, 1963, 1988 Margaretha Shemin Illustrations, 1963, 1988

Theresa Breslin *A Homecoming for Kezzie*

pp 73-77 from *A Homecoming for Kezzie* by Theresa Breslin (Methuen 1995) is printed by per-mission of the author and Egmont Children's Books Ltd

David Ian Neville *Across the Barricades*

pp 49-51 of *Across the Barricades* a play by David Ian Neville (1990) is reprinted by permission of Oxford University Press, Oxford UK

Acknowledgements for Belgian and Dutch extracts (in order of the anthology)

Louise van Santen *Chicken Coop*

pp 12-13 from *Op het puntje van mijn tong, Gedichten (On the Tip of my Tongue: Poems)* trans-lated from the Dutch by David Colmer. De Prom, 1998. ISBN 90 680 1620 2 (The Netherlands)

Daniel Billiet *Rwanda*

pp 14-15 from *Wat de ogen niet horen (What the Eyes Do not Hear)* translated from the Dutch by Nadine Malfait. Mechelen, Bakermat, 1995. ISBN 90 5461 0964 (Belgium)

Bisera Alikadic *The Bridegroom*

pp 30-33 from *Vertrouw nooit een draak (Never Trust a Dragon)*, stories and poems by writers from The Netherlands, Belgium and the former Yugoslavia, translated from the Dutch by Nadine Malfait. Leopold, 1997. ISBN 90 258 30374 (The Netherlands, Belgium and the former Yugoslavia)

Jan Terlouw *The English Pilot*

pp 32-37 from *Oorlogswinter (War Winter)* translated from the Dutch by Nadine Malfait. Lemniscaat, Rotterdam,1972. ISBN 90 60691180 (The Netherlands)

Daniel Billiet *Little Boy*

pp 20 from *Wat de Ogen niet Horen (What the Eyes Do not Hear)* translated from the Dutch by Nadine Malfait. Bakermat, 1995. ISBN 90 54610964 (Belgium)

Roger H. Schoemans *The Clay Stampers From London*

pp 14-19 from *Serafijns oorlog (Serafijn's War)* translated from the Dutch by Nadine Malfait. Averbode, 1998. ISBN 9 031 7133 41 (Belgium)

Tardi *Armageddon*

pp 112-119 from *Loopgravenoorlog 1914-1918 (Trench War 1914-1918)* translated from the Dutch by David Colmer. Casterman, 1993. ISBN 90 303 8467 0 (Belgium)

Martha Heesen *Star And Joe Join The Army*

pp 45-49 from *Sterre en Joe (Star and Joe)* translated from the Dutch by Nadine Malfait. Querido, 1997. ISBN 90 214 6557 4 (The Netherlands)

Ed Franck *The Birch Tree*

pp 50-54 from *Uit de loop van een geweer (From the Barrel of a Gun)* translated from the Dutch by Nadine Malfait. Hasselt, Clavis, 1991. ISBN 90 682 2124 8 (Belgium)

Herman de Coninck *Last Post*

pp 23 from *Vingerafdrukken (Fingerprints)* translated from the Dutch by David Colmer. Arbeiderspers, 1997. ISBN 90 295 1160 5 (Belgium)

Rita Verschuur *That's How It Was*

pp 101-111 from *Hoofdbagage (Head Luggage)* translated from the Dutch by Nadine Malfait. Van Goor, 1996. ISBN 90 00 031125 (The Netherlands)

Judith Herzberg *1945*

From *Is dit Genoeg. Een Stuk of Wat Gedichten (Will this Do? A Few Poems)* compiled by Cees Buddingh and Eddy van Vliet, translated from the Dutch by David Colmer. Elsevier-Manteau, 1982. ISBN 90 100 4291 X (The Netherlands)

Bart Moeyaert *The Spring Of '39*

pp 14-15 from *Holle Bolle Gijs II (Fatso II)* translated from the Dutch by Nadine Malfait. Querido, 1996. ISBN 90 214 6662 7 (Belgium)

Willy Spillebeen *Escape Across The Water*

pp 123-127 from *Een pluisje van de zee (A Piece of Fluff from the Sea)* translated from the Dutch by Nadine Malfait. Houtekiet, 1989. ISBN 90 52 40021 0 (Belgium)

Herman Van Campenhout *The Red Cross Delegation Is Coming*

pp 74-76 from *Petr Ginz (Peter Ginz)* translated from the Dutch by Nadine Malfait. Davidsfonds-Infodok, 1994. ISBN 90 656 5647 2 (Belgium)

Roger Vanhoeck *The Orchestra*

pp 66-71 from *Sonate in Auschwitz (Sonata in Auschwitz)* translated from the Dutch by Nadine Malfait. Bakermat, 1995. ISBN 90 5461089 9 (Belgium)

Remco Campert *A Time Of Killing*

pp 185 from Dichter, Remco Campert, De Bezige Bij 1995, ISBN 90 234 4743 3 Gedicht (Netherlands)

Karlijn Stoffels *Courier For The Resistance*

pp 158 from *Mosje en Reizele (Moshe and Reizele)* translated from the Dutch by Nadine Malfait. Querido, Amsterdam, 1996. ISBN 90 214 8353 X (The Netherlands)

Ruud van der Rol and Rian Verhoeven *Dear Kitty*

pp 80-83 from *Anne Frank Beyond the Diary* translated by Tony Langham and Plym Peters. Penguin, London, 1993. ISBN 0 14 036926 0 (The Netherlands)

Theo Olthuis *For Anne F*

pp 47 from *Het geluid van vrede (The Sound of Peace)* translated from the Dutch by Nadine Malfait. Ploegsma, Amsterdam, 1993. ISBN 90 216 1464 2 (The Netherlands)

Els de Groen *Antonia*

From *Tuig (No Roof in Bosnia)* translated by Patricia Crampton. Spindlewood, Barnstaple,

Devon, 1997. ISBN: 0 907349 73 0 (The Netherlands)

Ted van Lieshout *Why I Came To Hate War*

From *Mijn Botjes Zijn Bekleed met Deftig Vel (My Bones Are Covered with Decent Skin)* translated from the Dutch by David Colmer. Leopold, 1990. ISBN 90 258 3960 6 (The Netherlands)

Imme Dros *Tiger Man Is Leaving*

pp 27-31 from *Dag Soldaat, Dag Mooie Soldaat (Hi Soldier, Hi Handsome Soldier)* translated from the Dutch by Nadine Malfait. Querido, Amsterdam, 1996. ISBN 90 214 6040 8 (The Netherlands)

Anne Provoost *Lucas Meets Benoit*

pp 62-67 from *Vallen (Falling)* translated from the Dutch by Antwerpen. Houtekiet / Fontein, 1994. ISBN 90 5240 2787 (Belgium)

Paul Kustermans *The Decision*

pp 104-106 from *Land in Oorlog (Country at War)* translated from the Dutch by Nadine Malfait. Averbode, 1994. ISBN 90 317 1066 0 (Belgium)

Acknowledgements for the Portuguese extracts

Fernando Silvan *Boys And Girls*

pp 115 from *Primeiro Livro de Poesia* from the anthology compiled by Sophia de Mello Breyner Andresen, translated from the Portuguese by Amanda Booth. Ed. Caminho, Lisbon, 1991. ISBN 972 21 0597 3

Fernão Mendes Pinto *The Sack Of Nouday*

pp 123-125 from *The Travels of Mendes Pinto* translated from the Portuguese by Rebecca D. Katz. University of Chicago Press, Chicago and London, 1989. ISBN 0 226 66951 3

Alice Vieira *My Grandad And The Brass Band*

pp 57-67 from *Lote 12–2 Frente (Block 12-2F)* translated from the Portuguese by Amanda Booth. Ed. Caminho, Lisbon, 1980, 7th edition. ISBN 972 21 0038 6

Sergio Godinho *Song Of Fire And War*

From *Song Lyrics*, musical interpretation by José Mario Branco translated from the Portuguese by David Brookshaw

Ilse Losa *Uncle George's Death*

pp 171-178 from *Rio sem ponte* translated from the Portuguese by Amanda Booth. Edições Afrontamento, 1988. 2nd edition No. ed.: 311.

Sophia de Mello Breyner Andresen *Two Men Who Just Couldn't Talk*

pp 48-57 from *O Cavaleiro da Dinamarca (The Knight from Denmark)* translated from the Portuguese by Amanda Booth. Ed. Figuerinhas, 1988, 21st edition.

Daniel Filipe *Let's Fight My Love And We Must Find Them Before It's Too Late*

pp 33-37 from *A Invenção do Amor (The Creation of Love and Other Poems)* translated from Portuguese by Jaine Beswick. Editorial Presenca, Lisbon, 1972.

Every effort has been made to trace copyright holders, but in a few cases this has proved impossible. The editor and publishers apologise for these cases of unwilling copyright transgression and would like to hear from any copyright holders not acknowledged.